Contents

Foreword by the Series Editor

This volume on Australian theatre's long-standing and evolving relationships with its traditional imperial centre is the ninth in the series 'Australian Playwrights' commenced by Ortrun-Zuber Skerritt of Griffith University, Brisbane. Since 1985 eight monographs or edited collections and eight video interviews have been produced. The book studies are *Louis Nowra* edited by Veronica Kelly; *Patrick White* by May-Brit Akerholt; *Jack Hibberd* by Paul McGillick; *David Williamson* edited by Ortrun Zuber-Skerritt; *John Romeril* edited by Gareth Griffiths, *Alma De Groen* by Elizabeth Perkins, *Our Australian Theatre in the 1990s* edited by Veronica Kelly and *Body Show/s: Australian Viewings of Live Performance* edited by Peta Tait.

The recent publications in the series are focussed less on author studies and more upon industrial developments, contemporary theorisations and the works of specific artists and theatre companies, thus mapping the cultural and industrial contexts in which Australian theatre-making occurs. It provides information about the general theatrical field and documents and analyses the work of specific groups. This covers a broad range of drama, performance, dance and physical theatre devised both inside and outside the now problematic fields of text-based or authored writing. The illustrations are a major feature of the series, allowing readers to glimpse Australian theatre and its performers in front of their varied audiences.

Future plans for the 'Australian Playwrights' series include author studies and further historical, thematic and theoretical studies.

The following video programmes where playwrights speak about their work are available.

Louis Nowra *(1985)*	36 min
Dorothy Hewett (1986)	52 min
Jack Hibberd (1986)	42 min
David Williamson (1986)	50 min
Stephen Sewell (1986)	59 min
Alma De Groen (1990)	44 min
Michael Gow (1991)	49 min
John Romeril (1992	54 min

My thanks are due to the artists, editors and contributors for their scholarly work, patient collegiality and enthusiasm for Australian theatre-making in all its aspects.

Veronica Kelly
Australian Drama Studies Centre
University of Queensland, February 2003

Acknowledgments

It gives us great pleasure to thank the institutions which sponsored the conference where many of these papers were first delivered: the Drama Department at Royal Holloway, University of London; the Menzies Centre for Australian Studies, King's College, University of London; the Theatre Museum, London; the Australian High Commission; TNT; Stoll Moss.

For help with photographs we would like to thank the Theatre Collection, Bristol University; the Theatre Museum, London; the Victoria State Library; the State Library of New South Wales; the British Library; Lisa Montgomery at Belvoir Street Theatre; Bronwyn Klepp at the Queensland Theatre Company; Judy Seeff at the Sydney Theatre Company; Bob Anderson.

We are particularly grateful to the Society for Theatre Research for a subvention towards the costs of obtaining and reproducing photographs, and we would like to thank the Faculty of Arts at Royal Holloway, University of London, for help towards the costs of transcribing interviews. The Australian Drama Studies Centre, University of Queensland, gave financial assistance for editing and production costs.

Many people have helped this book on its journey and thanks especially go to Carolyn Pickett, Lynette Goddard, David Bradby, Ali Hodge, Kate Matthews, Marie Blount, Stephen Johnson, Rita Fitzpatrick, Margaret Leask, Libby Worth, Rosemary Schafer, and Heather Nimmo. Vincent Jones contributed computer expertise and intellectual rigour. James Bradley supplied expert editorial advice and other crucial support. Jeanette Champ assisted with formatting and Catherine Vaughan-Pow with indexing.

We would especially like to thank the practitioners who gave so generously of their time and shared their expertise with us in interviews: Cate Blanchett, Wayne Harrison, David Williamson.

Finally, sincere thanks to the contributors to this book, to the cover designer Amanda Lynch, and to our general editor, Veronica Kelly.

Elizabeth Schafer
Susan Bradley Smith
December 2002

Contributors

MICHAEL BILLINGTON has been theatre critic for the *Guardian* since 1971 and has also written for *Country Life, New York Times* and *Vanity Fair*. He broadcasts regularly on British radio and television and has written books on Ken Dodd, Peggy Ashcroft, Alan Ayckbourn, Tom Stoppard, and the staging of *Twelfth Night*. He has also published a collection of theatre criticism, *One Night Stands*.

SUSAN BRADLEY SMITH is senior lecturer in English at South Bank University, London. She is co-author (as Pfisterer) of *Playing With Ideas: Australian Women Playwrights from the Suffrage to the Sixties*, editor of the anthology *Tremendous Worlds: Australian Women's Drama, 1890-1960*. *Griefbox*, a collection of her own plays, was published in 2001.

RICHARD CAVE is Professor of Drama and Theatre Arts at Royal Holloway, University of London. He has written extensively on aspects of renaissance drama (especially Jonson and Webster), nineteenth-century and modern theatre, Anglo-Irish drama, forms of dance theatre and the study of the body as a medium of expression.

SUSAN CROFT is Curator of Contemporary Performance at the Theatre Museum. Her publications include *She Also Wrote Plays: an International Guide to Women Playwrights from the 10th to the 21st Century* (Faber 2001). She is completing a Critical Bibliography of English Language Women Playwrights 1360-1914 for Manchester University Press.

HELEN GILBERT teaches drama and theatre studies at the University of Queensland where she also directs experimental performance work. Her books include the award-wining *Sightlines: Race, Gender, and Nation in Contemporary Australian Theatre* (1998), *Post-colonial Drama: Theory, Practice, Politics* (co-authored with Joanne Tompkins 1996), and the edited anthology *Postcolonial Plays* (2001). She is currently working with Jacqueline Lo on a study of Asian influences in the Australia performing arts.

MARGARET HAMILTON is a consultant for the Australia Council, the Federal Government's arts funding and advisory body, in international arts market development and based at the Australian Embassy, Berlin. She is undertaking a PhD in the School of Theatre, Film and Dance, University of New South Wales and is an Australia/Germany Educational Development Fellow. Her research has been published in Australian and German journals, and she lectures at Potsdam University.

VERONICA KELLY is a Reader in the School of English, Media Studies and Art History, University of Queensland and Director of the Australian Drama Studies Centre. She is the General Editor of the 'Australian Playwrights' series and co-editor from 1982 of the journal *Australasian Drama Studies*. Her books include *The Theatre of Louis Nowra* (Currency 1998) and the collection *Our Australian Theatre in the 1990s* (Rodopi 1998). She publishes widely on colonial and contemporary Australian drama and theatre history.

JULIAN MEYRICK is currently Associate Director at the Melbourne Theatre Company and an Honorary Associate of La Trobe University's Drama Program. A professional director and a theatre historian, he has also published in the arts policy and theory/practice areas and his book on Sydney's Nimrod Theatre, *See How It Runs: Nimrod and the New Wave: 1970-1985* was published by Currency Press (2002). As a director he has staged numerous productions in Sydney and Melbourne, including *Who's Afraid of the Working Class?* for the Melbourne Workers Theatre and Joe Penhall's *Blue/Orange* for the MTC. He was the 1998 recipient of the Green Room Award for Best Director on the Fringe.

KATHERINE NEWEY has taught theatre and women's studies at universities in Australia and the UK. She currently lectures in Theatre Studies at Lancaster University. She has published widely on nineteenth-century popular theatre and women's playwriting.

ELIZABETH SCHAFER is Professor in Drama and Theatre Studies at Royal Holloway, University of London. She is the author of *MsDirecting Shakespeare* (1998), co-author of *Ben Jonson and Theatre* (1999) and co-editor with Peta Tait of *Australian Women's Drama: Texts and Feminisms* (1997/2000). She has written the stage history *Shakespeare in Production: 'The Taming of the Shrew'* (2002) and is currently working on a biography of Lilian Baylis, and the *Twelfth Night* volume for the Cambridge University Press *Shakespeare in Production series*.

PETA TAIT is a Senior Lecturer in Theatre and Drama at La Trobe University, Australia and publishes on bodies in circus performance and gender identity and emotion. She is author of *Performing Emotions: Gender, Bodies, Spaces, in Chekhov's Drama and Stanislavski's Theatre* (2002), *Converging Realities: Feminism in Australian Theatre* (1994), *and Original Women's Theatre* (1993). She is co-editor with Elizabeth Schafer of *Australian Women's Drama: Texts and Feminisms* (1997/2000), and editor of *Body Show/s: Australian Viewings of Live Performance* (2000).

Photographs

Cover

Cate Blanchett and Geoffrey Rush in the 1993 Sydney Theatre Company Production of *Oleanna*. Photograph: Tracey Schramm.

Photo 1

Poster for *White Australia*. Courtesy of the La Trobe Picture Collection, State Library of Victoria.

Photo 2

Robert Helpmann as Petruchio and Katharine Hepburn as Katherina in the 1955 Old Vic production of *The Taming of the Shrew*, which toured Australia, directed by Michael Benthall. Courtesy of the University of Bristol Theatre Collection.

Photo 3

Kevin Smith as Bottom in Noel Tovey's 1997 production of *A Midsummer Night's Dream*, Sydney Theatre Company. Deborah Mailman is in the background. Photograph: Tracey Schramm.

Photo 4

Deborah Mailman as Rosalind and Kirstie Hutton as Celia in Neil Armfield's 1999 production of *As You like It* at Belvoir Street, Sydney. Photograph: Heidrun Löhr.

Photo 5

Margaret Harvey as Ariel and John Stanton as Prospero in the Queensland Theatre Company's 1999 production of *The Tempest*, directed by Simon Phillips. Photograph: David Kelly.

Photo 6

Photograph identified as Ella Zuila. Courtesy of the State Library of New South Wales.

Photo 7

Sketch by May Holt for scene design for *Every Man for Himself*. Courtesy of the British Library.

Photo 8

Haddon Chambers. Courtesy of the London Theatre Museum.

Photo 9

Herbert Beerbohm Tree as the hero of Haddon Chambers's play *Captain Swift*. Courtesy of the University of Bristol Theatre Collection.

Photo 10

Sybil Thorndike in Gilbert Murray's translation of *The Trojan Women*. Courtesy of the London Theatre Museum.

Photo 11

Portrait of Inez Bensusan by Sir Cecil Rea (1924). Courtesy of the Art Gallery of New South Wales.

Photo 12

Cloudstreet. Courtesy of Belvoir Street Theatre. Photograph: Heidrun Löhr.

Photo 13 and **14**

Tap Dogs. Courtesy of the Sydney Theatre Company. Photograph: Frances Andrijich.

Introduction

Susan Bradley Smith
and
Elizabeth Schafer

... I think that there is universal appeal about the disadvantaged, everyone wants to hear the hard luck stories, and in colonial societies it is the indigenous people that have fantastic hard luck stories to tell, stories that are inherently dramatic. In Australia it's guilt, over in the UK it might be seen as the exotic or other, but it's also about social issues that they have that they can deal with at a distance.

Wesley Enoch

I suppose there is a lingering feeling in Australia of cultural isolation. Like any small country, we like to get noticed in bigger cultures, like England's and America's. I'd be silly to say that it isn't part of my psyche, too. So, yes, being in the West End means a great deal

David Williamson ('The Aussies').

How do we account for the range and nature of the various voices that constitute Australian theatre and drama, its history and its international manifestations? Do shifts in cultural stance and critical taste tell the whole story? Precisely what is dominant in or characteristic about Australian theatre is an ongoing debate, a debate that is sensitive to problems that postcolonial theory postulates about most settler colonies like Australia when it comes to considering culture. The issues central to that consideration raise questions about the relationships between social and artistic practices, between indigenous and settler populations, and between old and new worlds and their value systems (Ashcroft et al. 133). Part of that process, for those of us who are Australian, involves not only looking at ourselves as Australians, but interrogating how others view our cultural renderings of ourselves.

In 1892, the London *Dramatic Year Book* paid tribute to Australian drama, claiming that 'there is perhaps no country in the world where the drama has made such rapid strides and attained such a high standard in so short a period as in Australasia' (Kippax 7). In the century and more since then Australia has become a highly developed brand and selling Australia has never been easier – that is, so long as you are peddling genuine 'Australia-as-paradise' products like sport, soaps, wine and tourism. The rapid strides made and high standards set by Australian cultural products have not necessarily abated, but in the contemporary global marketplace it seems that Australia suffers from being dominantly imagined more in geographical, natural and physical terms rather than conceptual and creative ones. *Playing Australia* wonders why.

This book is also concerned to explore what is special about Australian theatre, and what insights and developments it offers international theatre communities. It worries over such issues as why a nation like Australia, where old and new worlds collide producing a distinctive theatre history and style, still suffers from imperfect cultural dialogues with old colonial powers like Britain. It suggests that the pressures of participating in global communities insist on increasingly meaningful and sensitised dialogues whereby performing Australianness becomes less than ever a parochial event.

The chair of the British Council, Helena Kennedy, said in 2001 in a lecture on cultural diversity to the Royal Society of Arts that 'Culture is what distinguishes us as nations ... but it is also through culture that we can understand each other as individuals'. She argued that 'all major geopolitical issues are, in a broader sense, cultural' which is why 'cultural pluralism within nations and cultural dialogue across nations is more urgent than ever' (Kennedy 4). *Playing Australia* engages directly with the urgency of these sentiments. Collectively, the essays in this book ask what Australian drama is, has been, and might be, both to Australians and non-Australians, when performed both in national and international arenas. Careful attention has been paid to the complexities of nationalism versus internationalism and the power of culture: while most Australian practitioners realise (and in many cases have long realised) that they do not need to defer to 'the mother country' to approve its cultural products, it is nevertheless acknowledged that 'we do need to convince others to buy it' to participate in the global market (Ball). This is not always an easy task when, as leading international theatre critic Michael Billington admits, 'the UK has an arrogant parochialism theatrically ... we don't know much about what's going on in new writing' with the majority of British theatre being 'inward looking'. The task is complicated again by the fact that Australians are not famous, it seems, for the kind of introspective plumbing of interior worlds that is thought to produce interesting cultural products: 'what problems could Australia possibly have that couldn't be solved in a half-hour episode of *Neighbours?*' (Ball). *Playing Australia*, on the theatre and drama front at least, goes some way to answering that question.

Playing Australia also seeks to raise a wide range of questions by playing with the notion of what 'playing Australia' might be, including playing in Australia; Australians playing away from home; playing with Australian stereotypes; and the relationship between culture, politics and national identity; all insisting on the complexities of Australian experiences. One of the most useful arenas for looking at a range of negotiations of what 'playing Australia' might mean is that of Anglo-Australian theatrical exchange, a subject scrutinised in several essays in the collection. It is unsurprising perhaps that Australian contributions to British theatre have often traditionally been undervalued – high achievers for example often become elided into Britishness – and great tensions still exist based on assumptions of superiority by the old imperial capital, still an acknowledged major centre for theatre. David Williamson, Australia's leading playwright, confirmed this when interviewed for the June 2002 West End opening of *Up For Grabs* (which starred Madonna): 'it's a great bonus when you have a production in the Birthplace of English-speaking Drama' (Williamson, 'The Aussies').

Anglo-Australian theatrical exchange is not the only arena surveyed here however, and the collection opens with a series of reflections on what it can be to play Australia to itself, or within Australia. In two of the essays – those by Helen Gilbert and Elizabeth Schafer – whiteness, otherness and negotiations of racial identities are discussed (issues that are further pursued elsewhere in the book). These discussions inevitably raise the always troubling topic of what satisfactorily signifies Australianness in the theatre and in different localities. The question 'What can be read as Australian?' confronts us with the disturbing thought that a performance may be deeply, even some might say authentically, Australian, and yet if it is not read as such then is its Australianness negated? And does this matter?

Much of the traffic of British-based theatre practitioners going to Australia to participate in and influence Australian theatre has been well documented; particularly the visits by stars whether they be Australians returning home, such as Oscar Asche, or visitors from England such as Laurence Olivier and Vivien Leigh. What is less often documented is the large number of Australia theatre practitioners who have made a contribution to British theatre, and because this book seeks to redress that balance and look particularly at expatriate Australians (possibly reflecting expatriate experiences amongst the writers) there is something of a bias in favour of examining those neglected contributions. This neglect is still puzzling. Luke Jennings suggests that Britain is sanguine that a 'kangaroo mafia' dominates the British dance scene. The British cinema-going public are confident that Australians make excellent films. And yet there still remains a gap in knowledge, a simple ignorance of Australian drama and theatre, despite the sudden increase in Australia theatre on view in the UK during the period 2000-2002. This book hopes to complicate the discussion. Meanwhile Britain is still exporting theatre to Australia but many of these events now say something very complex about what it is to play Australia.

The range of critical approaches in the collection is as wide as the range of authors and there has been no attempt to impose coherence in terms of methodology. Rather, this collection hopes to provoke even more various thinking on what playing Australia might mean. The authors who have contributed to this book could also all be situated at different points along a continuum of experiences of Australianness. Some have lived in Australia most of their lives, some in Britain. Most have alternated between the two countries, have experienced expatriation for long periods, and are acutely conscious of how the lens through which Australianness is viewed changes quickly and radically. Different registers are used – some essays are highly theorised, others are more meditative – but this reflects the diversity and range of the authors, theatre practitioners, periods, and subjects considered.

Playing Australia to Australia

The subject of how Australia has enacted Australianness on its own stage constitutes an enormous area of study and could include nineteenth-century melodramas and pantomimes filled with local detail; the Pioneer Players' attempts to create a national Australian drama; the realistic portrayals of Australia after the success of *The Summer of the Seventeenth Doll*; the displaced visions of Australia in work ostensibly set elsewhere; and the psychic as well as geographical divides within Australia that are embodied in different places and people (most apparent in indigenous theatre playing to white Australia). Then there is the question of 'whose Australia is being enacted?' and at different periods in Australian theatre history different versions of Australia have been dominant. In terms of live performance, for example, women and Aboriginal people have only had their versions of playing Australia enacted on the high-profile stages comparatively recently. Rather than attempt coverage of this enormous and almost infinitely varied subject, the writers here have focussed on areas that have previously been neglected in writing on Australia's own theatre history. Helen Gilbert offers a consideration of a group of widely divergent plays where white Australianness plays alongside Aboriginal and Asian identities 'as agonistic elements in the constitutive field of Australian nationalism' and suggests that the challenge for theatre of the new millennium is 'to create paths through' the ideological impasse of racism and nationalism and 'to dilute the cultural power of whiteness by embracing heterogeneity and difference'. Susan Croft then examines the often completely neglected area of school and college drama and focuses on the versions of Australia played out in texts performed by girls in an educational and presumably formative context. Julian Meyrick takes a new approach to examining the well-worn topic of the influence of British theatre on how Australia played out versions of Australianness and non-Australianness in the theatres of the post-World War Two period. By focussing on the professional theatre magazines, written for and often by practitioners themselves, Meyrick complicates the general picture of British dominance in Australian theatre of this time. Finally Elizabeth Schafer examines productions of Shakespeare in Australia which have used Aboriginal identity to rewrite and newly politicise Shakespeare's plays, and which have appropriated these canonical texts to play a version of Australia that Shakespeare palpably could not recognise, while producing a Shakespeare that is distinctly and uniquely Australian.

Playing Australia abroad: colonial enactments

This section focusses on playing Australia overseas, in particular in the UK, often in London. For most theatre artists discussed here, success in British theatre would have been simply satisfying: Britain, compared with Australia, offered a bigger audience base, more opportunities, more theatres. Although it was a very long way from Australia in terms of the time it took to travel there, so that relocation to Britain was a very serious move, these artists were not subject to the rhetoric of loyalty/disloyalty towards their native country which was sometimes mobilised against expatriate theatre workers in the later twentieth century. For these artists playing Australia abroad was an achievement to be celebrated, something perhaps most spectacularly illustrated by Gilbert Murray's vision of his own trajectory from the boy from the bush to Oxford don and British aristocrat (by marriage). The discussion begins with Peta Tait's analysis of the career of Ella Zuila, 'the Australian Funambulist' whose high-wire career lasted decades, while her 'Australian identity evoked an exotic geography of untamed margins away from the European centre of culture'. Tait comments that in the world of circus 'Zuila ... found it advantageous to be billed as Australian since the remoteness and the newness of her nationality could be emphasised and played upon to publicise her act'. Katherine Newey then examines the multiple identities of Anglo-Australian May Holt, whose work is much neglected and whose career is often hidden in the shadow cast by the successes of her father Clarance and her brother Bland Holt. Newey uses the particulars of May Holt's career to raise crucial questions about women's theatre work, and how it is assessed now by theatre historians. She argues for a more inclusive vision which would allow for imagining 'an interchange between Britain and Australia without having to see this in terms only of an oppressive colonialist ideology or an Australia cultural cringe'. Susan Bradley Smith then discusses the career of Inez Bensusan, the multi-talented expatriate playwright, producer, actress and women's suffrage worker who relocated to London and became a central figure in the agitation to secure women the vote. This essay raises wider questions about the impact of expatriate Australian theatre practitioners and their influence on the development of British theatre, and in Bensusan's case suggests that British feminist theatre has not yet fully acknowledged these significant developments. This section concludes with Elizabeth Schafer's assessment of the importance of their Australian heritage in the careers of two extremely successful Australian playwrights of the colonial period: Haddon Chambers and Gilbert Murray. Both negotiated versions of Australianness via the London stage and yet Chambers's work is largely forgotten today and Murray is rarely thought of in terms of his Australianness.

Playing Australia abroad: the late twentieth century

This section opens with a meditation by Michael Billington, the *Guardian* theatre critic, whose championing of Australian theatre and drama is longstanding. Billington is clear that the best Australian drama he has encountered contemplates the subject of Australian identity and his respect for Australia drama and theatre causes him to consider the difference between the critical reception of Australian theatre in the UK and the critical reception of a related performance art – Australian cricket. Billington's discussion is particularly instructive because of his wide experience of theatre, although his knowledge of Australian theatre in Australia itself may be circumscribed by the fact that in Australia he is a visiting luminary – invited to events such as the

Adelaide Festival – and likely to be encouraged to see predominantly what Australian cultural policy makers want him to see. Billington's discussion is followed by Richard Cave's analysis of one of the biggest Australian theatrical successes in the last decade: *Tap Dogs*. This event raises particularly interesting questions about what it is to play Australia, and one might speculate that this show's success may relate to its ability to market stereotypes of Aussie blokes. Cave however, goes further and considers the show's gay dynamics, and how these changed and were modified over years of touring. The juxtaposition of Cave's analysis with a discussion of *Tap Dogs* and its success by the show's producer, Wayne Harrison, generates a particularly multi-faceted assessment of this event.

The theme of a self-conscious notion of playing Australia abroad continues in Margaret Hamilton's discussion of the marketing of Australianness in the context of Germany. In the hard-hitting field of international marketing, the booking and promotion of Australian acts is not only a matter of 'translating cultural forms and differences in an international context' but 'What ... are the venues presenting and/producing international work ... interested in programming?' and 'how are Australian cultural policy makers "playing Australia" on the continent as distinct from Britain?' When complex products such as the Australian/Indonesian piece *The Theft of Sita* tour Europe they raise important issues about what is and is not Australianness, issues which would be seen very differently in the context, for example, of the Adelaide Festival for which the piece was first commissioned. The question of what may happen to a production when it tours away from the community that originally produced it is something which is also addressed in Susan Bradley Smith's discussion of the British tours of *Cloudstreet*, and the fare of the HeadsUp festival, an examination that suggests that British audiences continue to read Australia within a colonial paradigm whereby the exotic 'other' prevails as the preferred mode of relationship. Finally, in interview, Cate Blanchett reflects on her experience of playing, in the sense of acting, in Australia and in the UK, and what her Australian theatre training brings to her global performances.

Tonal differences and faultlines

I remember going over [to England] and seeing what was being offered in contemporary English writing at the time my play was going on there and knowing I was out of step with the tone of English theatre, which was incredibly rarified ... our stuff was raw by comparison. It was talking about direct

emotions directly expressed, it wasn't stuffing three layers
into the subtext ... the pattern of social behaviour we were
capturing as Australian playwrights on stage was truthful to
our culture, but was thought to be gauche by an English
culture ...(Williamson, Interview)

All of the contributors to this book have been forced to consider what is
of significance about Australian theatre, theatre history, and
contemporary performance, not only for Australians but the rest of the
world. So writing now, in late 2002, it is only fair that we offer a
summary of that significance, and in so doing argue for the not
insubstantial future of Australian theatre, for its historical importance,
and for it being paid due attention in these professedly postcolonial
times. We offer four claims.

The first is that Australian theatre is of central importance to any
history of Australian cultural expatriation in London. Australian theatre
in London is also a story of British theatre, and could become
increasingly so. As historian Stephen Alomes argues 'It was after all the
cultural practices of Expat Aussies, that can be said to be responsible
for shocking England out of its imperial condescension to the colonies'
(79).

The second claim could be described as a more temporary
phenomenon, but one that arguably places Australian political theatre,
particularly indigenous theatre, at the very centre of global
considerations of what is currently most fashionable. If anything will
focus the world's attention on the dire need for reconciliation in
Australia, then it will be the export of Australian culture, perhaps most
importantly Aboriginal culture, and theatre plays a central role in that
process. It is, as a genre, vital; and any contemporary theatre
practitioners or academics who teach contemporary political theatre
cannot do so without seriously considering recent indigenous
Australian theatre history. There is a lot at stake there.

The third claim, more to do with adapting our ideas of theatre
history, argues for the inclusion of Australian theatre history into
mainstream considerations about what is and has been important in the
development of western theatre over the last two centuries. It is absurd
not to include Australian experiences of suffrage theatre, for example,
when Australian women were emancipated citizens decades ahead of
their British and American counterparts. Anglo-centred theatre
histories that claim to be universal histories of Shakespeare, for
example, will have less credibility in this new century the more they
ignore global experiences.

The fourth claim for the significance of Australian theatre centres on theorising performance practice. In writing about English acting traditions, Simon Trussler assesses how style is relevant to English theatre practice, and explores ways in which national identity, 'Englishness', has been both reflected in and influenced by the ways it has been rendered on stage. This research could be expanded by considering what happens to English style when it meets Australian style, either directorial or acting. As Wayne Harrison has said, Australian acting styles are 'very different from British acting styles ... you can see what Australian society actually does to acting styles' (see 165). So this fourth claim is perhaps the most interesting one, as it presents an opportunity for analysing how nations 'listen to' and 'feel' each other in that most intimate of arenas, the arts, in that most intimate of spaces, the global stage of the twenty-first century.

In David Malouf's play *Blood Relations*, an Australian version of *The Tempest*, the characters are sitting around feeling the effects of the strong home brew. Kit, Malouf's homosexual Ariel, suddenly announces that he can feel the dark closing in, and the earth trembling. 'That's the empire shaking' (63) he announces gleefully. Part of the task of this book is critically to evaluate the shared history and cultural relations between Britain and Australia, and to recognise common values and traditions that have informed the development of our theatre histories. But this is not a book about 'tugging our forelocks'. Rather its gaze is postcolonial in that while it acknowledges our relationships, professional and cultural, it wonders at the lack of mutual respect, and worries about the quality of our business and creative relationships. It looks hopefully to the future confident that it has contributed a significant dialogue to cultural history, one that has by necessity, done a bit of 'empire shaking'.

References

Alomes, Stephen. *When London Calls: The Expatriation of Australian Artists to Britain*. Cambridge: Cambridge University Press,1999.

Ashcroft, Bill, Gareth Griffiths, and Helen Tiffin. *The Empire Writes Back: Theory and Practice in Post-Colonial Literatures*. London: Routledge, 1989.

Ball, Ben. 'They Like Our Wine and Our Soaps, So Why Not Our Books'. *Sydney Morning Herald* 30 June 2000.

Billington, Michael. Concluding Panel, Playing Australia Conference, London November 1999.

Enoch, Wesley. Interview with Susan Bradley Smith. London, August 2000.

Jennings, Luke. 'Leaping Wizards of Oz'. *Evening Standard* 23 October 2001.

Kennedy, Helena. 'Globalisation Cannot Suppress Our Human Diversity'. *Independent Review* 4 December 2001: 4.

Kippax, H.G. 'Introduction'. *Three Australian Plays*. Melbourne, 1980.

Malouf, David. *Blood Relations*. Sydney: Currency Press, 1988.

Trussler, Simon. 'English Acting, Interactive Technology, and the Elusive Quality of Englishness'. *New Theatre Quarterly* 45 (1996): 3-5.

Williamson, David. Interviewed in Daniel Rosenthal, 'The Aussies Are Coming'. *Independent Review* 1 May 2002.

Williamson, David. Interview with Susan Bradley Smith. Byron Bay, NSW, August 1999.

Part I

Playing Australia to Australia

1.
Millennial blues: racism, nationalism and the legacy of empire

Helen Gilbert

Stage performances of whiteness function to both reveal and neutralise threats to Australia's race-based hegemonic nationalism, and theatrical representations of race over the last century have been inextricably tied to wider anxieties about the formation and maintenance of a robust Anglo-Celtic society in a seemingly hostile geo-political region. Selected colonial and modern plays are deployed to sketch a range of responses to cultural diversification, focussing on the ways in which whiteness has been delineated in relation to the flexible signifiers of Asianness and Aboriginality, and re-assessing images of Australian identity in reference to recent political events that seem to have crystallised millennial anxieties about the country's cultural and political future.

On 6 November 1999, when the majority of Australians answered a resounding 'no' to the question of whether we should change our current system of government from a constitutional monarchy to a republic, international observers, particularly those writing for the British tabloids, were somewhat bemused at our apparent attachment to a foreign monarch whose importance within even British politics had waned considerably. The issues at stake in the referendum were, of course, much more complex than this superficial reading of the result – as indicative of a backward-looking loyalty to the Queen – implies, since many Australians who voted 'no' in fact supported the switch to a republic but not one modelled on the only option given on the ballot papers.[1] Nevertheless, the tabloid response does point towards an important and unresolved issue, not only among the fence-sitters but also in both monarchist and republican camps, in the intense debate leading up to the referendum: the issue of what role Anglo-Celtic[2] culture could and should play in an increasingly multiracial Australia. This question, though by no means new, had gained urgency (if not clarity) at the cusp of the new millennium in the lead-up to the Sydney 2000 Olympics and in the wake of events such as the rise of Hansonite politics, Australia's conflict with

Indonesia over East Timor's independence, and the stalling, under John Howard's conservative government, of the official reconciliation process between Aboriginal and non-Aboriginal Australians.

While the referendum seemed to approve the continued hegemony of Anglo-Celtic culture within our nation, David Malouf's assertion that the 'no' vote was 'a cry from the heart of those who did not feel like full participants in the new Australia' (Davie 241) should alert us to the intricacies of the situation. For instance, despite their original dispossession by British settlers, many Aboriginal Australians felt that indigenous interests would be better served by a system of government that retained links, however symbolic, with the British monarchy. This position emphasised the need for Aborigines to maintain an international avenue of appeal against local injustices such as mandatory sentencing for minor property offences. Other groups voted not to embrace constitutional change because they saw little benefit to be gained from what political editor Paul Kelly has termed an 'impoverished brand of republicanism', which, like earlier radical nationalist movements, defined itself by 'anti-British assertion' (23) while still championing an unproblematised model of Anglo-Celtic identity as the preferred Australian norm. Both responses signal rejection of a political system that did not propose to address in any significant way the on-going privileges of white (or white-thinking) Australians. At the same time, the 'no' vote was bolstered by those opposing more inclusive versions of republicanism seen, in some circles at least, as pro-Aboriginal and pro-Asian.

These conflicting notions of what agendas might (not) be served by an Australian republic suggest key points of connection *and* disjunction between racialised subjects in discursive formulations of the nation as articulated at a specific historical moment. Yet, the occasion inevitably invoked other historical moments at which debates about national identity dominated public discourse in anticipation of, or response to, certain political events, notably the 1901 Federation of Australian states, the 1970s implementation of multiculturalism as an official strategy for cultural development, and the 1988 bicentenary of Anglo-European settlement/invasion. Such discourse has long been characterised by a strategic mobilisation of race and ethnicity as flexible signifiers in hegemonic narratives of nationhood. In this respect, the recent republican debate was not especially progressive, even though its opinion-making elite may have prided themselves in being more informed, more cosmopolitan, more postcolonial, than their predecessors.

To consider ways in which issues of identity left unresolved by the referendum have figured within Australian theatre over the last century, this essay examines a limited selection of texts that stage Englishness, Aboriginality and Asianness as agonistic elements in the constitutive field of Australian nationalism. My primary aim is less to catalogue the paradigmatic modes of representation that mark Aborigines and Asians as racial Others against which white Australians have been defined, though that is part of the process, than to draw attention to those normative (Anglo-Celtic) figurations of national subjectivity that tend to pass as racially *unmarked*. This interest in images of Englishness – be it in metropolitan or (post)colonial guises – and its correlative discourse of whiteness derives from Richard Dyer's argument that to understand whiteness as a racial category is to dislodge its centrality, since white power 'reproduces itself regardless of intention, power differences and goodwill, and overwhelmingly because it is not seen as whiteness, but as normal' (10).

Randolph Bedford's melodrama, *White Australia, or The Empty North* (Photo 1) provides a telling portrait of colonial anxieties about establishing and maintaining a robust Anglo-Australian society in a seemingly hostile geo-political region. First performed in 1909,[3] this play fits quite neatly into a broader category of Asian invasion narratives that began in Australia in the late 1880s and intensified in the early years of the twentieth century as the newly independent nation began to define its cultural, political and economic position within the Asia-Pacific region. In generic terms, David Walker argues that the invasion narrative is a 'discourse on the relationship between national strength, military capacity and the patriotic spirit' (98). Whereas British invasion narratives of the period were commonly anxious meditations on the decline of imperial power and Britain's consequent vulnerability at a time of intensifying European rivalries, Australian versions of this genre expressed fears of not being able to sufficiently establish coherent identities (Walker 98-101).[4] As well as being geographically compromised because of its proximity to Asia, the fledgling Australian nation was also apparently at risk because of the effects of Britain's commercial and political links with Asian countries.[5] Hence, a sense of betrayal on the part of the mother country often permeated accounts of colonial nation-building. At the same time, some sections of the populace worried that continental decadence and complacency might spread to Australians, leaving them unprepared for a foreign invasion. It is not surprising, then, that nationalist intellectuals such as William Lane and Kenneth

Mackay figured the 'shining purity of a white Australia and the dirty compromises of British capitalism' as a powerful juxtaposition 'between symbols of youth, cleanliness and purity and those of age, decay and exhaustion' (Walker 106).

I offer this brief cultural history as a way of anchoring the character constructions and narrative trajectories evident in Bedford's play. *White Australia* dramatises attempts by a squatter and an engineer to repel an invasion by an alliance of 'coloured' races that have declared war on Australia. This alliance is led by an English-educated Japanese spy who is assisted by a few of his own countrymen, various slavish Chinese supporters and, crucially, a treacherous Anglophile Australian (Cedric), whose bravery and loyalty have clearly been eroded by too many years spent in Britain. Most of the action is set in the so-called 'empty north' even though more populous areas such as Sydney are the predictable targets of the Japanese naval invasion that forms the spectacular climax of the play. The setting reflects strong contemporary concerns that the vast, sparsely populated areas of northern Australia were an open invitation to millions of Asians who might usurp land that white Australians had failed to develop.[6]

Bedford uses a predictable array of stereotypes to convey the moral battle between good and evil that is well recognised as one of the hallmarks of melodrama. The Japanese villain, Yamamoto, is cast as a ruthless, duplicitous tyrant bent on annihilating Australians and stealing their land; he is also aristocratic and dangerously well-versed in the white man's ways, almost admirable, provided he remains in his own country. The Chinese, on the other hand, are portrayed as lascivious, dirty, servile nuisances, threatening in numbers but individually lacking in the tactics to plan a successful assault. Pitted against these 'yellow' villains are two main kinds of white Australians: likeable but lazy, gambling drunkards too complacent to guard against attack; and resourceful, virtuous and energetic patriots whose valour and ingenuity eventually save the day when they bomb the Japanese fleet in Sydney Harbour from the vantage of a revolutionary airship balloon. In the finest of melodrama traditions, the winning side's glorious victory is only made possible by the intervention of two comic servant types, in this case Aborigines, who rescue the 'goodies' from certain death after they have been captured by their foes. Although the Aborigines do get some credit for their valour, naturally it is left to the romantic hero, Jack, to reiterate the play's moral message:

Brother Australians! Today by some intelligence, with the aid of a strengthening love (*turns to* Vic) and by much of that luck which belongs to the drunkard and the fool, Australia has decisively routed its present enemy. Be we shall have more. Our rich and empty land is a permanent temptation to the poor and overcrowded world and if we would hold Australia we must be strong. No more unpreparedness – no more mad devotion to vicarious sport – arm yourselves and think, get guns and resolution. (85)

Of course, there is much in this play that invites, indeed compels, deconstructive analysis. In particular, one might critique Bedford's overt racism by examining ways in which the narrative uses carefully differentiated manipulations of racial otherness to demonise Asians and yet commend Aborigines even while displacing them from the imaginary space of the nation. This kind of analysis might be usefully informed by Homi Bhabha's work on the destabilising functions of the colonial stereotype, a hegemonic knowledge formation – or rather (de)formation (Lo 193-94) – that continually reveals its biases and slippages through a process of anxious repetition.   Bhabha's formulation could also illuminate our understanding of Cedric's role as an imperialist traitor in thrall to the Orient and unable to withstand its corruptive power. Yet, ultimately, this particular kind of racism seems something of a soft target, and perhaps not the most useful focus for my purposes.   More compelling areas for investigation are the play's incredibly anxious reiteration of whiteness and the question of how that may have functioned not only to normalise Anglo-Australian versions of national identity, but also, and in a perverse way, to de-naturalise notions of an organically white Australia.

The second part of my proposition is counter-intuitive, I know, and biased by a late twentieth-century recuperative impulse, but perhaps not as outlandish in this context as it might seem. Following Veronica Kelly's lead in reassessing the potential of colonial popular theatre to deliver powerfully subversive performances of empire (40-52), I would argue that the play, *White Australia*, in fact 'alienates' whiteness in at least two ways.   Firstly, what I am claiming as a kind of accidental Brechtian *verfremdungseffekt* occurs through the extraordinary focus on what Dyer has called 'extreme whiteness', a form distinct from the unmarked whiteness that generally underpins the hegemony of Anglo-Australia.   For Dyer, the whiteness of most people is ordinary, unspectacular or plain and this is what allows whiteness to imagine that it is able to speak on everyone's behalf – to be broadly representative. In his formulation, 'Extreme whiteness coexists with ordinary whiteness [but] it is exceptional, excessive, marked. It is what whiteness aspires to and also ... fears' (222). Thus extreme whiteness leaves a residue through which whiteness becomes visible as a racial marker rather than simply passing as an invisible, disinterested and normative category.

In Bedford's play, the mode of excess in representations of whiteness begins in the first few moments with an audience aside by Kate, one of the heroines, as she reveals her distrust of Yamamoto: 'I don't like that man ... Green's my eye but white's my colour' (2). This kind of obvious racial self-fashioning is adopted time and again by virtually all of the other Anglo-Australian characters, though it has different inflections according to gender and circumstance. The women are, of course, paragons of virtue whose whiteness is rhetorically intensified as they prove their allegiances to the national ideal of racial purity. Ironically, Victoria,[7] the romantic heroine, is even willing to endure sexual violation rather than reveal strategic military secrets to the Japanese, though, predictably, this threat of inter-racial rape is averted at the eleventh hour. The paradox here is that the promised submission to racial contamination actually makes Victoria whiter since she would lose her virtue to protect white Australia. Extreme whiteness thus constitutes itself in the field of racial otherness, deriving ontological power from the threat of that which is 'not white'. The already fallen white prostitute, Paw Paw Sal, provides an even more overt example of the improbable power of extreme whiteness when she is found, mad and dissolute, in the opium dens of the Port Darwin Chinese community:

MAC: You are a white woman.

SAL: I was – Gord forgimme, I was. (52)

Spurred by her countryman's verbal recognition of her whiteness to rebel against her Chinese pimp, Sal manages to stab her oppressor, exclaiming, 'White's my colour, you yeller dog' (53). Moments later she dies but not before uttering a refrain: 'I'm all white again, an' gord forgimme, all white' (53). Here the anxious repetition of a re-appropriated whiteness suggests it is less an essence than an aspiration (Hage 20), something that can, to a certain point, be accumulated.

The play's versions of Australian masculinity are similarly punctuated by numerous vocal iterations of whiteness, delivered either as a form of self-reference, or as a way of interpellating others into the dominant discourse. From playful, approving expressions such as 'Ah, mate, you're a white man' (29), to assertions like 'I'll show that I'm white when I'm wanted' (25), to the jubilant battle cry of 'First blood to the white man' (24), the sense of whiteness is intensified to the point of radical excess. Whiteness is represented as the organising principle of colonial Australian society and the moral touchstone of its male patriots. In an elegant paradox, Australian masculinity draws on Englishness as a form of white patrimony but also defines itself against the emasculating Englishness that Cedric, the traitor, has accumulated. As a male parallel to Paw Paw Sal, Cedric is the figure who plays out the instability that radical excess makes possible. He emphasises his whiteness as a marker of difference from his Asian collaborators – who constantly refer to him as 'the white man' – yet, among members of his own race, he has lost his claim to whiteness by dint of his treachery.[8] The choice of an Anglophile but Australian-born traitor as the play's villain serves Bedford's patriotic purpose well because it allows him to take a shot at Britain's pro-Asia policies as well as at those Australians whose slavish imitations of Englishness were seen to weaken the national type. In this respect, Cedric's characterisation reflects one of the central contradictions in the constitution of white Australian identity: that it is commonly defined in terms which suggest both an extension of and a radical break from the British imperial centre.

In one version of Bedford's script, whiteness also registers as a constructed rather than natural category through a comic set piece where Terribit and Minimie, the two Aboriginal characters, play at being their white masters. Using a surcingle (corset) and stays, along with affected upper-class manners, Minimie fashions herself as 'White Mary' and then demands all the privileges, including the vote, that her new status is supposed to afford. Terribit, meanwhile, takes on the role of the white suitor, albeit somewhat reluctantly because he fears it will compromise his own masculinity. After a considerable amount of stage business, they discard their disguises and resume Aboriginal modes of behaviour as Minimie paints Terribit with ochre to prepare him for war. This kind of cross-cultural transvestism, overtly staged as a self-reflexive performance, seems to me perfectly to fulfil Brecht's demand for a historicised treatment of social relations. Terribit's comment, 'White's the best trick of all but I'll back black against yeller till the cows come home'[9] shows that he is fully aware of the ways in which Aborigines are positioned relative to Asians and Anglo-Australians in the social hierarchy. That Australian melodramas typically used white actors in blackface to play Aboriginal characters, a convention likely familiar to colonial audiences, further stresses the possibilities for a wayward signification of whiteness in Bedford's play.

If we agree with Dyer that to make whiteness noticeable as a racial category is to take the first step in dismantling its authority, then it would seem that the generic modalities of melodrama – the mode of excess, the overt polarisation of moral categories, the comic performativity – mesh quite well with the postcolonial critical project of dismantling racial privilege. I am not suggesting here that *White Australia* was deliberately written to engage critically with the racist discourses of the time, but rather that both its text and dramaturgy open up possibilities for such a project. Support for this stance is evident in reviews of the premiere performance, since at least one commentator (from the nationalist *Bulletin* of 1 July 1909) complained that the 'talk of White Australia from the word "go"' strained credibility and that the political purpose of such 'verbiage' was 'too glaringly obvious' (8). In a more contemporary context, it might be possible to argue that the mode of excess that has characterised Pauline Hanson's vitriolic diatribe against Aborigines and Asians also serves to put whiteness on the public agenda in a way that problematises its earlier invisibility as the Australian norm. Hanson's 1996 maiden parliamentary speech 'Australia, Wake Up!' reads as the classic invasion narrative in the melodramatic mode, except that it is missing the comic set piece: implicitly addressing her fellow *white* Australians, Hanson warns of an imminent takeover by Asian hordes abetted by villainous local multiculturalists, the latter troped as traitors to the nation. Aborigines, according to this narrative, are responsible for a fatal disunity within Australian society and so weaken our ability to repulse the Asian enemy. We are warned that time is of the essence, so we must come to our senses before it is too late to steer the nation unswervingly towards its right (white) destiny. From this kind of perspective, it is not surprising that events such as the East Timor crisis were constructed in some sectors of Australian society as a timely wake-up call. In a complicated chain of signification, Australia's conflict with Indonesia over East Timorese independence was also used to bolster the monarchists' case for a 'no' vote in the constitutional referendum, the logic being that decreasing constitutional ties to Britain would make us more prone to Asianisation and, in particular, to adopting bad republican models such as that of Indonesia.

Whereas Bedford's melodrama synthesises anxieties undergirding the sedimentation of the White Australia Policy as a form of racial management, Mona Brand's 1948 social realist play *Here Under Heaven* turns on a discourse of tolerance that anticipates the 1970s policy switch to official multiculturalism. This discourse of tolerance is played out through various characters' responses to the surprise appearance of a Chinese woman, Lola, in a tightly-knit southern Queensland sheep-grazing community. Lola gains entry to rural Australia at the invitation of the upper-class station-owners who never consider that their soldier son's new wife, whom he met in Singapore during the war, might not be white. The play's narrative project is clearly to show how racial prejudices get in the way of productive cross-cultural interaction, and yet the implied proposition that tolerance will lead to a genuinely democratic nation troubles me in a number of ways. Preston King points out that 'if one concedes or promotes a power to tolerate, one equally concedes a power not to tolerate' (6). Taking up this argument, Ghassan Hage sees racial tolerance as the flip side to racism in so far as it is 'never a passive acceptance, a kind of "letting be"', but rather an action that always presupposes control over an object of tolerance (89). In the Australian context, Hage insists, multicultural tolerance is therefore 'a strategy aimed at reproducing and disguising relationships of power in society ... a form of symbolic violence in which a mode of domination is presented as a form of egalitarianism' (87).

There is evidence in Brand's play to support this argument as the power of the arch-racist, Mrs Hamilton, gradually gives way to the will of her more tolerant son, Richard. Lola is not passive in this transaction, but neither is she fully agential, since Richard's rebellion against his mother seems on one level at least to represent a proper resumption of patriarchal power after a brief and unwanted interregnum. Mrs Hamilton's intolerance, despicable though it may be, nonetheless positions her as a manager of national space, an empowered subject rather than an objectified Other to be tolerated or not tolerated according to the imperative of a race-based society. At the spectatorial level, the Asian Other is firmly positioned as the object of the viewer's racial tolerance, which limits an otherwise brave political project, at least read in contemporary terms. Try as she might, Brand is unable to construct a fully-developed Asian character without resorting to cultural stereotypes; as a result, Lola, in her exquisite cheong sam, excites our exoticising gaze while the white Australians in the play are never racially marked. The implied world view of the younger Hamiltons – a view that absorbs difference back into unity at the level of family cohesion – is in fact epistemologically consistent with the very subtle hint of nostalgia that seems to pervade the play even as it looks forward, in a way quite revolutionary for its time, to a different kind of nation. For me, this nostalgia is located primarily in Mrs Hamilton's lament for a pioneer past that does not seem entirely to lose its mythopoeic force even though it is conjured through the racist dialogue of a character we are encouraged to critique.

Where Brand is more successful in dislodging the authority of whiteness is in her treatment of class issues. The Hamiltons' full access to white nationhood as a privileged social space depends not only on their visible racial features but also on their upper-class attributes, which are aligned with Englishness at various points. Hage notes that certain markers of class capital such as economic riches, education, manners, accent and religion, function to signal whiteness in so far as they allow their possessors to claim certain forms of dominant national belonging (56). As Brand's narrative unfolds, the Hamiltons' class capital is shown to be at risk, both from the drought that threatens their livelihood and from a historical weakening of class barriers, which Lola seems to exacerbate. That she is cultured, highly articulate and clearly more knowledgeable about world affairs than the insular Australians unsettles the fixity of class/race hierarchies. Moreover, it is Lola who deliberately transgresses social boundaries by bringing a sick Aboriginal child to the homestead so that she can tend her. This particular juxtaposition of racial subjects signals an oppositional social orientation whereby the Asian migrant seeks to establish national belonging in reference to Aboriginal rather than Anglo-Celtic society. Such orientation represents a signal moment in the national imaginary, even though in the world of the play that moment can only be fleeting since the Aborigines are ultimately figured as a dying race.

Here Under Heaven also puts whiteness at risk via its focus on miscegenation. Cross-racial sexual desire highlights the notion that 'heterosexuality is the means of ensuring, but also the site of endangering, the reproduction of [racial] differences' (Dyer 20). Dyer maintains that if white bodies cannot 'guarantee their own reproduction as white', then they are 'no longer indubitably white bodies', and 'the "natural" basis of their dominion is no longer credible' (25). This is why white women's virginity has been such a site of anxiety within British imperial projects. In Brand's play, it is the men rather than the women who sexually compromise their whiteness. Two of the Hamilton sons have ignored the social prohibition on interracial sex – one with an Asian the other with an

Aborigine – transgressions that cannot be overlooked since both result in hybrid offspring, though in the case of Australia's liaison with Asia (figured by John's marriage to Lola), hybridity is only foreshadowed by Lola's pregnancy. Thus the hypothetical 'Eurasian' and the bastard 'half-caste' stand as images of a refigured nation. Nonetheless, it seems that this play's potential intervention in the hegemonic nation-building process is considerably weakened by the absence of assertively visible signs of such hybridity. The figure of the Eurasian is only anticipated at some point in the narrative future and the part-Aboriginal child haunts the margins of the stage, appearing briefly as a mute and virtually lifeless form almost completely obscured by the blanket in which she is wrapped.

Whereas Brand's capacity to unsettle racial categories may have been limited by the scarcity of suitable actors at the time, forty years later Louis Nowra was able to assemble a large multiracial cast in his epic adaptation of Xavier Herbert's *Capricornia* as a special bicentennial project in 1988. In my book *Sightlines* I argue that this play, particularly in its performative articulations of hybridity, celebrated miscegenation to the point of dislodging racism as the central narrative subject.[10]   Rather than reiterating this line of analysis, I want to examine briefly *Capricornia*'s treatment of Anglo-Celtic versions of whiteness and their functions within a counter-hegemonic narrative of nationhood that had particular significance at a time of celebratory national self-imagining occasioned by the Bicentenary.   Set in Port Zodiac (Darwin) in the 1930s, Nowra's epic play isolates and critiques mechanisms of racial privilege by making visible the rhetorical strategies through which the typical colonialist invasion narrative unfolds.   A key tactic of this counter-discursive project is to dramatise the feared decline of the white races that the invasion narrative attempts to avert. Hence, the play abounds with abject or degraded forms of whiteness embodied in characters who use addictive drugs, go combo, commit violent crimes or simply succumb to the tropical heat. When whiteness is not always already degraded, it is positioned as fundamentally at risk. This inherent instability is figured primarily through the anxiety surrounding Marigold, the colonial belle, who is eligible for marriage but not safely removed from the moral and physical temptations of Port Zodiac's degenerate society until close to the end of the play.   There are also a number of scenes that invoke Englishness as a signifier of whiteness only to dismantle its discursive power vis-à-vis the management of racial categories.   A case in point is the pseudo-English tea party during which Mrs Hollower (a missionary) and Dr Aintee discuss eugenics while the Aboriginal servant girls Tocky and Christobel parody their table manners and general attitudes in a running meta-commentary for the audience.

Nowra juxtaposes all these images of acutely visible whiteness to a chaotic transitional society where signs of Asian and particularly Aboriginal national belonging are increasingly the norm. At one point Norman, the 'half-caste' protagonist is left to run the formerly white-owned cattle station with the help of Tocky, now his lover, a handful of black stockmen and a Chinese cook. While Tocky's pregnancy briefly signals a hopeful future for those formerly positioned as the underclasses of imperial modernity's progress in Australia, the fact that she dies before her baby can be born suggests that the historical moment depicted was not ripe for the acceptance of a re-racialised northern society where negotiations between Asian and Aboriginal Australians could be more pivotal than those anchored by the white mainstream. Nowra's vision, however, means to be taken seriously as a contemporary model of the nation, not only in broader cultural terms but also in the more specific context of current Australian theatre. As part of a productive counter-bicentennial discourse aimed at interrogating the 'explosion of populist nationalism, commercialism and Eurocentrism' (During 179) that erupted during our year-long public celebration of imperial conquest, *Capricornia* staged an alternative image of the nation, one inflected by an acute awareness of the ways in which racial tensions have shaped our history.

In the past two decades, with the increasing momentum of theatre that stages a variety of Aboriginal and Asian-Australian identities, the hegemony of whiteness as a performative signifier of Australianness has diminished to some extent. Nevertheless, plays still emerge that appear to engage critically with our past and present racism while ultimately reiterating the fantasy of a white nation. My symptomatic (mainstream) example of this trend is David Williamson's 1997 play, *After the Ball*. Styled as an intimate family drama, this text seems to touch only tangentially on the issues of national identity, Hansonite politics and republicanism since Williamson's characters – all white Australians – are primarily enmeshed in the kinds of conflicts that reflect deep-rooted family disharmony. Yet it seems to me that the play is as much about a dysfunctional nation as a dysfunctional family. Through a series of flashbacks designed to convey the history of filial antagonisms, Williamson also supplies a telling political retrospective. For instance, Judy's pro-Asian stance is set against her father's fears of being over-run and outclassed by Asians in a dialogue reminiscent of the early 1980s debates about Asian immigration, an issue which has resurfaced with a vengeance since the rise of Pauline Hanson's One Nation Party.

In *After the Ball*, the race debate unfolds so that Ron, the father, expresses his outmoded racist views in ways that invite a critique, but one that is inevitably muted by a number of sleights of hand. The first is neatly effected through the play's gender politics, which generate considerable sympathy for Ron by developing his character against a powerful foil: his shallow, nagging, uneducated, socialite wife. The Sydney Theatre Company production emphasised this contrast by portraying Kate, the wife, as every bit the shrew while Ron presented as a kindly if old-fashioned father figure – just the kind of 'dinkum Aussie' that formed the bedrock of the post-war generation. The second trick, a rhetorical one, is achieved by citing Asian ingenuity/intelligence as part of a commonsense rebuttal of racism. Hence Ron maintains:

> I'm not a racist. A racist believes his lot's superior. I don't. *They're* superior. Year after year, the top students are always Asians ... Asians are brighter than whites. In fifty years time, all we'll be doing is collecting their garbage. (59)

This disavowal is uncannily similar to Hanson's much-quoted protestation: 'I am not racist. I know in my heart I am not racist ... I take people on who they are' (Hage 183). But whereas Hanson leaves herself open to attack because of her overtly 'redneck' politics,[11] Ron (and by implication Williamson) covers himself to some extent by tapping into a more subtle and persuasive discourse: the discourse of 'Anglo decline', which Hage has identified as the 'sense of Australia's dominant ethnocultural grouping being under siege' (181). Elsewhere in the play, the sense of decline is detached from the immigration debate to become a more general lament for the changes wrought by modernity and late capitalism (Barcan). It is this detachment, intensified in the Sydney Theatre Company production by an appeal to nostalgia via projected sepia-toned photos used to illustrate the flashback sequences, that invites Williamson's predominantly middle-class audience into thinking race is *not* one of the play's real vehicles of hegemonic nationalism.

In contrast to their parents, the younger generation in *After the Ball* seem to offer progressive and inclusive visions of contemporary Australian identity. Judy, the daughter, embraces the idea of a multicultural society, but her position is not all that far removed from Ron's in so far as her take on multiculturalism is based on discourses of enrichment and productive diversity that never really dislodge Anglo-Australians from the centre of the cultural map. Her stance illustrates Hage's argument that, 'rather than being imagined as a crucial part of the national body, multiculturalism is imagined as an object performing a function for that body' (149). Judy's particular kind of pluralism cedes no national or governmental space to Asian or other migrants but rather envisions a society/nation of ethnic enclaves clustered around an Anglo-Celtic centre. Not surprisingly, her views are never really scrutinised because they benefit from a broader construction that creates an ontological gap between multiculturalism and racist intolerance (Hage 77). And because Judy believes passionately in that gap, she can assert with confidence in relation to the 1997 Queensland state elections that One Nation political candidates will not win substantial support. (Many like-thinking Australians were proved wrong on that count.)

Within Williamson's conservative view of a multicultural society, Aboriginality hardly figures except in a throwaway line that praises Aborigines for having been responsible custodians of the land before the arrival of white settlers. Englishness, on the other hand, features prominently as that which Australians must reject in order to come of age as a modern nation. The narrative of the nation's filial journey towards full independence from the imperial centre unfolds through the son, Stephen, who initially leaves Australia for Europe in protest against the 1975 constitutional crisis when Prime Minister Gough Whitlam was sacked by the Governor General. We are compelled, or at least I am, to read the family argument on this political crisis as a commentary on the republican debate leading up to the 1999 referendum. In so far as Stephen galvanises the discourses of maturity and independence to stress the failure of Australia's democratic process in its deference to a distant and irrelevant political figurehead, the play stresses a need for a constitutional break with the monarchy.

What is interesting about Williamson's conjunction of republicanism and the discourse of Anglo decline in face of the increasing Asianisation of Australia, is that it perfectly captures the ambivalence and confusion that characterised many Australians' approach to the referendum. This ambivalence continues to be evident as we lumber, inevitably, towards the next constitutional debate and, according to most analysts, an eventual republic of some kind. Meantime, the continuation, almost ad nauseam, of the so-called race debate in both political and public arenas confirms Ien

Ang's argument that 'the ideological work necessary to actively *disarticulate* racism and nationalism ... has remained undone' (125). Our theatre's challenge for the new millennium is to create paths through this ideological impasse, to dilute the cultural power of whiteness by embracing heterogeneity and difference.

References

Ang, Ien. 'Asians in Australia? A Contradiction in Terms'. *Race, Colour and Identity in Australia and New Zealand*. Ed. John Docker and Gerhard Fischer. Sydney: University of NSW Press, 1999. 115-30.

Australian Journal of Political Science 36.2 (2001).

Barcan, Ruth. 'Hansonism, "Caring" and the Lament for Modernity.' *Meanjin* 57.4 (1998): 749-58.

Bedford, Randolph. *White Australia (or The Empty North)*. Unpublished TS. National Archives of Australia , CRS A1336/2, item 931. Copyright reading at Protestant Hall, Exhibition St, Melbourne, February 1909.

Bhabha, Homi. 'The Other Question ...' *Screen* 24.6 (1983): 18-36.

Brand, Mona. *Here Under Heaven. Tremendous Worlds: Australian Women's Drama 1890–1960*. Ed. Susan Pfisterer. Sydney: Currency Press, 1999. 143-208.

Davie, Michael. *Anglo-Australian Attitudes*. London: Secker and Warburg, 2000.

During, Simon. 'Australia 1788(?) – Foundling of the Enlightenment.' *Meanjin* 47.2 (1988): 179-93.

Dyer, Richard. *White*. London: Routledge, 1997.

Gilbert, Helen. *Sightlines: Race, Gender, and Nation in Contemporary Australian Theatre*. Ann Arbor: University of Michigan Press, 1998.

Gilbert, Helen, ed. *(Post) Colonial Stages: Critical and Creative Views on Drama, Theatre and Performance*. Hebden Bridge, Yorkshire: Dangaroo, 1999.

Hage, Ghassan. *White Nation: Fantasies of Supremacy in a Multicultural Society*. Sydney: Pluto, 1998.

Hanson, Pauline. 'Australia, Wake Up!' Maiden speech delivered to the Australian Federal Parliament, 10 September 1996. <www.satcom.net.au /freedom/ maidensp.html>

Kelly, Paul. 'Child of the Empire.' *Weekend Australian*, 10-11 March 2001: 17, 22-23.

Kelly, Veronica. 'Hybridity and Performance in Colonial Australian Theatre: *The Currency Lass*'. Gilbert, 1999. 40-54.

King, Preston. *Toleration*. London: George Allen and Unwin, 1976.

Lo, Jacqueline. 'Return of the "Native" in K.S. Maniam's *The Cord*'. Gilbert, 1999. 190-200.

Nowra, Louis. *Capricornia*. Sydney: Currency Press, 1988.

Perera, Suvendrini. 'Whiteness and its Discontents: Notes on Politics, Gender, Sex and Food in the Year of Hanson.' *Journal of Intercultural Studies* 20.2 (1999): 183-98.

Untitled review of *White Australia, or the Empty North. Bulletin* 1 July 1909, 8-9.

Walker, David. *Anxious Nation: Australia and the Rise of Asia 1850–1939*. St Lucia: University of Queensland Press, 1999.

Williamson, David. *After the Ball*. Sydney: Currency Press, 1997.

Notes

1 For detailed analyses of the referendum's results, see *Australian Journal of Political Science* 36.2 (2001). Commentators featured in this special issue discuss the varying roles of national identity, political affiliation, and partisanship and populist protest against politicians in defeating the proposal for a republic.

2 In this essay I use the term 'Anglo-Celtic' as a marker of ethnic origin, regardless of current geographical location. 'British' pertains to the broad geo-political entity of the British Isles and, at times, its erstwhile empire. It is not synonymous with 'English', which is used as a more limited descriptor to refer to things identified with England itself (as distinct from Scotland, Wales, Northern Ireland and so forth). These terms often have specific connotations and histories in the Australian context but all evoke whiteness in their most common usages. 'Anglo-Celtic' is the more neutral term and has been appropriated to categorise the dominant white culture while Britishness and Englishness often signify ambivalently as traits that both constitute and contrast with Australianness.

3 There is some debate over which of two extant versions of the script was used for this premiere. Unless indicated otherwise, references given here are to the copyright reading version titled 'White Australia – The White Man's Land, or, For Australia' held by the National Archives of Australia, CRS A1336/2, item 931. The play was performed under the title *White Australia; or, The Empty North* on 26 June 1909, at the King's Theatre, Melbourne.

4 It is worth noting that invasion narratives still persist in Australian popular culture, albeit in much diluted forms. Their continued purchase is evident in the recent support for the federal government's refusal to allow asylum seekers (mostly of Middle Eastern and Afghan origin) to be processed on Australian territory.

5 Walker's account of Asian-Australian trade in the period explains that these effects were not always clear or detrimental to Australian interests; nevertheless the general fear of being overrun by Asians often led Australian opinion-makers to paint political events pertaining to Asia in a negative light (68-84).

6 In this respect, the Northern Territory was regarded as only nominally an Australian possession during the early colonial era. The small Anglo-Australian population had failed to make the land productive and thereby stake a legitimate claim on it, and the local Aborigines could not always be trusted to defend white interests. Moreover, the significant numbers of Chinese already living in the area were figured, quite literally, as further 'chinks in the armour' (Walker 113-26).

7 The name is not incidental but, in all likelihood, chosen to evoke positive aspects of British character in the young Australian heroine (by dint of reference to Queen Victoria) as well as to signal eventual victory for her side.

8   In the script version held in the Library of Congress, Washington (D21455, deposited in 1910), Cedric becomes the focus of a redemption narrative when, in a compressed climactic moment he reclaims his whiteness (and thus his birthright) by double-crossing Yamamoto in a belated effort to take his proper place in the nation.

9   Library of Congress script (50).

10   This argument is based on the production's costuming codes, its embodied visual ironies, racial slippages and self-conscious character constructions, and on the performative virtuosity of a multi-racial cast playing across a spectrum of racialised characters (Gilbert 1998, 112-14).

11   Suvendrini Perera discusses at length the ways in which Hansonite politics have been affiliated with the working and rural classes with the result that 'redneck' has become an explanatory label for the versions of whiteness supported by Hanson's philosophies. In this formulation, class politics operate to distance normative Anglo-Celtic whiteness from the more extreme versions (191).

2.
'A new untravelled region in herself': women's school plays in late nineteenth- and early twentieth-century Australia

Susan Croft

Women's plays written for school performance in turn-of-the-century Australia exhibit a wide range of feminist politics which deserve critical attention. In addition these plays rewrite existing narratives and become a space to propose specifically Australian models of womanhood, drawing on a discourse of pioneering colonial development as distinct from British models.

Feminist scholars such as Susan Bradley Smith, in this volume and others, have begun to trace the history of Australian women's suffrage theatre and the Australian feminist playwrights of the late nineteenth and early twentieth centuries whose work was produced on the professional stage. Elsewhere in this volume Katherine Newey asserts the need to break down the binary division between Australian high and popular culture and quotes Helen Day on the inclusiveness and rejection of imposed hierarchies characteristic of women's theatre history. This essay begins to address a yet more marginal and feminised space within the hierarchies of cultural and theatrical history, a space not only of amateur performance but of performance primarily by and for children and young people: the community pageant, the school play.[1] In the process, however, it adds new names to the list of Australian feminist playwrights and explores how feminism begins to inform the girls' school play in this era (hence giving clues as to how it had begun to inform girls' education in this era). It addresses how the public performance of the school play or college pageant, a context in which aspirations and images of womanhood are enacted, becomes a space to propose models of Australian womanhood. Other essays in this volume discuss the received image of nineteenth and early twentieth-century theatrical 'Australianness' as 'masculine, working class, contemptuous of the coercive regimes of bourgeois respectability' (Newey 95) and propose more complex models for women where a broader model of 'Australianness' and 'respectable femininity' combine.

The focus on some of the contexts in which such feminine models, respectable or otherwise, were being developed, and on their relations to the 'centre' – the mother country and its dominant culture – re-writes existing narratives and proffers new models and representations of identity.[2]

However not all models proffered in this area of work are new or radical. While accounts of Australian theatre on professional stages have emphasised the emergence of home-grown drama, hailing the currency lad or lass and the bushranger drama, there were of course other home-grown varieties – or perhaps more accurately, locally-grown hybrids of British transplants, which celebrated Australia as colony and its relationship to the mother country as one of loyal devotion. The pageant is one form which becomes particularly prominent in the late nineteenth and early twentieth centuries throughout the English-speaking world. It was one expression of the burgeoning amateur theatrical movement, and was fuelled by a variety of factors including the export of cheaply-produced scripts, the desire of communities, geographic or other, to celebrate their endurance, their history and to entertain themselves, and the growth of a middle class with increased leisure time. Other pageants are primarily educational in intent, designed to inculcate patriotic values in young minds. The pageant is a usefully elastic form, providing large numbers of roles for groups of characters as well as individual speaking parts, and the opportunity for others to be involved in making the set and costumes. Published pageants are no doubt the exception and many more went unpublished but are documented in local newspapers.

While pageants in Australia – and indeed elsewhere the British colonies – may share with other more radical native-grown varieties of drama a discourse of pioneering development, sturdiness, dynamism, progression, it is not one of opposition to the metropolitan centre or political radicalism. It is primarily territorial and imperial and constructs national colonial identities through encouraging loyalty to, and identification with, the imperial mother country, often by exclusion of the unacceptable Other. In Australian Helen Ashton's *The King's Colonists: a Little Play for Little Australians*, the characters are introduced by the allegorical figure of Australia herself, who recounts the discovery of the country by the King's colonists.[3] It features allegorical characters representing the spirits of the country and its natural features (though with no mention made of Aboriginal myths of the landscape) and groups of children representing famous Australian 'types': Surf Maidens, Tennis Players, Stockmen who salute with their whips, Swagmen, Cricketers and Scouts. The Aborigines who appear are presented as a comic turn, speak in pidgin English and are presented as rueful but accepting of their lost status, rightfully ceded to the whites whose time has come. 'King Billy of the Blacks, with dog and gin' is eager to join the whites' 'budgeree' and recounts to his wife how: 'Me an' you own all this country one time, before white faller come. Now me ole man – no more 'possum, no more wallaby. *(Laughs)* No matter! Bimebyme go to sleep blackfeller, jump up white feller!' (6). Gertrude Latham's 1910 missionary pageant, *Australia's Past*, asserts more liberal values. Australia, seated on a throne, is presented by the allegorical representatives of her Wealth in Metal, Bushland, Sheepfold, Ocean and so on with exemplary gifts, but is rebuked by Faith for failing to see that her duty is to 'Pour out your wealth in teaching these to live' (4). 'These' are her unfortunate neighbours, New Guinea, Japan, China and India, who are now presented to her. Australia then accepts her God-ordained role to preach the gospel, a mission which includes a feminist element when she accepts the task set her by Freedom to rescue her Indian sisters from the misery of purdah, 'who chained from birth / Know not the meaning of friendship or mirth', and to 'Raise India up to a place by your side – / No longer a slave, but a Christian bride!' (5). The final image of the piece is unusual in the role it offers Aboriginals, as Australia invites the little Aboriginal Boy to sit side by side with her on her throne as 'Loved by one Father we will share the land'. Notably though, while Australia is portrayed as a grown white woman, he is merely a child. In Australian Enid Derham's pageant *Empire* (1912) each colonial power appears as a hand-maiden kneeling to Empire. Similar imperialist identifications are enacted theatrically in such Canadian works as Edith Lelean Groves's 1900 pageant *Canada Our Homeland*, celebrating the country's natural resources and, following the outbreak of war in 1914, in fiercely patriotic pieces like *The War on the Western Front*, where representatives of the Allies in the First World War speak of their role in overcoming the savage Hun; and *Britannia*, where the countries of the empire, Canada and her provinces foremost among them, pay homage to their patroness Great Britain.

However while the accepted discourse of colonial celebration may be marked by an emphasis on empire, expansionism, riches, loyalty to the mother country, duty, racial supremacy and identification between the colonies, a number of these qualities remain present in more radical discourse. Feminists arguing for the increase of women's rights within the colonies might hitch their argument to a familiar rhetoric of colonial vision, and while (sometimes) ignoring or rejecting appeals to loyalty to the mother country or racial supremacy, they shared the patriotism, sense of possibility, growth and expansionism of more reactionary discourse, or exploited its rhetorical potential allied to a radical cause.

Within the professional theatre, images of what would shortly afterwards be called New Women in Australian women's plays of the colonial period of around 1874-1910 are also marked by a particular identification of the emancipated woman's independence with her position as *colonial* woman. This draws on the discourse of colonial pioneering development, dynamism and progression, and the theatrical discourse of witty, inventive Australian currency lasses, and uses it to reinforce the campaigns for women's rights. Even where women's rights are not the primary concern of the work, in many Australian plays of the period, there is a celebration of female independence which is represented as typically and proudly Australian, far removed from traditional helpless womanhood and sometimes specifically contrasted to English female behaviour. This valorisation of the independent colonial woman can operate even where her actions fail to confirm the rhetoric of independence. In Australian Helen Benbow's *For £60,000!!!* (produced Sydney 1876), a classic melodrama with an Australian setting, the heroine Emma protests her sturdy Australian womanhood and is much criticised by her English Aunt Honora. While, in fulfilment of traditional melodramatic plot demands, Emma becomes suitably helpless when the action starts (fainting when her father is shot and being carried off by the villainous Tradby) Emma's Australian difference from Englishwomen is central to her intended appeal as a heroine. Even plays by Australian women that do not specifically identify their heroines as Australian tend to present their heroines as particularly physically boisterous and independent; examples here include Edith May Magarey's *True Love Runs Smoothly* (1896), and Mrs E. S. Haviland's *On Wheels* (1896). In plays by British women too, Australian women, for whom the key right, the suffrage, was attained relatively early, figured as pioneers and representatives of independent womanhood, showing the way forward to their British cousins. In British suffragist Catherine Dawson-Scott's play *Cousin Mary*, Mary is a medical student, is used to 'roughing it and coping as a single woman' and the play ends with her influence beginning to tell on her repressive English aunt.

It is also useful to compare school or college plays with pageants as creations which may be individually or collectively written but aim to express, inculcate and enact community values, with the majority or a large number of the school community performing. While all the plays discussed below were performed by the schools or colleges in question and published, thus enabling their survival, they represent different relationships to the school or college authority. The first comes from a tertiary or college level institution and was directly produced – she describes her role as 'overseer' – by the Principal of the college in question. The play is sometimes attributed to her, though the actual script was written by three others, identified only by their initials, who were in fact male. The second was written by a teacher but appears to have been constructed with specific pupils in mind, suggesting that their representation as characters on stage had a close relationship to their actual views and public personae within the school. The third, chronologically the earliest, and in content the most radical, is an adaptation from a well-known narrative and was actually written by students who, in the published version, are identified only by their initials.

A Mask (1913) is sometimes listed under the name of its director Louisa MacDonald who was the first College Principal of the Women's College of Sydney University from 1892-1919. A liberal principal with feminist views, she also ran its Women's Literary Society and supported endeavours like Janet Achurch's Australian tour of *A Doll's House*. The piece is a pageant written for the college's twenty-first anniversary, and aimed to 'show in symbol our hopes and aims'.4 In a brief foreword MacDonald writes that she was only one of several collaborators, the others being the writers Christopher Brennan and John LeGay Brereton, while MacDonald directed and designed the piece. Like other campaigning feminist works of the period, such as British suffragist Cicely Hamilton's *A Pageant of Great Women* and other pageants performed at women's colleges in Britain, the USA and elsewhere, which often expressed the 'aspirations of womanhood'.5 *A Mask* employs mythical and historical figures to symbolise women's achievements and potential. The cast of names may change but the intention stays the same: the celebration of women's achievements, their range and variety.6 Here the Sibyl, the wise woman who can see past, present and future, reads their names from the book of riddles. They include the familiar heroines – Joan of Arc, Florence Nightingale, Mary Queen of Scots and Penelope – plus the comic Sairy Gamp from Dickens, but also more challenging characters like Medea, Madame Curie, Charlotte Corday, and Angelica Kauffman. Patient Griselda is presented equivocally as one 'who for many men is still / The lovely model of subservient will'.

Most developed of any scene, however is that which most figures the play as Australian: the presentation of the prison reformer Elizabeth

Fry. She is given a lengthier introduction than most other figures by 'Rumour', and is then described in a long speech by a woman convict who speaks in a working-class accent. This section stands out from the rest of the piece as a vivid, realistic account, where the heroine is not enacted for the audience but discussed in the third person by a very down-to-earth admirer, a Woman Criminal. Despite the capital letters of her generalised title, this character is represented as an individual and given a voice, and in her own representation of Elizabeth Fry in the speech that follows is concerned to present Mrs Fry in non-idealised terms, with individuality and as a woman, not a saint:

> They jaw about Mrs Fry – yes 'er, an' be 'anged to them –
> Cockin' their eyes as if they thought she was sainted;
> She was no saint, I tell yer; she was a woman.
> I was in Newgate the first time ever I seen 'er,
> Where three 'undred women an' Lord knows how many kids
> Slept an' cooked an' ate an' quarrelled an' pigged
> In two old cells an' a couple o' wards, God help 'em ... (17)

In the respectable context of an Australian woman's college, the scene tacitly acknowledges the less than respectable beginnings of White Australia. Among all the 'universal' images of womanhood who appear in flowing robes in pageants from Middlesbrough, England to Rome, Georgia, this scene suddenly shifts class, style, accent and location to present and evoke real women, not mythical heroines. It contrasts jarringly with the subsequent return of the action to more conventional fare that occurs immediately following with the interlude where 'To the tune of "My Lady Greensleeves", the maidens dance a minuet' (18).

Madame Juliette Henry's play *The Birthday of the Headmistress* was written in French for performance by her pupils at a Hobart girls' school, where she appears to have been a probably temporary French mistress. It was published in pamphlet form in both French and English translation by Henry's patron Lady Hamilton, from which the quotations below are taken. Henry also published a volume of lectures (1894) she had given in Tasmania covering subjects including art, *Hamlet*, playwrights Corneille and de Musset, as well as 'The Education of Woman by the Mother'. Most interesting is her discussion of Ibsen's *A Doll's House*, which, she felt, though it showed great talent and dramatic power, was 'illogical, unnatural and dangerous', and compares Nora unfavourably to Octave Feuillet's Suzanne, a heroine who underwent a similar trial in which 'pure womanhood and dignity' won. Lady Hamilton apparently wrote an answering paper defending Ibsen, suggesting that this was an active intellectual exchange and debate.

Despite Henry's critique of Ibsen, her own play does encourage female ambitions beyond the domestic sphere.

The piece concerns preparations for a recitation to celebrate the headmistress's birthday, the conceit being that the play is set in a school in France, though pupils and teachers play versions of themselves. The piece emphasises throughout the importance of girls' education: thus Margaret, whose family have apparently lost all their money, can at least rejoice that she has now learned enough to go back and teach her little brothers and sisters. This will provide consolation for her mother as 'No real mother suffers for herself. She only suffers through her children' (11). While promoting ideals of female education as supporting the role of dutiful daughter, the play also suggests that new opportunities for women are opening up. The girls, congratulating themselves on the success of their arrangements for the party, joke that they will 'soon be equal to being members of Parliament', a joke that Mary Hamilton (presumably the daughter of Henry's patron and translator) takes seriously, celebrating the fact that women will soon be able to vote and then become MPs and ministers. While the other children mock her, they also acknowledge her status and she is given the most prominent position in the presentation and the role of reciting the 'most important piece … Victor Hugo's poem, about what an attentive mind can hear on the Mountain heights' (11,13). Even the servant Jane is swept up in this celebration of female possibilities, though she is perplexed at the question of who would be the servants if everyone became learned. The play ends with a reprieve for Margaret's family, when it is announced that her brother has achieved success in a country called Australia 'about which we know so little, I am ashamed to say', but 'where a young man can make his way quickly if he is but hard-working and temperate in his habits' (14). While the opportunities specifically referred to in Australia are offered to the young man, the references to women's imminent achievement of suffrage rights are in fact to Australia, where South Australian women won the vote in 1894 with other states gradually following, and all Australian women (except Aboriginal women who had to wait until 1967) gaining the vote in 1902, suggesting this as the context for pioneering female achievement as well as male.

In 1876 students of Presbyterian Ladies College, a secondary rather than university-level institution in Melbourne, produced a stage adaptation of Tennyson's *The Princess: a Medley*. It was adapted by four students who, in the published version, are identified only as: 'L.B., E.B., A.C. and B.McL'. Originally written between 1847 and 1851,

Tennyson's poem narrates a story in which a Prince and his two friends disguise themselves as women to enter the women's college which his betrothed, Princess Ida, has established and decreed to be off-limits to men. The men are discovered and battle breaks out between the Prince and Princess' countries. The Princess' side (her brother and his cohorts do the actual fighting) win but it is the women who are brought to submission, not by force but by vulnerability, as the experience of nursing their wounded enemy arouses their womanly love. By 1876 the poem had gained iconic significance and was already the site of controversy. As Gilbert and Gubar have explored in *No Man's Land*, *The Princess* rapidly became a key text for Victorian readers, critics and other writers in exploring the literal 'battle of the sexes' around women's rights and in particular women's higher education. Gilbert and Gubar identify a division that persists from the earliest critics to the late twentieth century 'betwixt the mockers and the realists', as the poem itself puts it, that is, between those who read it as misogynist mockery and those who see feminist celebration. The poem excited several dramatic adaptations or parodies, including W. S. Gilbert's play *The Princess* (1870), and in 1884 the most famous adaptation when Gilbert collaborated with Arthur Sullivan on the comic opera *Princess Ida*, which is clearly on the side of the mockers, pointing up the absurdity and grotesquerie of female intellectuals and their aspirations.

By contrast, in Britain in 1905 the pseudonymous woman writer Marnie=Charlon[7] published a version, *Ida*, in a volume with another play *The Queen's Degree*. *Ida* is designed to be performed between the first two scenes of Act II of *The Queen's Degree*, which is set in a fictional 'Angleria' and deals with the struggle of women students to be granted university degrees at the end of their studies. News is brought at the end of the piece that the Queen intends to confer on all female students who have passed the University Honour Examination the Degree of Bachelor of Arts. In fact, despite lengthy campaigns of which Marnie=Charlon's play is an exemplar, women were only admitted to Oxford University degrees in 1920, to Cambridge ones in 1923 and to full membership of Cambridge University only in 1947. Marnie=Charlon's *Ida* represents Tennyson straight and approvingly, reading celebration not mockery, endorsing the possibility of equality and quoting from Tennyson's original the Prince's assertion that 'either sex alone / Is half itself, and in true marriage lies / Nor equal, nor unequal: each fulfils defect in each' (28-9).

Predating Gilbert and Sullivan's opera but not Gilbert's play, the Australian version fits into neither tradition – or perhaps into both – as it mocks the absurdities of the original poem but also takes seriously the arguments around women's rights at its heart. The Presbyterian Ladies College piece adapts, 'develops' and, in effect, subverts the original. While borrowing most of the dialogue from Tennyson in the early scenes, the Australian students' version adds new material and departs radically from the original in the ending. Tennyson's emphasis on rivalry between the Princess's two seconds-in-command, Lady Psyche and Lady Blanche, is much reduced; the battle itself disappears; while the importance of Psyche's infant child in awakening the Princess's tender feelings, which caused one 1884 critic of the poem, S. E. Dawson, to describe the baby girl as 'the conquering heroine of the epic',[8] is quite absent, leaving only a scene where Cyril vows to bring the child back to her mother, thus cementing his bond with Psyche. Instead the men are court-martialled and banished and the scene which follows becomes a confrontation between the two Kings as Ida's father, Gama, and the Prince's father, Phogoeus, argue with the Princess as to whether she should submit and do her duty by marrying her betrothed. While Phogoeus' arguments in Tennyson are told to his son while Ida's are recounted in a letter, the Australian version, though drawing on Tennyson for Phogoeus' arguments such as his famous 'Man for the field, and woman for the hearth, / Man for the sword and for the needle she ...', presents Gama as mediator, proposing that the Prince remain in the college on probation for three months:

> If at the end his teacher's satisfied,
> And light dawns on him, do not cast him off;
> Time and yourself can conquer any man. (27)

The 'Commencement Day in the Women's University' scene that follows is an entirely new addition and parallels the earlier additional scene (iv) 'Lady Blanche's Examination-room'. In that scene, as the disguised men try to gain admission to the college, they are quizzed on their knowledge of history and literature and found wanting because of the masculinist bias of the papers they have submitted. Cyril, expecting approbation, gets pity for his foolishness in submitting a history paper full of references to male rulers with no mention of the queens Boadicea, Elizabeth or Anne, while Florian demonstrates his shameful ignorance of the Princess' publication, 'The Woman Shakespeare'. The authors show a nice self-mockery of feminist theories (with resonances today), while also endorsing them. Most pointedly the Prince's paper on the theme 'For woman is not undeveloped man, But diverse –' is dismissed as an idle jest, 'In truth, we thank you for the compliment' (15), says Lady Blanche, sarcastically. The title is a direct quotation from the Prince's concluding speech in Tennyson's original, where he accepts the Princess in marriage while emphasising the equality but difference of the sexes. In the Melbourne students' version the men merely demonstrate a 'healthy ignorance / [Which] Promises virgin soil' (15). In the Commencement Scene the Prince eventually passes his degree with an eighty-page essay on woman from which Ida has him read 'to testify his altered views' (28). The central thesis, to Phogoeus' disgust, is that 'Time's noblest offspring is its last ... each new race

> Stands king-like on the graves of older men
> Greater than they: and women opening up
> A new untravelled region in herself,
> Summing up all humanity hath known
> Most perfect. (29)

This is a doctrine not of sexual equality but female superiority! The Princess, approving his thesis in her capacity as examiner, agrees to marry him, envisaging their future shared task of showing men the way. Together they:

> Will clear away the vain pretence of power
> That seems to keep him up but drags him down;
> Will place him somewhat lower as is meet,
> Than the angel of his hearth; yet leave him space
> To climb the shining pathway after her. (30)

The play ends with a wedding ceremony in which the men swear to love and honour and obey. 'Faith in womanhood / Beats in his blood, and though he sink and fall, / Her smile shall comfort him, her hand shall raise' (29), concludes the speech, reinforcing the imagery of strength and female leadership which suggests its roots in narratives of pioneer endeavour.

The adaptation refers to its Australian context directly only once, when in the examination room scene the disguised 'female' would-be initiates, asked if they have learnt at all at the universities in their own land reply 'We thought to enter Melbourne, but the men / Who rule it write "No women study here"; / So much the green-eyed monster jealousy / Hardens the hearts of the authorities' (30). Yet, Florian goes on to say that when examined they passed with credit. These are direct allusions to the admissions policies of Melbourne University, which also serve to equate the men's benighted country (whose most vocal representative is it ruler, Phoegoeus) with Australia. Less directly the imagery of 'women opening up / A new untravelled region' suggests a discourse of new frontiers, possibilities and horizons, an image reinforced later in a speech where, along with 'the Grecian sense of art', 'the Roman power to rule' and 'Parisian grace', 'English purity' is situated as part of 'all that humanity hath known'; the past ground, already trod, on which the new generation of women stand to confront the new untravelled region. 'Happy man with such a partner' (30). It is a remarkable piece for a group of young women to write, subverting and rewriting the patriarchal authority of the poet laureate and supplanting his vision of marriage of newly gentle and submissive females with kind and courtly men with a more radical one, in which men are literally re-educated to prepare them for marriage as a mutual departure to create a new society in untravelled regions; a much more Australian vision of partnership and shared endeavour.

Rose Seaton's play, *Hatshepset Or Maat'ka-Ra, Queen Of Egypt, B.C. 1516-1481*, is another school play which, in a reversal of the accepted direction of trade where British models are exported from the metropolitan centre to the colonial outposts to be adapted to local circumstances, was written by a British emigrant to Australia. It was commissioned by her former employer, Cheltenham Ladies College (a British secondary level institution where she had taught drama and elocution) for performance by the pupils. Seaton's earlier published dramatic work *Andromeda: The Promised Gift* (1891), features a heroine who, without her knowledge, is promised as virgin priestess to the Goddess Diana as substitute for her mother, and when she inadvertently breaks the pledge, thus bringing about her younger brother's death, goes disguised to her father deliberately causing him to kill her. In contrast to this sad, victimised and self-sacrificial heroine, Seaton's 1906 piece traces the career of Queen Hatshepset, who rebels against her father's decree that she reign with her weakling half-brother Thothmes II. She is described as 'A woman of vigourous mind and eager fancy' (9), dresses as a man for part of the play, becomes a great queen and then regent as her son grows up, and ends the play looking back over her accomplishments.

According to the Introduction and Preface to the published version, by 1906 Seaton had moved to 'the antipodes' and the Cheltenham Ladies College magazine for Spring 1905 carried an item copied from the *Walcha News* in Sydney giving an account of recitations and a concert given by Seaton in aid of funds to relieve 'the distress caused by recent bush fires'. Seaton's former colleagues wrote to her in Sydney to commission her to write a play based on historical works on ancient Egypt, which she duly did. Despite Seaton's quoted personal 'circumstances of great anxiety and sorrow' (11) it is a much less sorrowful piece than *Andromeda*, and it is tempting to read the two pieces as emblematic of a change in consciousness. The former is a late-Victorian Old World piece, pre-occupied by a father-daughter relationship; a seam obsessively worked by Victorian women. Endless versions of Jeptha's daughter and similar myths celebrate filial duty and piety and female self-sacrifice, and many melodramas feature cruel but later repentant patriarchs and their misunderstood children; plays much occupied by the death of women, children and the same fathers, frail and remorseful. *Hatshepsut* is a new-century New-World piece presenting an image of proud independent womanhood, confident, optimistic and lively. It represents, like the Australian New Women heroines of other women playwrights, a role model and ambassador to the mother country for the cause of pioneering womanhood, bold and boisterous independent heroines, aspiring graduates and future career women.

References

Anon ['L. B., E. B., A.C. and B. McL']. *The Princess: a Drama of Woman's Future. Adapted and developed from Tennyson's 'Princess'.* Melbourne: Fergusson and Moore, 1876.

Adelaide, Debra. *Australian Women Writers: A Bibliographic Guide.* London: Pandora,1988.

Ashton, Helen. *The King's Colonists: a Little Play for Little Australians.* Sydney: W. Brooks, 1910.

Benbow, Helen. *For £60,000!!!: A Sensational Comedy in Four Acts.* Castlemaine, Victoria: n.p., 1874.

Blair, Karen J. *The Torchbearers: Women and their Amateur Arts Associations in America 1890-1930.* Bloomington: Indiana University Press, 1994.

Daley, C. and M. Nolan eds. *Suffrage and Beyond: International Feminist Perspectives.* Auckland: Auckland University Press, 1994.

Dawson-Scott, Catherine. *Cousin Mary. Carpet Plays.* London: J.M. Dent, c.1912.

Derham, Enid. *Empire: a Morality Play for Children.* Melbourne: Osboldstone, 1912.

Gardner, Viv. 'Introduction'. *The New Woman and Her Sisters: Feminism and Theatre 1850-1914.* Ed. Viv Gardner and Susan Rutherford. London: Harvester Wheatsheaf, 1992. 1-14.

Gilbert, Sandra and Susan Gubar. *No Man's Land, Volume 1: The War of the Words.* New Haven: Yale University Press, 1988.

Gilbert, W.S. *The Princess.* London: Samuel French, c.1870.

Gilbert, W.S. and Arthur Sullivan. *Princess Ida* (1884). *The Savoy Operas.* London: Wordsworth Reference, 1884. 255-312.

Groves, Edith Lelean. *Canada Our Homeland.* Toronto: William Briggs, 1900.

– *The War On The Western Front.* Toronto: William Briggs, 1916.

– *Britannia.* Toronto: McClelland, Goodchild and Stewart, 1917.

Hamilton, Cicely. *A Pageant of Great Women.* London: The Suffrage Shop, 1910.

Haviland, E.S. *On Wheels: a Comedy in Three Acts.* Sydney: C. Haviland, 1896 and ed. Susan Pfisterer. Women and Theatre: Occasional Papers 4.

Henry, Juliette. *The Birthday of the Headmistress.* Trans. Lady Hamilton. Hobart: Tasmanian News Office, 1892.

– *Lectures.* Hobart: Tasmanian Press Office, 1894.

Lake, Marilyn. 'Between Old Worlds and New: Feminist Citizenship, Nation and Race and the Destabilisation of Identity'. Daley and Nolan 277-94.

Latham Gertrude. *Australia's Past: a Mystery Play.* Fremantle: Peter and Salmon, 1910.

MacDonald, Louisa. *A Mask*. Sydney: n.p., 1913.

Magarey, Edith May. *True Love Runs Smoothly: a Short Comedy*. Adelaide: J.H. Shearing, 1896.

Marnie=Charlon. *The Queen's Degree and Ida*. London: Women's Printing Society, 1905.

Pfisterer, Susan. 'Australian Suffrage Theatre'. Unpublished PhD Thesis, University of New England, 1996.

Pfisterer, Susan and Carolyn Pickett. *Playing with Ideas: Australian Women Playwrights from the Suffrage to the Sixties*. Sydney: Currency Press, 1999.

Seaton, Rose. *Andromeda: The Promised Gift: A Dramatic Poem. Romances and Poems*. London: Simpkin, Marshall, Hamilton, Kent & Co. Ltd, 1891.

Seaton, Rose. *Hatshepset or Maat'ka-Ra, Queen Of Egypt, B.C. 1516-1481 with Scenes from Egyptian History*. Cheltenham: Thomas Hailing, c.1906.

Stange, G.R. ed. *The Poetical Works of Tennyson*. Boston: Houghton Mifflin, 1974.

Van der Water, Manon. 'Constructed Narratives: Situating Theatre for Young Audiences in the United States.' *Youth Theatre Journal* 14 (2000): 101-13.

Williams, Margaret. *Australia on the Popular Stage 1829-1929*. Melbourne: Oxford University Press, 1983.

Winn, Edith Lynwood. *A Vision Of Fair Women: A Dramatic Paraphrase Based Upon Tennyson's 'Dream of Fair Women'*. Boston: Baker, 1891.

Notes

1   See Manon van der Water for a discussion of 'how and why the field obtained and maintains a marginalized image' which is also highly relevant outside the US, the country she addresses.

2   Elsewhere I have explored the relationships between colonies in terms of their several imagined relations to each other and the centre, as expressed in women's plays of the period ('And shall Macaulay's proud New Zealander / Thus sit on me?': Sweet Girl Graduates and Bold Colonial Women in Canadian and Australian Women's Plays 1874-1910' at the Women and Texts conference, University of Leeds, 1997).   The comparisons with other plays from the English-speaking world and my assertions of the rarity or otherwise of finding a theme treated in a particular way is based on the larger research project involving reading several thousand plays written between 1837 and 1914 by women from Britain, Ireland, the USA, Canada, New Zealand and Australia, for a *Critical Bibliography of Women's Plays Published till 1914* (in preparation for Manchester University Press).

3   No biographical information is available, as far as I am aware, about Ashton or Gertrude Latham.   Enid Derham was a Melbourne-born poet, editor and academic 1882-1941 (Adelaide 49).

4   Foreword to programme for *A Mask*, quoted in Pfisterer (96), to which I am indebted for biographical details on MacDonald.

5   Hamilton's pageant was performed by suffrage societies at rallies and other events all over Britain and in Ireland between 1909 and 1911.   In the US, suffragists like Inez Milholland and later Hazel Mackaye staged feminist

pageants and processions from 1912 onwards. Karen Blair describes Mackaye's first commission by the National Women's Suffrage Association in 1913 to create a political entertainment in which 'Maidens blowing trumpets, dressed in flowing white Grecian robes, heralded the hour-long Allegory' (137). This was followed by a parade of floats representing countries where women had gained the vote, those who had won partial suffrage and those still in struggle and then the full procession of 5-10,000 marchers from women's groups who passed before an audience of around 250,000.

6   Hamilton's pageant features up to ninety prominent women from myth and history depending on the production. American Edith Lynwood Winn's *A Vision Of Fair Women* originally presented in Rome, Georgia as part of a suffrage campaign and published in 1891, features great women of story and history from Boadicea to Grace Darling, Bo Peep to Portia, Patient Griselda to Pocahontas together with the Goddess of Night, the Gypsy Queen and Bertha the Spinner. The piece is loosely Tennyson's poem *A Dream of Fair Women* but Winn's heroines are generally more active than his, where victims of love or self-sacrifice are to the fore: Fair Rosamond, Jeptha's daughter, Iphigeneia, Helen and Cleopatra.

7   This is the typographical layout of the name as given on the cover.

8   S.E.Dawson's *Study of the Princess*, Montreal, (1884) quoted from Stange in Gilbert and Gubar.

3.
Sightlines and bloodlines: the influence of British theatre on Australia in the post-1945 era

Julian Meyrick

*Since 1945 the impact of Britain on Australian theatre has swung between extremes of enthusiastic emulation and fierce rejection, marbled by a complexity not captured by simple notions of cultural dominance and/or subservience. However, unpicking the Gordian knot of this relationship is difficult given the ubiquity of many of its crucial manifestations. One way of avoiding gross generalisation is to focus on one type of empirical referent: articles in professional theatre magazines ('the trades'). By examining publications such as **Trust News**, **Theatre Australia** and **RealTime** for both the kinds of articles carried and their quantity, conclusions can be drawn about the nature and degree of British influence on Australian theatre in the post-War period.*

In 1947 Brian Jones, a young British Council administrator, was part of a team invited to Canberra by Dr H. V. Evatt, then Minister for External Affairs in the Chifley Government. Despite a reputation for being difficult, Evatt proved surprisingly receptive to plans for reviving Australia's Depression-ravaged theatre by bringing out a 'first class' British company to give performances of the classics around the country. The team established itself at the Hotel Canberra, then a hang-out for Liberal party big-wigs including the illustrious ex-Prime Minister Billy Hughes:

> When he was hard-up for someone to play with, Billy Hughes would summon me to a game of billiards. 'The British Council,' he asked me one day, 'what exactly is it?' Since the council began, in 1934, it has proved impossible to find a brief answer to this question. Its name gives no clue. The fact that my reply had to be injected into Billy Hughes' famous ear trumpet did not make things easier. I said something about cultivating closer cultural relations between Britain and Australia. 'Cultivating closer cultural relations,' he repeated. 'But why? And why officially? Haven't they been going on

naturally and satisfactorily for 150 years or so? Tell me. What
is the real purpose of the council? Trade? Secret Service?'
(*Sydney Morning Herald* 4 September 1982)

Billy Hughes's reaction signals both the revisionist historian's task and
the problems of carrying it out. For first-world ex-settler colonies like
Australia, not only are cultural values imposed by the colonising power,
but foundational categories (like 'cultural values') are handed down
with them in the process. Grids of force co-opt local trajectories to the
centre to such an extent that terms like 'ideology', 'hegemony', and
especially 'influence' cease to illumine specific relations and point
instead to generalised states of domination difficult to analyse because
rarely presenting fixed boundaries.[1] It would be easier, and less time-
consuming, to say where Britain and Australia diverge, where
Australian theatre assumes an autonomous self-identity. But even here
– in the welter of 'coming of age' metaphors describing Australian
drama during the 1970s, for example (see below) – doubts linger. Just
what kind of 'maturity' did Australian theatre attain? And if the answer
is (as it was), one founded on notions of a 'national voice' which was
'discovered' and allowed to speak, what anterior process of auricular
construction dictated that Australia should have a national voice to
discover in the first place?

This chapter attempts to address this problem – a familiar one to
postcolonial performance theorists (Gilbert and Tompkins, Gilbert
1998) – by relocating it. It would not be difficult to construct a
plausible account of British theatre's impact on Australia by looking at
what are, from the outside, peak moments of cultural influence. The
British Council accomplished one such in 1948 when it brought to
Australia Laurence Olivier, his wife Vivien Leigh and forty actors of the
Old Vic company. Designed to ameliorate the strong anti-British
feeling after the war (particularly in Melbourne, which had experienced
heavy casualties) the tour is almost too good an image of altered
political relations: on the one hand, Olivier as latter-day *pater familias*;
greeted like royalty, inspecting troops, making speeches on behalf of
King and Empire to an adoring public and unctuous press. On the
other, Olivier and Leigh abusing each other behind the scenes, drink,
neglect and lovelessness subsumed by an image of perfect partnership.
When the gap between public and private proved too much, Olivier was
shipped home with a poisoned foot, Leigh on the brink of nervous
collapse. But by that time the tour had been deemed a 'success', thus
clearing the path for illustrious (and not-so-illustrious) British
companies (Holden 224-45).[2]

Colourful though such episodes are, the valency of their meaning is ambivalent. For all the enthusiasm which greeted the Old Vic tour, there was a notable absence of support for Tyrone Guthrie's suggestion the following year that Australia pay to have its theatre artists trained and (a revealing choice of word) 'finished' in Britain (Guthrie 80). Nor is the Old Vic's metamorphosis into a national theatre paralleled by the wayward twists and turns of Australia's own 'national theatre debate' (Kirby-Smith 396-434). Fierce inter-state rivalries and an entrenched scepticism of the public benefit of high cultural production ensured that whatever imperial influence was exerted was mediated through a miasmatic web of local conditions. The processes of symbolic annexation are liable to swift and sudden reversals. Cultural codes and relations, established in an aura of mystifying dominance, provide, by definition, the means for their own subversion and re-appropriation. Who benefited from the renewed 'cultural relations' between Australia and Britain? If it seems on the surface that it was the latter, closer examination points to a more complex exchange that defined in a negative sense the very thing it apparently excluded. The tours, the reports, the endless comparisons with British efforts in the post-war period united feelings in a common direction. If there was one thing everybody agreed about Australian theatre, it was that it was *not* like Britain's.

This chapter therefore takes a different tack to the panoptic overview, instead keeping low, to the ground of concrete theatrical practice. It focuses on one type of empirical referent: articles in professional theatre magazines. 'The trades', as they are sometimes called, are an ephemeral field in Australian publishing. Nevertheless enough continuity exists between different journals to give a sense of Australian theatre's developing self-identity.[3] The advantage of such material is that not only was it written for practitioners, it was frequently written by them too. Mission statements, post-mortem reviews, cultural analyses, biographical sketches and shameless plugs take a self-consciously 'inside' view of the theatre scene. It is therefore possible to examine the texture of the ties that existed between British and Australian theatre by noting the accounts given of these by practitioners themselves. If the notion of cultural influence is to be more than a chasing of Hegelian *Zeitgeists,* such cognitive analysis is vital. This is particularly true of post-War Australian theatre where overseas travel and television were the harbingers of an expanded cultural awareness stretching beyond the binary wastes of postcolonial domination/resistance.

1945-1968: British theatre as ideal-type

The influence of British theatre in Australia in the three decades following the end of World War II can be summed up simply: the 'repertory idea'. This configured the development of Britain's own non-commercial professional theatre from the days of Annie Horniman and the Vedrenne-Barker Royal Court experiments in the 1900s. Rowell and Jackson give an overview of the movement's core values:

> Repertory ... from the very beginning [was] an idea in the minds of its advocates as much as it [was] a practical method of presenting plays. Already at the turn of the century, the idea of repertory – as a form of theatre opposed in every way to the dominant commercial theatre of the time – had become ... inseparably linked to such other central issues as the need to establish a state-subsidised national theatre organised on repertory principles, the need to encourage new... playwrights, and the need to raise the general standards of production. At the same time, awareness was growing of the theatre's potency as an educative as well as artistic or entertainment medium, and therefore of its importance in the cultural life of the country as a whole. (2)

There were four aspects to establishing repertory companies and these crop up repeatedly in the literature surrounding Australian theatre of the period: the need for appropriate buildings, for ensembles of non-star actors, for a national playwright base, and for an 'educated' (i.e. non-commercial theatre-loving) audience. When in 1955, after tours by the Stratford Memorial Company in 1950 and 1953, the Menzies government established the Australian Elizabethan Theatre Trust as a means of delivering state support to the arts, its first newsletter posted objectives in every way consonant with these goals. 'The aim of the Trust (AETT) is to make the theatre in Australia the same vigorous and significant force in our national life as it was in England during the reign of the first Elizabeth', it announced in imperial cadences echoing those of SMC's director, Anthony Quayle (cf. Neill 164-66). '[It] will seek the co-operation of kindred organisations overseas such as the British Council, the Stratford Memorial Theatre and the Old Vic Theatre' ('AETT Letter To Members' 21 April 1955). Unsurprisingly, its first act was to appoint an Englishman, Hugh Hunt, as Executive Director, and he promptly declared his determination to set aside the 'amateur' values of the Australian scene and replace them by his own 'professional' approach to play production (Hunt). By way of example he offered a production of *Medea* with the ill-tempered expatriate Judith Anderson in the title role, which at staggering cost toured the state capitals. If it did not have the hoped-for galvanic effect on audiences, it perhaps did bring home that the vastness of the Australian landscape complicated Euro-centric notions of stock companies. While the rest of Hunt's tenure was punctuated by classic-looking productions with a touch of the Old Vic Theatre School about them, a different course of action gradually outlined itself as the way forward for state-supported theatre. This did not subvert the repertory idea as it was handed down, essentially as a model to follow, by British theatre. But it did refashion it to local conditions and, in the process, expose the limits of its applicability.

The first problem lay in the fact that Australia, unlike Britain, was a political federation of nominally equal states. Early AETT circulars reflect the regional, as opposed to the national, focus of its concerns. In April 1959 appeared a more substantial broadsheet, the first *Trust News*, citing as its *raison d'être* the need to keep people informed of what the AETT was up to in other states (1). By 'people' the Trust meant anyone with a strong interest in the performing arts and it is significant that for the first years of its life there was little attempt to distinguish between sponsors, subscribers and practitioners. All were assumed to have an equal stake in the development of the performing arts industry. And, in a financial sense, this was not far from the truth. Despite constant agitation by the Trust's Chair, 'Nugget' Coombs, and withering comparisons with Canada and Britain, money from the federal government remained niggardly. Significant contributions came from the states, or from sponsors and subscribers who were perforce state-based, and expected to get their money's worth. Tension was particularly acute between New South Wales and Victoria, with their strong metropolitan centres of Sydney and Melbourne; and South Australia, Queensland, Tasmania and Western Australia.[4] Each Trust initiative had to be weighed in the balance of state self-interest. The upshot for theatre was the gridlock of plans for a national company that in Australia, as in Britain, had been the major focus of public discussion since 1945. Whereas both ballet and opera established companies that were, in theory at least, national in scope, the Trust was forced twice to abandon initiatives for a national touring theatre and continually justify its financial outlays in terms of regional impact.[5] As a result, the glory of British repertory theatre's institutional entrenchment was not replicated in Australia. The *Trust News* shows instead a demotic collection of part-funded ventures struggling to escape the embrace of commercial theatre and its best-known face, J. C. Williamson's ('the Firm'), still the major purveyor of theatre in the country. When, in time, state-based repertory theatres were established, each had quite different *personae*.[6]

The second limitation of the repertory idea was that in itself it was not a prescriptive model to be slavishly copied. Australian critics heaped enthusiastic praise on yet more tours by the Old Vic: 'every woman gently sighed when [Miss Leigh] turned to reveal in the trailing skirt a startling inset of white ruffles' (*Daily Telegraph* 29 September 1961); Katharine Hepburn was 'chucklesome, lively and, the true test, feminine withal' (*Sun* 23 August 1955 – see Photo 2); or the Royal Shakespeare Company, 'one of the few really great theatre companies in the world' (*Sydney Morning Herald* 24 March 1970). Nonetheless there was no agreed template for ensuring such 'standards' could be locally reproduced. Again this can be seen in the national theatre debate, whose proponents could never agree on priorities. Though the Trust had started by declaring that it would neither capitalise buildings nor provide on-going funds for permanent companies, these, in practice, became the chief calls on its budget. The 1960s in Australia saw the non-commercial professional theatre struggling to equip appropriate theatres, seed acting companies and develop subscriber audiences against a backdrop of snail-like increases in state support. While in Britain a strongly interventionist Labour government under Harold Wilson achieved an even expansion in the performing arts sector, the impact of subsidy in Australia was piecemeal and divisive. The residual structure of the pre-war 'little theatres', largely amateur but with complex 'professional' aspirations, clashed rhetorically and industrially with an emergent state-supported system, with every institution appealing to different precedents: the Abbey Theatre (Hunt), the Moscow Arts Theatre (the Independent), the Group Theatre (the Ensemble), the Berliner Ensemble (the Emerald Hill Theatre), the Old Vic (the Melbourne Theatre Company and Old Tote).[7] The response of the Trust under its second director, Neil Hutchinson, was to pull in its horns. Significant failures (of a Sydney Union Repertory Theatre in 1962, for example)[8] placed it under financial pressure. It sought a way out, to the disgust of the industry, by entering into arrangements with J. C. Williamson and Garnet Carroll to co-produce West End and Broadway hits. Thus by 1968, the date at which the Trust was superseded by the Australian Council for the Arts as the country's major subvention agency, the configuration of the industry was almost a parody of British theatre with its neat stratifications between amateur, professional and commercial sectors.[9]

Table 1

	MTC 1953-55	Old Tote 1963-65	SATC 1965-67
No. of plays produced	40	14	13
No. of overseas plays produced	37	14	10
No. of British plays produced	26	7	6

If the British experience was more aspiration than realisation for the structure of Australian theatre, then where was its influence felt? Table 1 provides repertoire information for the MTC, the Old Tote and the South Australia Theatre Company for the first three years of operation – and the answer to the question: British influence meant British plays. Each company program shows a 90%+ percentage of overseas drama, and of this over half represents works from Britain. This in turn reflected the tastes of a body of Trust-nominated theatre managers rapidly acceding to positions of program control in the new state-supported industry. Many of these practitioners were British by birth and training (Robert Quentin, John Sumner, James Mills, Elsie Beyers, Alan Edwards). Even when they were not (Tom Brown, Robin Lovejoy, John Clark, John Tasker) they had invariably spent time in Britain absorbing its production methods and sensibilities. They turned to Britain as a source of plays – 'properties' in commercial parlance – as a matter both of professional contacts and cultural preference. With drama by local writers such a small percentage – with Lawler, Beynon, Coburn, Locke-Elliot and Seymour overseas, and Patrick White twice rejected by the Adelaide Festival – this influence was accentuated. The *Trust News* shows the 'social fund of knowledge' of its readership (in Norbert Elias's phrase) as heavily Anglo-centric: plugs for Trust productions of *Salad Days* and *Look Back in Anger* (1958), *Rape of the Belt* (1960), *A Taste of Honey* and *A Man for All Seasons* (1962), and *Henry V* (1964); coverage of the *Summer of the Seventeenth Doll* in London (1957), *The Bastard Country* in Birmingham (1964) and *One Day of the Year* in Nottingham (1967); and a 'Theatrelover Crossword', with clues like 'Loan's better half character who needs entertaining on the stage' (9/65); 'Author of Royal Hunt of the Sun' (12/65) and 'Opening scene of Man and Superman' (Spring/66). Such intimacy with British drama was all the more telling because it was not especially self-conscious.

By the end of the 1960s Australian theatre was thus a compounded paradox: an industrial structure both heteromorphic and unstable; underfunded given the scope of its activities, but unique, deep-rooted and resilient. This structure was freighted with a drama largely culled from Britain, whose mores seeped into stage production lending the results an Anglophone gloss. It could not last, and while it did it was deeply resented. The visceral effects of British influence were plainly visible for all to see – or rather, hear. 'Playwrights Have Not Had the Final Words on Australian-ness', Eunice Hanger observed in an article for *Theatregoer,* a short-lived 'trade' from the early sixties:

> Producing an Australian play five years ago, I was asked by a girl who was playing a young married woman of average education whether I wanted her to assume an Australian speech. 'No more than you're using', I said, without thinking. She laughed, and drew attention to my answer as a joke. I had implied that she normally spoke Australian, since she had not been assuming any difference from her ordinary speech. She found this amusing because she had been teaching speech for years. On her own implication, she had not been teaching Australian. (Hanger 52)

1968-88: British theatre as fraternal co-worker

Table 2[10]

	Nimrod Theatre 1970-73	APG 1970-73	Playbox Theatre 1976-79
No. of plays produced	29	25	28
No. of overseas plays produced	8	2	8
No. of British plays produced	4	1	3

Table 2 shows the play programs for the first years of operation of three major 'New Wave' theatre companies of the 1970s: Nimrod Theatre (Sydney); the Australian Performing Group and Playbox Theatre

(Melbourne). It demonstrates a striking change from the repertoire of the state theatre companies: 70%+ Australian work, with at best, 13% British drama (and this mainly Shakespeare). Such a reversal reinforces the belief, loudly trumpeted at the time, that New Wave theatre was a unique irruption, throwing over an enervated colonial sensibility and releasing a flood of creative energy rooted in the sensory experience of 'being Australian'. Some of these clarion calls are well-known and stand as orthodox sign-posts for the 'national' drama they both described and exhorted into being (Hibberd, Hewett, Brisbane, 'Not Wrong').[11] Others are less frequently quoted, perhaps because they hint at an essentialising, even racialised mentality lurking at the edges. 'Every Australian is aware of wearing the outback on his shoulders', argued Sydney critic for the *National Times* Kevon Kemp in a 1973 issue of the *Elizabethan Trust News:*

> The big spaces haunt us all; our economy and politics as well as our arts all mirror the vast spaces and the empty light and heat of the big country ... I suggest that this sort of awareness of the physical effects of space and heat – the hot weather that leads to an utmost economy of gesture and movement and the need for 'air' around people – are some clues to the acting style we are after. The Australian is also possessed of a vitality and physical handsomeness beyond most other lands. On the Australian Ballet's overseas tours, the sheer health of the company and the beauty of its dancers' bodies are always remarked on. Even such a specialised judge as 'Playboy' magazine gave a verdict after a photographic study of Australian girls that they were the most beautiful in the world.

While it is not entirely fair to judge the New Wave by its more dubious supporters, it is striking how the term 'Australian', which in the 1950s and the 1960s acted as a simple mark of origin, returned as a positive category of order in the 1970s. So complete was this return rhetorically (so saturated is the use of national descriptors) that the result almost overnight was an entirely different frame of reference for theatrical activity. A 'reality disjuncture', as sociologist Melvin Pollner has called it, was achieved; a shift not just in cultural effects but in structural values, which brought in its wake a new vision of theatrical past and future.[12] In this British theatre again played a part, but now as an antipole against which 'real' Australian drama had to struggle to define itself:

> Because we are *not* a European nation, tempered by millenniums of war and civil strife, with a history riddled with kings and peasantry and class warfare and Christianity and a culture we are proud to call our own: we are barbaric, working

class, provincial, ignorant nation of understimulated slobs ... And if instead of inventing an Australian theatre ... we continue to put on reverent examinations of foreign classics, so that bejeweled furry old women can sit through them bored stupid but glad to make the sacrifice for the sake of their cultural jingoism ... we may as well give up the fight. Australian theatre is Australian plays: we must not only write them or perish, we must recognise them or perish (Ellis 43).

In 1976, the *Trust News* was superseded by *Theatre Australia* as the major professional theatre magazine in the country. The hand-over was elaborately self-conscious, with the new 'trade' strongly declaring its national(ist) credentials: '*Theatre Australia* is the first truly national and comprehensive theatre magazine to be published in Australia... It will carry nationwide reviews of professional productions and a full range of articles on Australian theatre practice and its evolution' (*Theatrescope* 2, September 1976). Issued monthly, the new magazine provided, as had the *Trust News*, an inter-state survey of the industry. But the felt-meaning behind it was different. Where for the *Trust News* Australian theatre was the sum of state-located parts, for *Theatre Australia* it was an ideal stretching beyond different regional expressions. Throughout the late 1970s and early 1980s *Theatre Australia* embroidered its approach with the rich tones of national assertiveness; its reviews, articles, published letters and 'quotes and queries' and 'whispers, rumours and facts' sections all showing a marked inward turn. Vestiges of the past such as the Trust itself found themselves the object of attack (over its unsuccessful commercial co-production strategy, for example), while an avowed Anglophobia fuelled a pro-Australian editorial stance to both repertoire programming and industry appointments.[13]

It is above all the sense of direction in Australian theatre that changes. *Towards an Australian Drama* (Rees) becomes *After the Doll* (Fitzpatrick); the hankering after a distant point of coherence replaced by the confident genealogising of a body of dramatic work recognisably, if not uncontentiously, 'Australian'. The critical debates of the period – about the 'social reportage' feel of writers like Williamson and Buzo, for example, or (the reverse) the lack of 'characterisation' in New Wave plays – are predicated on the existence of a homogenised sensibility which needs only elaboration. The violent collisions that ensued – between critics and practitioners, between practitioners and bureaucrats, between older practitioners and younger ones – took their force not from antagonistic points of view but from a dispute over shared territory. No-one questioned the construct of Australian drama as such, or showed much awareness that it *was* a construct – an invention of the profession, not a 'found' cultural object. And most *ex-post facto* accounts have not questioned it either, however much they might deplore the limits of its thinking (Radic). The New Wave remains largely what it was to those who bore witness to it thirty years ago: an exemplary and privileged expression of a 'national' drama.

To provide a critical reappraisal of such an 'ideological complex' is beyond this analysis. Nevertheless it is interesting, turning back to the *Trust News, Theatre Australia,* and other short-lived trades like *Masque* and *Australian Theatre News,* that the 'renaissance' of Australian drama, while acknowledged, is tempered by evidence of continuity with its Anglo past casting it in a more partial light. The flow of British companies continued: the RSC, out in 1970, 1973 and 1976 (the last encompassing, thanks to Britain's hyperinflation and the company's desperation for dollars, even the most remote country areas); the Prospect Theatre, successor to the Old Vic, out in 1971 and 1979; and a steady stream of Anglo pot-boilers piggy-backing their marketing on the penetration of BBC television programs and the consequent celebrity of the 'stars' involved.[14] References to British theatre, if drowned out in volume by references to Australia's, are still easily familiar. Numbers of British practitioners regularly arrived to present before the local industry: John Arden, playwright-in-residence at the University of New England in 1974; Albert Hunt, founder member of Brisbane's Popular Theatre Troupe in the same year; William Gaskill, directing for the Old Tote in 1975; and Martin Esslin, Dorothy Heathcote and John Osborne, out for National Playwrights Conferences in 1974, 1975 and 1976 respectively.[15] And while interest in overseas theatre broadens to include Asia and Eastern Europe, it is still articles on the 'London Scene' that are carried most regularly.[16]

Such strong residual concerns speak of a network of cross-cultural associations by no means displaced or voided by the language of national resurgence. A stint in Britain, for example, was still part of the Grand Tour for Australia's numerous tertiary-educated baby-boomers taking their place on the ground floor of the theatre industry. And their experience was often strongly positive, even while it was acknowledged it had to be transposed into an Australian context. John Romeril, a leading New Wave authorial voice, spent six months in Britain on a Churchill scholarship in 1972, sending back two detailed reports on his experience of companies such as Inter-Action, Cockpit Theatre and Oval House:

> London... [is] a monopoly board ... of vigilant, vociferous community groups. A staggering number of people are concerned with issues of power and control. Trade Union

action is more and more action precipitated by the rank and file. Once unrepresented powerless sections of society ... are organised to secure their rights ... This ground swell is what I mean by grass roots politics revitalised ... Theatre too – or part of it – has taken the great leap forward. Inter-Action and groups like it are experiments in shared decision-making, one theatre-worker ... one vote. From that the jump to jointly conceived, collaborative projects has not been great. Roles and traditional hierarchies have been broken down. Actors, writers and directors have begun to work so closely they're virtually inter-changeable and in fact often function all three ways.

Romeril hints at the area where British theatre exerted most influence in the 1970s: 'alternative' company structure and operation. Though the number of British plays programmed declined at all levels, key British ventures provided pathfinder models for their Australian New Wave counterparts. A remarkable homology exists between the Nimrod Theatre and the English Stage Company (ESC), for example. Philip Roberts's history of the Court, based closely on primary source material, details aspects of the company which find exact parallels at Nimrod: an avowed commitment to new plays (and consequent rocky relationship with critics); a contemporary approach to classics, particularly Shakespeare; a duumvirate or tripartite artistic directorship, not always harmonious; an unstable relationship between Board and staff; and a split between 'aesthetic' and 'political' orientations in the programming. That Nimrod took the ESC as a model, particularly in the mid-part of its life, is admitted by the company's leaders.[17] And though there are divergences – the Court was involved in battles against censorship that in Nimrod's case had largely been won by the time it opened its doors – nevertheless the professional links between them were strong. Nimrod's production of *The Removalists* won the George Devine Award in 1972, while the ESC went on to stage plays by Buzo and Williamson in 1971 and 1975 respectively.

Despite the nationalist rhetoric, then, many aspects of New Wave theatre can be seen to be British in origin if not application: the empowering of artistic directors at the expense of management boards; the functional specialisation between artists, administrators and technical support staff; the increasing reliance on state subsidy; above all the belief in the cultural value of 'high art' – or 'critical' – drama. The Australian and British scene converge not, as in the past, for reasons of cultural subjugation but out of a sense of shared professional concern. Australian alternative theatre synchronises with British (and US) equivalents as part of a transnational wave of politically progressive, aesthetically radical, cultural activism. To argue that Australian theatre was similar to Britain's because it sprang from similar industry structures is to miss the point. It is those very industry structures that practitioners struggled so hard to instantiate, and thus the reason why the British experience continued to provide Australian theatre with its subtext, albeit an unacknowledged one throughout the 1970s and early 1980s.

1988 and beyond: UK theatre as non-comparable professional Other

> The Bicentennial year of 1988, with its plethora of plays critiquing or celebrating various versions of Australian nationalism, appears to have marked some sort of determining moment in the subsequent confidence of playwrights in interpolating a unified or inclusive national narrative. The challenge of Aboriginal land-rights claims and the presence of a large migrant multicultural population have rendered problematic older versions of Australian history ... In the following decade more regionally-based and identity-focussed work has come to the fore, and Aboriginal writing and theatre-making have become major components of a theatrical endeavour which adopts new modes of historical enquiry. *(*Kelly 2-3)

Though, as Vaughan points out, the present is more difficult for historians to contextualise than the past (217), contemporary Australian theatre seems to take its cue from a decline in nationalist energy which so strongly marked it up to the late 1980s. Thereafter, as the essays in *Our Australian Theatre* make clear, in the 1990s different on-stage concerns – with gender, ethnicity, and regional and Indigenous perspectives – marry with different political conditions to seed an industry at once more diffuse and more fluid than in preceding decades. Open questioning of the New Wave's blithe nationalism is only one aspect of such a change. Other dimensions include a decline in real levels of subsidy, a rise in capital costs, a drop in audiences and an on-going erosion of the category of 'high art' in an economy increasingly marked by global trends in the consumption of cultural goods. The surface results of this are clear enough, even if the deeper causes remain harder to discern: state theatre companies have softened in their support for new drama; 'alternative' companies have repositioned themselves in niche markets catering to self-contained audiences; and community and regional theatres, flourishing so strongly in the 1980s, have either died away or reinvented themselves as administratively light-weight enterprises working on a project-to-project rather than program-oriented basis.   It is no longer possible to talk about Australian theatre as either homogenised ideal or practical whole exhibiting intellectually centripetal features.   For the time being at least, the fragmentation that has marked the sector over the last ten years looks set to continue as the mark of its identity.

1989 was the year in which *New Theatre Australia,* the successor to *Theatre Australia* (which ceased trading in 1982), put out its last issue. Thereafter, Australia was left without an on-going nationally-focused professional theatre magazine.[18] In August 1994 the first regular issue of *RealTime,* a cross-art form magazine with a performance focus, appeared. The format of this broadsheet reinforces the impression that, just as select repertoire statistics are unlikely to provide an accurate snapshot of contemporary dramatic concerns, so the industry itself is hard to gloss. Articles show the idea of 'theatre' being challenged, if not subsumed by, broader notions of 'performance' and the resulting mixed-media and hybrid understandings of the field; while these categories, in turn, are reflected in subsidy structures and artists' self-imaging.   And while sections like inter-state reviews used in earlier magazines are still employed, 'straight' theatre articles currently comprise less than 5% of content. The concerns of practitioners from the mid-1990s onwards seem at once more wide-ranging, more eclectic and more 'theory-literate' than those from earlier decades.

With national sensibility no longer the chief locus for intervention in Australian theatre, the influence of British theatre as a model, either conscious (as in the 1950s and the 1960s) or unconscious (as in the 1970s) has likewise declined.   The picture of the industry sketched recently by Fotheringham, for example, is one in which a renovated commercial sector strategically allies with local initiatives (part amateur, part professional), while international festivals challenge both the cultural hegemony and the resource dominance of mainstream non-commercial theatre.   Fotheringham concludes that an important exclusionary mechanism has been destabilised and new stage voices and new ways of getting them heard effected:

> As long as professionalism was a term centrally defined by the training institutions and the major state companies whose practices, repertoire and control of the market was the perceived goal, ragged edges could be ignored or at least minimized. The emergence of both venue managers and of annual festivals as entrepreneurs challenged this hegemony, and the rise of independent or sub-contracting organisations which tour artists and shows further eroded it ... This has created new opportunities for artists (particularly young artists) and companies to shift the boundaries even further ...

Whereas a decade ago a NIDA hegemony/state theatre monopoly seemed the most accurate way to characterise the dominant force in Australian theatre, the different agendas of other major agents are starting to reshape the field, not principally from without but from within. ('Boundary Riders' 36)

Only time will tell if this cheery assessment of the 'collapse of the centre' – and the progressive impact of resurgent commercial imperatives in particular – is correct. Fotheringham's analysis is not inapplicable to Britain. The disillusionment with established companies as the proper frame for new work is echoed by Bull in his overview of British mainstream theatre in the period, while the Thatcher government's economic rationalism generally, and its savage arts cuts in particular, as outlined by Pick and more recently Peacock, point to the deregulated conditions which both countries have experienced in the last twenty years. Yet, while the economic situations are similar, it is harder to line up the two theatre cultures isomorphically. Greater sensitivity to international pressures on the one hand and a renewed local focus on the other have stretched both industries between super and sub-national magnetic poles – and taken them further from each other.

Yet as we have seen, the impact of British theatre on Australian theatre was always complex. Unpicking the Gordian knot of these 'cultural relations' is especially difficult given the ubiquity of many of its crucial manifestations. The influence of British theatre may be seen not only at peak moments of cultural display but in the ebb and flow of everyday industry relations: the contours and values of rehearsal practice, production practice, company organisation, marketing styles, approaches to audience development and so on. The relationship between the two cultures has been at its most profound when it has been least remarked (or effectively disguised). So whether Britain's influence in the post-1945 period was in retrospect hegemonic – and whether it has entirely disappeared today – is a question which needs to be treated with care. Australian theatre is a nebula of artistic influences draped around a loose industry frame. Trying to identify a core identity prior to its engagement with outside cultural influences is a useless task. Negotiating outside cultural influences is not only what Australian theatre *does,* it is what it *is.* When, in turn, it hands back products of its own theatre – whether in the shape of touring companies like Circus Oz, or cross-media cultural events like the opening ceremony of the 2000 Olympic games, or in a migrating stream of actors, directors and designers to both Britain and the US – these should be seen as expressions of a fully-fledged artistic sensibility. That this sensibility is capacious rather than narrowly defined, permeable at the boundaries and demotic, does not indicate a lack of specific cultural gravity. The influence of British theatre on Australian theatre becomes, through a series of Archimedian intellectual pulleys, the retooling of a European artistic legacy to service an at times anxious, at times energetic, rethinking of national imaging and related cultural activism.

References

'Australian Drama Special.' *Theatre Quarterly* 7.26 (1977): 47-110.

Australian Elizabethan Theatre Trust Newsletter. 21 April 1955. Continued by *Elizabethan Theatre Trust Circular to Members* (17 May 1957-3 February 1970).

Australian Elizabethan Theatre Trust Broadsheet (7 March 1966-31 January 1969).

Australian Theatre Review 1.1 (September 1973).

Brisbane, Katherine. 'The Most Secret Shakespeare.' *Elizabethan Trust News* 2 (Autumn 1972): 2-5.

– 'Not Wrong – Just Different'. Holloway 91-96.

Bull, John. *Stage Right*. New York: St. Martin's Press, 1994.

Covell, Roger. 'The Role of Little Theatre.' *Hemisphere* 8.12 (December 1964): 2-7.

Elizabethan Trust News (see also *Trust News* and *Theatrescope*). 1.1-15.5 (December 1971-October-November 1989).

Ellis, Bob. 'Go Out and Write an Australian Play (It's Not Hard).' *Bulletin* (3 October 1970): 42-43.

Fitton, Doris. *Not Without Dust and Heat*. Adelaide: Harper & Row, 1981.

Fitzpatrick, Peter. *After the Doll*. London: Edward Arnold, 1979.

Fotheringham, Richard. 'Where the Hell is Camberley?' Review of *The Brass Hat* by Thomas Muschamp. *Theatre Australia* (November 1977): 39.

– 'Boundary Riders and Claim Jumpers: The Australian Theatre Industry'. Kelly, ed. 20-37.

Gallasch, Keith. Correspondence with the author, 21 November 2001.

Gilbert, Helen. *Sightlines: Race, Gender, and Nation in Contemporary Australian Theatre*. Ann Arbor: University of Michigan Press, 1998.

Gilbert, Helen and Joanne Tompkins. *Post-Colonial Drama: Theory, Practice, Politics*. London: Routledge, 1996.

Guthrie, Tyrone. 'Report on Australian Theatre'. *Australian Quarterly* (21 June 1949): 9-30.

Hanger, Eunice. 'Australian-ness.' *Theatregoer* 1.4 (May-July 1961): 52-54.

Hewett, Dorothy 'Shirts, Prams, and Tomato Sauce'. Holloway 108-18.

Hibberd, Jack. 'Wanted: A Display of Shanks'. Holloway 89-90.

Holden, Anthony. *Olivier*. London: Weidenfield & Nicolson, 1988.

Holloway, Peter, ed. *Contemporary Australian Drama* (Rev ed.). Sydney: Currency Press, 1987.

Hunt, Hugh. 'What is the Future for Australian Theatre?' *Voice* (4 September 1955): 25-6.

Hutton, Geoffrey. *It Won't Last A Week!* Melbourne: Sun Books, 1975.

Jones, Brian. 'How Olivier and Leigh Changed Theatre in Australia'. *Sydney Morning Herald* 4 September 1982.

Kelly, Veronica, ed. *Our Australian Theatre in the 1990s*. Amsterdam: Rodopi, 1998.

– 'Old Patterns, New Energies'. Kelly, ed. 1-19.

Kemp, Kevon. 'Towards an *Australian* Acting Style.' *Elizabethan Trust News* 6 (31 March 1973).

Kessell, Norman. Review of *The Lady of the Camellias* by Alexandre Dumas. *Daily Telegraph* 29 September 1961.

Kippax, Harry. 'Masterly Shakespeare.' Review of *The Winter's Tale* by William Shakespeare. *Sydney Morning Herald* 24 March 1970.

Kirby-Smith, Virginia. 'The Development of Australian Theatre and Drama, 1788-1964'. Unpublished PhD Thesis, Duke University Press, 1969.

Kruger, Loren. *The National Stage: Theatre and Cultural Legitimation in England, France and America*. Chicago: University of Chicago Press, 1992.

McConachie, Bruce. 'Using the Concept of Cultural Hegemony to Write Theatre History'. *Interpreting the Theatrical Past: Essays in the Historiography of Performance*. Ed. Thomas Postlewait and Bruce McConachie. Iowa: University of Iowa Press, 1989: 37-58.

Marr, David. 'The Peanuts Problem.' Article on the AETT's *Dead-Eyed Dicks*. *Theatre Australia* (July 1977): 58-62.

Masque. September/October 1967-May/June 1971.

Meyrick, Julian. *Nimrod and the New Wave, 1970-1985*. Sydney: Currency Press, 2002.

Neill, M. 'Post-Colonial Shakespeare? Writing Away from the Centre'. *Post-Colonial Shakespeare*. Ed. Ania Loomba and Martin Orkin. London: Routledge, 1998. 164-85.

New Theatre Australia. 1 -12 (September/October 1987-September/October 1989).

Peacock, D. Keith. *Thatcher's Theatre: British Theatre and Drama in the Eighties*. UK: Greenwood Press, 1999.

Pick, John. *Managing the Arts? The British Experience*. London: Rheingold, 1986.

Pollner, Melvin. *Mundane Reason: Reality in Everyday and Sociological Discourse*. Cambridge: Cambridge University Press, 1987.

Radic, Leonard. *The State of Play: The Revolution in the Australian Theatre since the 1960s*. Ringwood: Penguin, 1991.

RealTime. August 1994-August 2001.

Rees, Leslie. *Towards an Australian Drama*. Sydney: Angus & Robertson, 1953.

Roberts, Philip. *The Royal Court Theatre and the Modern Stage*. Cambridge: Cambridge University Press, 1999.

Romeril, John. 'Some Remarkable Institutions: Art and Socialisation.' *Elizabethan Trust News* 6 (March 1973).

Rowell, George and Jackson, Anthony. *The Repertory Movement: A History of Regional Theatre in Britain*. Cambridge: Cambridge University Press, 1984.

South, Josephine. *Ten on The Tote (An Illustrated History of the Old Tote Theatre 1963-1973)*. Sydney: Old Tote Theatre Company, 1973.

Sumner, John. *Recollections at Play*. Melbourne: Melbourne University Press, 1993.

Theatre Australia. August/September 1976-May 1982.

Theatregoer. 1.1-2.12 (Winter 1960-1962).

Theatrescope (see also *Elizabethan Trust News* and Trust News). 1-3 (June 1976-December 1976).

Trust News (see also *Elizabethan Trust News* and *Theatrescope*). April 1959-December 1967.

UNESCO 'Conference of Professional Repertory Theatres' (Proceedings). Adelaide, 21-25 March 1966.

Vaughan, Virginia.   *Othello: A Contextual History*.   Cambridge: Cambridge University Press, 1994.

Ward, Peter.   *A Singular Act: Twenty-Five Years of the State Theatre Company of South Australia*. South Australia: Wakefield Press, 1992.

Notes

1   For a discussion of problems in deploying 'ideology' as an explanatory term in theatre historiography see Kruger (8-11), and for a similar (though more positive) discussion of 'hegemony' see McConachie (37-58).

2   Holden's discussion of the tour makes clear its political intent and the high-powered forces behind its realisation (see especially 224-26).

3   The trade magazines examined for the purposes of this chapter are: the *Elizabethan Trust News* (also called *Trust News* and *Theatrescope*); *Theatregoer; Masque; Australian Theatre Review; Theatre Australia; New Theatre Australia*; and (very briefly) *RealTime*. Two broadsheets are also included: 'AETT Letters/Circulars to Members' and 'AETT Broadsheets', the first geared to theatre-goers, the second to practitioners.

4   Kirby-Smith gives a picture of the Trust in its first year of operation: 'By the end of June, 1955, when the first annual financial report was prepared, the Trust had accumulated a capital fund of £114,308/17/11, £29,831/3/6 of this sum coming from the federal government which gave £1 for every £3 raised through private subscription by the end of the previous August. From the first year of active operation... all the state governments and the city councils of Sydney, Melbourne and Brisbane (joined by Adelaide in 1956-57) granted annual support. Initially, however, there was no guarantee of federal subsidization beyond the original grant; assurance of continued support came only in 1957-58 when the amount of £20,000 was allotted to the Trust, this being increased to £47,100 for the following year.' (440-41).

5   The abandoned companies were the Australian Drama Company (1956-57) and the Trust Players (1959-62).

6   The Union Repertory (later Melbourne) Theatre Company, founded in 1954, started life as a two-weekly repertory and, despite its association with Australian plays like *Summer of the Seventeenth Doll* (1955), showed a semi-commercial propensity in its early programming (Hutton, Sumner). Its Sydney cousin, the Old Tote Theatre, opened in 1963, was allied to the University of New South Wales and the National Institution for Dramatic Art, drawing financial support from the first and (unwaged) student actors from the second (South). The South Australian Theatre Company, originally conceived as an adjunct to the 1965 Adelaide Festival of the Arts, was nationalised in 1972 by

Don Dunstan's Labor government, who saw it as one of the 'city-state' glories of the 'Athens of the South' (Ward).

7   For an overview of the 'little theatre' movement see Kirby-Smith (203-67). For examples of the kind of friction referred to here see actor/director Doris Fitton (especially Chapter 7 'The Trust') and for a worm's-eye view of the time see Covell: 2-7.

8   The failure of this little known but historically significant venture is covered in *Theatregoer* 2.1 (November 1961): 5 & 33-35; and 2.2-3 (December/January 1961/62): 5-7.

9   'What is Drama in the Australian Context?' asked David Bradley morosely at the UNESCO Conference of Professional Repertory Theatres in 1966: 'The basic paradox in which theatre in Australia is involved is largely a matter of our history and our distance from the great English-speaking centres. Theatre is an art of great cities, and unless our cities change character rapidly or we find some ingenious and indigenous new ways of reaching audiences; and barring the sudden appearance of some great national cause which will detonate our thinking playwrights and thinking audiences, the paradox will be with us for some years to come: namely, insufficient trained talent chasing a steadily declining popular audience' (7).

10   These figures are estimates only based on repertoire information supplied to the author by Geoffrey Milne, La Trobe University. Authoritative figures await compilation from the APG (Australian Performing Group) archives in the La Trobe State Library collection, Melbourne.

11   These three pieces are reprinted in Holloway's *Contemporary Australian Drama*. A list of relevant newspaper articles would be lengthy indeed, but should include Brian Hoad, 'Cultural Convulsions' (*Bulletin* 26 August 1972); Brisbane, 'Theatre Bigger and Healthier' (*Australian* 4 June 1974); and *Theatre Quarterly* 'Australian Drama Special' 7.26 (1977).

12   Similar to Kuhn's paradigm shift, Pollner explores in detail the way reality disjunctures are resolved in situations of potential social conflict. See especially Chapter 4 'Mundane Puzzles and the Politics of Experience' (69-86).

13   That *Theatre Australia's* editor, Robert Page, was an Englishman was an irony that did not noticeably softened its nationalist stance. For examples of Anglophobic articles see Fotheringham (1977) and Marr.

14   The bottom of the barrel was reached in a spate of commercial shows co-produced by the AETT in the late 1970s that were little more than British TV sit-coms in live performance formats. These included: *Doctor in Love* and *Man About the House (Trust News* May 1977); *Love Thy Neighbour (Trust News* March 1978); and *George and Mildred (Trust News* June 1979).

15   Some British practitioners stayed longer: Colin George, Elizabeth Sweeting and Richard Cotterill were all associated with Prospect: George became artistic director of the South Australian Theatre Company from 1977 to 1980, Elizabeth Sweeting Head of Arts Management at Flinders University from 1976 to 1981, and Richard Cotterill the last director of the Nimrod Theatre, 1986-87.

16   Early editions of *Theatre Australia* carry overviews of London theatre by expatriate playwright Alan Seymour. From May 1979 onwards articles by British critic Irving Wardle appear monthly, until the demise of the magazine in 1982. Editorials also show a strong awareness of developments in British theatre – presumably a reflection of editor Robert Page's knowledge of the British industry.

17   See Meyrick for further elaboration of the shared thinking between Nimrod, the New Wave and British first and second-wave theatre.

18   Other short-lived 'trades' include *Centrestage,* published by Showmedia International Pty Ltd, whose first issue came out in September, 1986, and thereafter appeared monthly for a further twelve; and *Theatre Australasia,* which appeared in 1994/95, putting out a small number of issues with a trans-Tasman focus.

4.
Reconciliation Shakespeare? Aboriginal presence in Australian Shakespeare production

Elizabeth Schafer

In the lead-up to the millennium several Australian productions of Shakespeare featured Aboriginal presence in ways that invited reflection on Reconciliation politics. These productions raise important issues about the history of Aboriginal participation in Shakespeare production, and Reconciliation Shakespeare can be seen to be a completely unique Australian contribution to the stage history of Shakespeare.

The notion of 'playing Australia' in relation to Shakespeare production has until recently received comparatively little critical attention from Shakespeare scholars. Yet Australian productions, adaptations and rewrites of Shakespeare are a particularly critical and high-profile arena for negotiating the subject of Australianness, as these productions can play against received notions of what Shakespeare is/should be in order to mark out, very forcibly, a different Shakespeare, one that is distinctively Australian.[1] Even more distinctive is Shakespeare production featuring Aboriginal identity, where Shakespeare readily becomes implicated in discussions of such complex topics as land rights and reconciliation. 'Reconciliation' is a highly politicised and difficult term to define in relation to Australia: it means different things to different people. Aboriginal playwrights Deborah Mailman and Wesley Enoch in their powerful text *The 7 Stages of Grieving,* ridiculed the entire concept by reducing the term to 'Wreck' 'Con' 'Silly' 'Nation' (Enoch and Mailman 295).[2] However, in this paper I want to argue that Shakespeare has provided Australian theatre with a useful space in which to dream of reconciliation – specifically between Aboriginal and Anglo-Celtic cultures – even while the reality is always of course much more complicated. In this, Australian theatre has produced a series of uniquely politicised productions which do not fit neatly in the dominant international debates about race and Shakespeare production, which tend to focus not on indigenous identities but on African-American or Black British performers.

The history of Australianised Shakespeare production in the professional theatre begins fairly recently, with a landmark production by Robin Lovejoy: his 1972 *Taming of the Shrew* for the Old Tote Theatre Company in Sydney was 'exuberantly Australian' (Leiter 673) and the first explicitly and confrontationally Australianised Shakespeare in mainstream theatre.[3] This *Shrew* helped establish a fashion in the 1970s for relocating Shakespeare productions to identifiably Australian contexts, a fashion which was to flourish particularly at the Nimrod theatre in the 1970s, and later in the work of the Bell Shakespeare Company. Lovejoy's production was a box office smash, toured to Canberra and was televised by the Australian Broadcasting Corporation. Lovejoy relocated Shakespeare's Padua to an unspecified country town in New South Wales at the beginning of the twentieth century, and substituted recognisable Australian types for the play's characters – Katherina was Miles Franklin's Sybylla without her brilliant career, Petruchio was a Digger back from the Boer War, and the tinker Christopher Sly became a 'freely ad-libbing drunken swagman' (Leiter 673-74). While Lovejoy's production set a fashion for playing Australia at the same time as playing Shakespeare, it was not until the 1990s that this was extended to include a clearly identifiable Aboriginal presence. Writing in 2001, John Golder and Richard Madelaine (9) comment that their discussion of Shakespeare in Australia 'would be brief indeed' if 'work by or featuring indigenous Australians were to be our sole criterion'. And yet in recent years Aboriginal theatre practitioners have made significant interventions in the staging of Shakespeare as directors and as actors. Wesley Enoch, one of the few Aboriginal theatre directors who has directed Shakespeare in the professional theatre in Australia, argues:

> It's still a political act when an Aboriginal person walks on stage ... You can't help but see their skin, and all the resonances that come with that at this point in time. (*Sydney Morning Herald* 26 May 1999)

The presence of identifiably Aboriginal performers in Shakespeare can thus be highly charged; raising the issues of land rights, discrimination and reconciliation politics, and using the attention that automatically accrues to a major Shakespeare production to increase public debate around these issues.

The productions discussed here all included significant Aboriginal presence, but it is as well to register the proviso that deploying an Aboriginal actor to inject a newly and overtly politicised meaning into Shakespeare may be provocative but has its limitations. Because the institutional context of all these productions was not Aboriginal – the theatre spaces, the production companies, the recorded reception by generally, although not entirely, non-Aboriginal reviewers – then certain constraints in addressing reconciliation would be always in operation. A production sponsored by, for example, the Sydney Theatre Company (STC), would inevitably be inflected by that company's institutional politics and perceived obligations. The STC is unlikely to use Shakespeare to present a case for reconciliation that involves major sacrifices for its predominantly non-Aboriginal subscribers.[4] However, while Gilbert (75-76) usefully reminds us that reconciliation must 'allow expressions of Aboriginality to serve the strategic interests of Aboriginal peoples rather than those of the mainstream theatre and its public'; she also adds that there is 'a good case for including "Aboriginalised" productions of classic texts as important sites of intervention in the historical processes that have stereotyped representations of indigenous peoples or simply erased them from our stages' (79). I would argue that 'Aboriginalised' Shakespeare is one such important site of intervention.

Contextualising my chosen group of Shakespeare productions is made difficult, however, because of absences and gaps in theatre history: when famous Aboriginal performers such as the Colleano circus family passed as Hawaiian in order to acquire more status than could ever accrue to them as indigenous Australians (St Leon), it is small wonder that there is little record of Aboriginal presence in Shakespeare productions before the 1970s. Gilbert argues:

> The visible signs of Aboriginality as ascribed to the performing body will of course vary from actor to actor and according to the theatrical contexts in which that body displays itself, but, if our performing arts culture is to address the historical stereotyping of indigenous peoples, it is strategically desirable to populate Australian stages with actors who identify as Aboriginal are recognised as such. (80)

The history of Aboriginal performers 'recognised as such' in Shakespeare begins, for me, in 1991 in a moment that underscores Australia's lack of an historian like Errol Hill, who has carefully documented Black American participation in Shakespeare production. In 1991 David Hough (*Bulletin* 8 October) commented of director Andrew Ross's production of *Twelfth Night* that he 'is not the first director to use Aboriginal actors in a Shakespearian play' but Hough speculates that Ross 'is the first ... to give them equal billing'. Hough gives no details and he may be referring to schools, youth productions and other areas traditionally ignored by historians, where Aboriginal theatre workers have been working with Shakespeare for a long time.

However in 1999 veteran Aboriginal actor Bob Maza felt that thirty years previously 'Casting Aboriginal actors in Shakespearean roles was ... unheard of' (*Sydney Morning Herald* 21 May 1999). One pioneer in Australian theatre was undoubtedly Brian Syron, who was probably the first Aboriginal director to direct professional Shakespeare in Australia. He directed *The Merchant of Venice* for the Old Tote during 1971-72 when he was an Associate Director for the company, and this production included the then little-known actress Helen Morse as Portia. Syron 'had acted in Shakespearian parts in the United States' (Chesson 178) but he did not act in Shakespeare in Australia, nor did he confront indigenous race issues in his *Merchant of Venice*.

Andrew Ross's 1991 multicultural *Twelfth Night* was made doubly significant because he chose it to open a brand-new Perth theatre company, Black Swan. Reviewers stressed 'the hot tropical colours of the north-west' (*Australian* 23 September 1991), which many felt sure was Broome, and the mix of guitar, flute, didgeridoo and hitting sticks for music. The *Fremantle Gazette* (8 October 1991) felt 'The director's choice of actors mirrors the cosmopolitan nature of our society and puts a particular spotlight on the theatrical talents of Aboriginal people'; however, the *West Australian* (21 September 1991) was worried that the casting decisions 'run the risk of underlining damaging racial stereotypes', and found 'notably an orientalist "Asian princess" and a brawling Aboriginal drunk'. While most reviewers commended Stephen Albert's drunken Sir Toby as extremely funny, the general tendency was to stress the multicultural and therefore non-confrontational mix of the production, and not to unpick specific meanings suggested by casting. Certainly in his flagrant, antisocial, and damaging alcoholism, an Aboriginal Sir Toby has the potential to be confrontational rather than simply amusing, and the discomfort created by casting Sir Toby as Aboriginal might be critical. By contrast the risk in stressing the multi-cultural dimension is that a production may lose its political bite. Jatinder Verma, in a discussion of British Asian theatre, offers a useful discussion of multi-cultural productions as:

> those productions featuring a racially-mixed cast which, by not seeking to draw attention to the racial mix of the producing team, are not generally attempting to confront the dominant text-based convention of British theatre. (194)

While Verma's analysis cannot be simply redeployed into the very different cultural context of Western Australia, his depiction of multi-cultural theatre as non-confrontational seems pertinent to the critical reception of this *Twelfth Night*.

Sue Rider's 1994 multi-racial *Taming of the Shrew* for La Boite in Brisbane was similarly received as multicultural, but arguably this production had more of an edge than it was generally credited with.[5] In the 1994 production Rider cast Aboriginal Deborah Mailman as Katherina, and in the 1996 revival cast Aboriginal Roxanne McDonald. If Rider's casting was in fact merely an example of multiculturalism it would not have been necessary to insist on Katherina being Aboriginal, a casting that inevitably upped the political stakes of the production. Penny Gay has explored how the narrative of *The Taming of the Shrew* can have extra nuances in a culture 'tamed' or subjugated by its colonisers, where the colonised are feminised by their defeat and political impotence.[6] Making Katherina the unfavoured and Aboriginal daughter coloured the undervaluing and indeed demonising of Katherina, and evoked the troubling histories of the taming/abuse of Aboriginal women in Australia. The sense of period in this production was also crucial; *Theatre Australasia* (May 1994) described it as 'post-World War II, with its rush of patriotism for Blighty, and British and Australian flags bound together in garlands' and the *Brisbane Review* (22 March 1994) commented appreciatively on the period detail: 'creme de menthe for the ladies at the wedding reception while the men drink cognac'. There was Glenn Miller music and Petruchio singing 'You Say Potato'. Thus Rider chose to place the action of the play in a time when Aboriginal people did not have the vote, even though they had been allowed recently to die for their country in the Second World War. This Petruchio was taking on a wife who *would*, in the historical context evoked by the production, be routinely discriminated against. Mailman's Katherina was certainly capable of looking after herself – the *Courier Mail* (19 March 1994) commented on her 'awesome half-nelson' – but her long final speech of submission reflected only too appropriately the comparative disempowerment of many Aboriginal people in contemporary Australia.

One reason reviewers downplayed the multicultural aspect was the playful cross-cultural, cross-gender casting of the ensemble of eight performers. For example, Baptista was played by an Aboriginal woman, Lesley Marller; Bianca was 'a WASP princess' (*Bulletin/Newsweek* 30 March 1994). However, Rider's Katherina, Mailman herself, believes her presence in Shakespeare cannot help but comment on contemporary race issues. She has argued that as a performer she constantly faces difficulties 'because of where we are as a country in terms of race relations and reconciliation' (*Sun-Herald* 2 May 1999) and that:

It's not just me on stage but it's the rest of my people too ... it can't only be Deb Mailman, it's Deb Mailman and a lot of history. It places a lot of weight on us as indigenous artists. The fact is, when we walk on to the stage it's still a political statement, whether the intention is there or not. (*Australian* 21 May 1999)

If this is true, then the ending of *The Taming of the Shrew*, traditionally read as Katherina submitting and reconciling herself to Petruchio, had a political edge in this production that has not been available in any other professional production of this play.[7] But once the Aboriginal Katherina had submitted to, and been reconciled with, the Anglo-Celtic Petruchio, this Petruchio woke from his dream and realised he was still the drunken tinker Christopher Sly, as he had been at the beginning of the action, and not married to a tamed heiress at all. He then uttered a single word as epilogue: 'Shit'. Rider's ending here suggested that reconciliation on the lines envisaged by the Slys/Petruchios of the world is only possible in dreams and plays.

After the *Shrew,* Mailman's next mainstream Shakespeare was Helena in the all Aboriginal *Midsummer Night's Dream* presented as part of the Sydney Festival of the Dreaming (12 September-4 October 1997, Photo 3); a festival which also included an Aboriginal *Waiting for Godot*.[8] This *Dream* was directed by Noel Tovey, an Aboriginal choreographer and director of international standing, and it followed the same director's production the previous year of *The Aboriginal Protestors*, an adaptation by Mudrooroo of Heiner Muller's play. In relation to his *Dream*, Tovey posed the challenge: 'Who understands the words dream and dreaming more than Aborigines?' (*Australian* 21 December 1996) and he chose to make the forest an Aboriginal space. A Rainbow Serpent covered the forest floor as well as the costumes of Titania and Oberon. Titania's bower was a giant waratah and spirits/fairies included Kangaroo (veteran Aboriginal performer Justine Saunders) and Lyrebird. Tovey, however, was also outspoken about the politics of his production; he wanted 'to show that, first and foremost, Aboriginal people can act as well as anybody else – and that there are many different ways of interpreting Shakespeare' (*Sunday Telegraph* 21 September 1997).[9] The mere fact that this production was cast as entirely Aboriginal made a strong statement, particularly following shortly after a tour by the RSC of a production of the same play directed by Adrian Noble, a production then already available as a film.[10]

Reviewers were mostly cautious but John McCallum felt an opportunity had been missed: the production was 'respectful to a fault' and there was 'no hint of radical revision or overtly political content'

(*Australian* 18 September 1997). This fails to consider that the very fact that the production happened at all was breaking new ground in terms of Shakespeare production, and it is important to acknowledge that once the STC had hosted Tovey's *Dream* a whole series of Shakespeare productions that foregrounded Aboriginality took place. While Tovey's declared point of entry to the play was dream and dreaming, *Midsummer Night's Dream* is in some ways a text that also readily alludes to reconciliation: the comedy ends in three marriages and a reconciliation between Oberon and Titania. However the cost is enormous: Titania has been humiliated by falling in love with Bottom, she has submitted to Oberon and given up her precious changeling boy; Demetrius is still technically under a spell and in that condition marries Helena; Hippolyta is war booty as well as a bride. Tovey's production of this troubling play can thus also be read as offering a reflection on the potential *costs* of reconciliation.

In 1999, however, reconciliation and Shakespeare really came together in the Australian repertoire, a year in which two *Romeo and Juliet*s, one *As You Like It* and a *Tempest* were all read as speaking to, and of, reconciliation. The Bell Shakespeare Company's 1999 touring *Romeo and Juliet*, which foregrounded race, was the only one of these productions directed by an Aboriginal director, Wesley Enoch. The play was substantially cut and edited by playwright Nick Enright and the production cast the Montagues as Aboriginal. It unapologetically sought to present a 'parable of reconciliation' (*Sydney Morning Herald* 26 May 1999). The play was set in the back streets of an inner city where Aboriginals still did not have citizen rights, and the two houses 'both alike in dignity' were probably not alike 'in terms of economic status, health care, educational opportunities and life expectancy' (*Sydney Morning Herald* 28 May 1999). Meanwhile Sue Rider at La Boite joined forces with Wesley Enoch's former company Kooemba Jdarra to produce a *Romeo and Juliet* (opened 26 April) which had the Capulets as Aboriginal. Kooemba Jdarra's artistic director Nadine McDonald was assistant director and her sister Roxanne McDonald, formerly Katherina in Rider's revival of her *Shrew*, played Lady Capulet, a role conflating Lord and Lady Capulet. Rider's director's notes to the cast stressed that:

> Juliet is Murri and Romeo non-indigenous. The prejudice they are fighting is race-based and their story, in pointing up the absurdity and tragic consequence of ignorance and intolerance, can become a powerful plea for reconciliation.

Romeo and Juliet has often been appropriated to discuss divisions between communities and Aboriginal presence in this play almost inevitably produces a stress on how much reconciliation can cost, since in Shakespeare's Verona reconciliation can only be achieved after the deaths of the young lovers, plus Mercutio, Tybalt and Paris.

In the same year *As You Like It* was also used quite explicitly used to discuss reconciliation and land rights, when Mailman starred as Rosalind in a production directed by Neil Armfield at the Belvoir Street Theatre, Sydney (Photo 4). By this stage in her career Mailman had become the first indigenous person to win the prestigious Australian Film Institute Best Actress award for her role in the film *Radiance,* and her track record in Shakespeare now also included Cordelia in a Bell Shakespeare *King Lear.* Although the spectacle of a pregnant and Aboriginal Cordelia is potentially very resonant, and the play speaks easily of dispossession and land rights, this production directed by Barrie Kosky was, in Jatinder Verma's terms, multicultural, and avoided what Wesley Enoch describes as a deliberate 'politics of skin' (*Sydney Morning Herald* 28 May 1999).

Mailman's Rosalind was much applauded and she was very much a focus for the production, with her image made up in clown whiteface featuring on the production programme and posters. As artistic director at Belvoir Street, Neil Armfield has often produced and promoted plays with significant Aboriginal content and he has led the way in casting Aboriginal performers in Shakespeare.[11] In this production Armfield cast Bob Maza, one of the few Aboriginal performers who has sustained a long standing and successful career in the theatre, as Duke Senior, and Aboriginal presence was also very much to the fore in Arden with both Silvius and Phoebe. The *Sydney Morning Herald* (21 May 1999) commented that 'casting an indigenous actor as Duke Senior, the original custodian turfed off his land by political chicanery, gives Shakespeare's comedy a different spin' and quoted Maza's dry understatement that 'It's an interesting political statement casting a Koori in the role'.

Armfield's production also queered *As You Like It,* and featured a transvestite Touchstone who paired off with a transvestite old queen Audrey. Celia was clearly, like Phoebe, settling for second best when she accepted she could not have Rosalind, and in the line up of married couples at the end, Rosalind was still the object of desire as far as Orlando, Celia and Phoebe were concerned. Consequently the play's final reconciliations were troubled. Most importantly, however, reconciliation – or lack of it – was very explicitly evoked by the fact that

Touchstone had the word 'Sorry' emblazoned across his backside: 'Sorry' being the word that the Howard Government had been asked but found it impossible to say to the stolen generations of Aboriginal people forcibly taken away from their parents.

An even more explicit discussion of reconciliation via Shakespeare appeared at the Queensland Theatre Company (QTC) 20 September-9 October 1999, in a production of the *Tempest* that explicitly confronted the white colonisation of Australia. It featured Aboriginal and Torres Strait Islander performers in the roles of Ariel, Caliban and the spirits of the island (Photo 5). This *Tempest* also rewrote the ending of the play to allow a very specifically Australian version of reconciliation to be suggested.[12]

The primary vision of this production was that of Anglo-New Zealand director Simon Phillips. This vision was articulated in an essay Phillips published in the production: he saw *The Tempest* as 'ripe for an interpretation based on Australian post-colonial history', and drew parallels with the white colonisation of Australia, citing contemporary Anglo-authored accounts of first contact that constructed and read Aboriginal people in ways uncomfortably close to the readings of Caliban voiced by Stephano, Trinculo, Antonio and Sebastian. In addition Phillips pointed out that the 'alcoholic corruption of Caliban cannot fail to ring a tragic note in the heart of the indigenous people of Australia'.

In order to embody his interpretation Phillips located *The Tempest* in terms of the First Fleet: the courtiers became 'white wigged officers' who 'in their resplendent late-18th-century clothes, resemble the European explorers who encountered the southern land during the age of rationalist geographical expansion'. The tempest, which interrupted the courtiers in the midst of a game of chess, landed Alonso and his companions in old Sydney Town, and the court servants were transformed into convict labourers: Trinculo (a woman) became 'a draggled tailed drab' and Stephano a 'bumptiously tattered gin-shop king' (*Australian* 27 September 1999).

Phillips' programme essay explained that he had 'subverted' the ending of the play to allow for a celebration of 'the diversity of cultural influences' of Australia, stressing that this was especially important in Queensland, which had given birth to the racist One Nation Party. This 'subversion' depended heavily on the representation of the spirit Ariel. Phillips saw Ariel, played by Torres Strait Islander Margaret Harvey, as 'hoping for time off for good behaviour' but also angry and chafing at her restraint.   That restraint, and Prospero's control of Ariel, was always visibly present in the European corset Harvey's Ariel was forced to wear over her emu spirit skirt of brightly coloured feathers (Haas).[13] At the end of the production, when Phillips wanted the wrongs of colonisation 'to be somehow acknowledged and ritualized', Ariel performed a ritual of cleansing and purification.   She divested herself of her corset, 'suggesting a culture released at last from the demons of colonisation' and providing 'the show's moving final image' (*Australian* 27 September 1999).   In addition Harvey spoke some of her lines in her mother's Torres Strait language (*Sunday Mail* Queensland Metro ed., 19 September 1999).

By contrast with Ariel, the Aboriginal Caliban (Glenn Shea) had no access to the spirituality of his ancestors, and he could not see the spirit world.   Degraded to a state even lower than the brutalised convicts Trinculo and Stephano, Caliban's memorable first appearance was in leg irons.   Phillips commented in interview:

> Caliban, whether or not he ever had [spiritual powers] at his disposal, has been deprived of these powers.   Along with the loss of the rights to his land, there has been a loss of access to that side of himself, this indigenous culture so rich in spirituality.   So he is a slave.   (*Courier Mail* 15 September 1999)

However, Caliban was able, by the end of the play, to hold out a hand to Prospero in reconciliation, and was, unhistorically, left in charge of the island.

The spirit world, which Phillips argued Caliban could not access, was presented as entirely Aboriginal.   The Jagera Jarjum Aboriginal Dance Group were dressed in kangaroo skins, in stark contrast with the formal court costumes of the invaders, and used dance and music to import traditional Aboriginal culture and ritual into Shakespeare.   The dance troupe themselves assertively recorded in the programme their view of what they were doing in the production:

> Jagera Jarjum believe in the strength and integrity of culture, drawing an unbroken line from Before Cook (B.C.) to the present day.   Culture is an integral part of life and they express the need to practise it and keep it strong.   Members of Jagera Jarjum are also painters, poets, storytellers and strong community advocates.
>
> THE TEMPEST represents a sharing and learning from two different performance languages to tell a story of colonisation and survival.

Sue Tweg has documented the protocols that were established to protect Jagera Jarjum's ritual performances when the production was revived in Melbourne and argues that the performance of a real ritual onstage could be read as disruptive to the tradition of mimesis on which so much Western theatre is based. The programme note also suggests that, like the Warlpiri women whose ritual performance are discussed by Holledge and Tompkins (72-85), Jagera Jarjum were confident that their ritual practice was not compromised by its performance away from the community it originated with. However Keiryn Babcock, reviewing the production for *Time Off* (6 October 1999), was concerned that the group were:

> equated with nature and the incomprehensible elements of the spirit world. They do not speak in language we can access, rather they present the audience with their culture – without any frame of reference from which we can understand it.

Babcock also highlighted the risk of reinforcing a 'romanticised view of Indigenous culture which has done much for tourism in this country', and certainly the performance of 'a corroboree around a real fire' (*Rave* 29 September 1999) can be read as looking back to nineteenth-century theatrical traditions in terms of the representation of Aboriginal people (Casey 86). Veronica Kelly, Brisbane reviewer for the *Australian*, commented: 'the indigenous presence is just that – a presence, with the whites getting most of the lines' (*Australian* 27 September 1999). While an Aboriginal spirit world might appeal visually to a predominantly Anglo-Australian audience, there is a risk that this may reduce spirituality/spirit awareness to decoration, mystical otherness, and cultural sampling. An Aboriginal takeover of the spirit world of *The Tempest* not only risks marginalisation in terms of today's dominant cultures, which take the material so much more seriously than the spiritual, but also leaves the Aboriginal performers to deal with what most modern audiences traditionally find the play's most tedious section, the masque. Gilbert (72-73) comments on the use of Aboriginal theatre making 'as an energiser' in relation to non-Aboriginal texts, with the attendant risks of this work becoming 'exoticised' and promulgating 'approved versions of Aboriginality'. While Jagera Jarjum clearly seized their chance to appropriate and reinvigorate *The Tempest*, Gilbert's analysis seems very apposite: 'For performing arts ... Aboriginal culture is often expected to provide an archive of so-called "traditional" forms which might extend the predictable repertoire of a transplanted Eurocentric theatre, and, at the same time, make that theatre more fully "Australian"'(72).[14]

Phillips' vision of Prospero was that he was a man who 'has managed to sufficiently tap into the belief system of the indigenous culture' to the extent that 'he has somehow usurped various dreamings to maintain power over them'. This might also be a criticism that could be levelled against the QTC production; that the director/Prospero has tapped into the belief system of the indigenous culture. The presence of Wesley Enoch as Associate Director complicates the debate here, but presumably his role was subordinate to the directorial vision of Phillips.

The Tempest is a particularly challenging text to place in relation to Australian history because British colonisation of Australia took place 170 years after Shakespeare's death, at a time when Shakespeare was becoming established as the Bard of Avon. David Garrick had celebrated Shakespeare's jubilee in Stratford, which helped to establish Stratford as a centre of quasi-religious pilgrimage, and Shakespeare production as well as texts were beginning to be widely used to articulate dominant cultural values in Britain and her expanding empire. Consequently it is possible to speculate that *The Tempest* may actually have impacted on how the white colonisers of Australia – or at least those colonisers who aspired to the high culture status then associated with Shakespeare – responded to the Australian indigenous populations. This was certainly not the case for the earlier first contacts with, for example, Canada and the US, which took place before Shakespeare had become such a cultural touchstone, and before *The Tempest* was in the public domain. While *The Tempest* has been much favoured as a vehicle for colonised peoples to 'write back', to tell their version of the story of colonisation and to register protests on behalf of Ariel and Caliban, the QTC production – directed by an Anglo-New Zealander with an Aboriginal assistant director – might seem compromised alongside more radical rewritings of the play.[15] However the QTC production was, perhaps surprisingly, the first mainstream Australian *Tempest* to address race issues with such clarity and determination. In his 1995 remounting of his original 1990 production of *The Tempest*, Neil Armfield cast an Aboriginal Caliban. Dymkowski (63) notes of this revival:

> Reviewers ... were powerfully struck by the new 'casting [of] Aboriginal actor Kevin Smith in the part' (James Waites, *Sydney Morning Herald*, 1/6/95). Armfield 'deliberately loaded the work with the politics of Australian colonialism' by the portrayal's evocation of the 'famous Aborigine ... Bennelong': 'to watch Smith [in loin cloth and tattered redcoat jacket] swagger around the stage like Jacky-Jacky, beaten, berated and plied with alcohol; to feel the power of his impotent anger at his dispossession; and to listen to him explain the music of his island to the drunken imperial clowns he has taken up with, is profoundly affecting' (Stewart

Hawkins, *Telegraph Mirror* 2 June 1995; John Trigger, *Capital Weekly* 16 June 1995; John McCallum, *Australian* 2 June 1995).

However in 1990, the year of Armfield's original production, *The Tempest* was also produced by two other major subsidised Australian companies, all of which ducked, or at least avoided foregrounding Aboriginal issues.[16] More recently, in 1997, Jim Sharman directed the Bell Shakespeare Company in *The Tempest* with an Aboriginal Miranda plus an Aboriginal (and female) Ariel, supported, as is the Bell Shakespeare Company's general practice, by a multi-cultural cast.[17] The QTC production is the first to carry through so tenaciously the full implications of casting Caliban as an indigenous Australian, and while by rewriting the ending of the play in relation to Ariel this production offered its audience a dream of reconciliation that was sentimental and unrealistic, it left them with a dream that was worth dreaming. Certainly when Phillips revived his production in Melbourne for the Federation festival in 2001 (opened 12 May) Martin Ball commented of the ending:

> As Prospero goes on his knees in supplication, it is a gesture of reconciliation. There will hopefully come a time when such a reading seems overly earnest, blinkered to the other possibilities of the text. But for today this remains a great production, a political, cultural and artistic triumph. (*Australian* 18 May 2001)[18]

Overall the 1990s saw a noticeable increase in Australian Shakespeare productions featuring Aboriginal presence, and in the lead-up to the millennium, Shakespeare seems to have offered a high-profile and yet also a helpfully alien context in which Australia theatre could speak of reconciliation. Of course it is important also to be pragmatic and to acknowledge that one reason that reconciliation Shakespeare began to flourish was because more Aboriginal performers like Deborah Mailman were coming through the performance academies, entering the acting profession, carving out careers for themselves, and demanding access to high-profile and challenging roles. Personally I welcome the ways in which in recent years Australian Shakespeare has been used to dream of reconciliation, and I would argue that international Shakespeare scholarship is significantly the poorer for its failure to investigate and even sometimes to acknowledge this distinctive take on Shakespeare production. Reconciliation Shakespeare offers a theatre practice that not only invigorates the texts with overt and confrontational politics, which indubitably plays Australia even as it plays Shakespeare, but also offers a unique contribution to the debates on Shakespeare and race, and what Shakespeare can mean in the new millennium.

References

Casey, Maryrose. 'From the Wings to Centre Stage: A Production Chronology of Theatre and Drama Texts by Indigenous Australian Writers'. *Australasian Drama Studies* 37 (2000): 85-98.

Chesson, Keith. *Jack Davis: A Life-Story*. Melbourne: Dent, 1988.

Dymkowski, Christine. *Shakespeare in Production: 'The Tempest'*. Cambridge: Cambridge University Press, 2000.

Enoch, Wesley and Deborah Mailman. *The 7 Stages of Grieving*. *Contemporary Australian Plays*. Ed. Russell Vandenbroucke. London: Methuen, 2001.

Gay, Penny. 'Recent Australian Shrews: the "Larrikin Element"'. *Shakespeare and the Twentieth Century. The Selected Proceedings of the International Shakespeare Association World Congress, Los Angeles, 1996*. Ed. Jonathan Bate, Jill Levenson and Dieter Mehl. Newark: University of Delaware Press, 1998. 168-82.

Gilbert, Helen. 'Reconciliation? Aboriginality and Australian Theatre in the 1990s'. *Our Australian Theatre in the 1990s*. Ed. Veronica Kelly. Rodopi: Amsterdam, 1998. 71-88.

Golder, John and Richard Madelaine. *O Brave New World: Two Centuries of Shakespeare on the Australian Stage*. Sydney: Currency Press, 2001. 103-120.

Haas, Lynette. 'Shakespearean Sea Change'. *Courier-Mail* 'Arts Section', 22 September 1999: 48.

Hill, Errol. *Shakespeare in Sable: A History of Black Shakespearean Actors*. Amherst: University of Massachusetts Press, 1984.

Leiter, Samuel L., ed. *Shakespeare Around the Globe. A Guide to Notable Post-War Revivals*. New York: Greenwood Press, 1986.

Parsons, Philip and Victoria Chance, ed. *A Companion to Theatre in Australia*. Sydney: Currency Press, 1995.

Phillips, Simon. 'Director's Notes'. Programme. *The Tempest*, Queensland Theatre Company, Optus Playhouse, Brisbane, 20 September-9 October 1999.

Rider, Sue. 'Director's Notes'. *Romeo and Juliet*, La Boite Theatre, Brisbane [April 1999]. Personal communication.

Schafer, Elizabeth. *MsDirecting Shakespeare*. London: Women's Press, 1989.

– *Shakespeare in Production: 'The Taming of the Shrew'*. Cambridge: Cambridge University Press, 2002.

St Leon, Mark. 'Con Colleano'. Parsons and Chance 152-53.

Tweg, Sue. '"Reconciliation" Tempests'. Paper presented at the 2002 Australia and New Zealand Shakespeare Association Conference.

Verma, Jatinder. 'The Challenge of Binglish: Analysing Multi-Cultural Productions'. *Analysing Performance: A Critical Reader*. Ed. Patrick Campbell. Manchester: Manchester University Press, 1996. 193-201.

Wild, Stephen. 'Australian Aboriginal Drama'. *Masks of Time: Drama and its Contexts*. Ed. A. M. Gibbs. Papers from the Australian Academy of the Humanities Symposium 1993. Occasional Papers 16: 177-95.

Notes

1   *Shakespeare Quarterly* used to carry reviews of Australian productions but now simply lists productions. The *Shakespeare in Production* volumes often cover Shakespeare in Australia, as do the Bell Shakespeare editions published in Australia. See also Golder and Madelaine; occasional articles in *Shakespeare Survey*; Schafer, *MsDirecting Shakespeare*; and Gay's discussion of *The Taming of the Shrew* in Australia. However, overall mainstream Shakespeare theatre history has not paid great attention to Australian and Australianising productions of Shakespeare, and outside of Australia it remains difficult to access details of Shakespeare in production in Australia.

2   For more extensive discussion of Reconciliation and theatre see Gilbert (72) who comments 'Although the early 1990s push for "reconciliation" between Aboriginal and non-Aboriginal Australians has been somewhat diluted since the Howard government gained power in 1996, there remains in many sectors of the community a general commitment to the movement, and a groundswell of support for Aboriginal cultural production'. See also Bradley Smith in this volume.

3   Lovejoy's production was staged by the Old Tote Theatre Company, Parade Theatre, Sydney 10 March-8 April 1972.

4   I would like to record my thanks to Carolyn Pickett for invigorating and challenging my thinking here. I am not intending to denigrate subscriber audiences, but they rarely include any Aboriginal presence . 'The subscriber audience' can usefully stand for a predominantly Anglo-Australian and thus limited response to theatrical discussions of reconciliation.

5   My observations are based on the 1994 production video (Brisbane: La Boite, 1994).

6   Gay also demonstrates that productions of *The Taming of the Shrew* now routinely Australianise it.

7   For a detailed stage history of *The Taming of the Shrew* see my *Shakespeare in Production: 'The Taming of the Shrew'*. There have been several black Katherinas and a few black Petruchios but Mailman and McDonald are the only *indigenous* black Katherinas playing opposite Anglo-Celtic Petruchios that I have discovered whilst surveying professional, mainstream productions in the UK, US, Canada, Australia and New Zealand.

8   This was performed at the Bangarra Studio Theatre, in the Bundjalung language in a translation by Mick Walker.

9   Tovey also spoke of how in the 1950s for him being Aboriginal and gay 'was to be twice cursed' (*Sydney Morning Herald* 28 June 1997).

10   Tovey's original concept, which had to be compromised, was that he wanted to present a '19th-century colonial pastiche: a group of Aboriginal actors in Elizabethan costume presenting a version of the play to the troops at Port Jackson. The colonial troops, in uniform, would occupy the best seats in the house' (*Sydney Morning Herald* 28 June 1997).

11   Armfield cast an Aboriginal actor Kevin Smith as Caliban in 1995 after casting him in *Hamlet* (opened 23 June 1994 and 14 September 1995) as Barnardo/ Reynaldo/ Grave Digger/ Captain/ Player.

12   Not all casting in this production was loaded in terms of the white invasion of Australia – Adrian, for example, was played by Asian-Australian Simon Chan.

13   Haas reports that the feathers were actually chicken feather as emu are important to Jagera Jarjum, the dance group participating in the production.

14   Gilbert (74) later comments 'All too often, white critics (and presumably audiences) deem Aboriginal performance to inhere in a limited range of signifiers – predominantly tribal dances, didgeridoo music, and dreaming stories – that express a commitment to "tradition"'. Wild's discussion of some of the problematics of defining 'traditional' Aboriginal performance is also apposite here.

15   Technically Caliban is not indigenous to *The Tempest*'s island as he was conceived by his mother Sycorax in Algiers but he is habitually read as standing for indigenous people whose land is taken by the white invader Prospero.

16   For a discussion of Gale Edwards's production of the play for the MTC see my *MsDirecting Shakespeare*. The other production that year was at La Boite, Brisbane, directed by Patrick Mitchell.

17   Tweg comments 'the director's interpretation settled on the mystical rather than the political, via a Borges story'. I would like to thank Sue Tweg for allowing me access to her work in progress on 'Reconciliation *Tempests*'.

18   The Bell Shakespeare Company also staged *Tempest* in 2001 directed by John Bell but this production avoided postcolonial politics and foregrounded 'youth, patriarchal authority and beach culture' (Tweg).

Part II

Playing Australia abroad: colonial enactments

5.
'The Australian Marvels': wire-walkers Ella Zuila and George Loyal, and geographies of circus gender body identity

Peta Tait

Solo high wire-walker Australian Ella Zuila performed extraordinary tricks. She was Australia's most famous female performer in London in the last quarter of the nineteenth century. Yet Zuila is notably absent from Australia's theatre history. This article investigates the cultural languages of gender and geographical body identities in death-defying performance spaces. Zuila was performing an idea of Australia within the British Empire. Her act was timely given a cultural imaginary that associated Australia with the risky frontier stretches of the Empire, and ideas of conquering new territory. Her act was an overt challenge to Victorian beliefs about the inferior physicality of the female body and even nature, and her husband-manager and partner, George Loyal, probably cross-dressed in her act.

Australia's most famous female performer in London in the last quarter of the nineteenth century performed a unique, dangerous act on a high wire. She played her Australian nationality as part of her aerial act. This was a golden age for female aerialists in circus. A number became internationally famous for performing at height and at speed — as if in defiance of the laws of gravity, that is, the natural laws for physical bodies. Record-breaking feats were done by both muscular male and female bodies, and some female aerialists outdid their male counterparts. These performances directly challenged beliefs about the innate gender difference of bodies. They contravened social ideas that set limits to nature and its physicalities. This is an investigation of the cultural languages of gender and geographical body identities in death-defying performance spaces.

The Australian wire-walker Ella Zuila

gets quickly to work. With pole in hand she glides out upon the wire and makes her way steadily to the opposite haven, while the gazers below watch her progress with quickening breath. It is true that a net is stretched below to catch the performer should she fall, but such a long distance seems to intervene between the figure above and the net below, and the net itself appears so frail and small, that the consequences of a slip or a false step seem almost as inevitably fatal as though this protection were not there. ('Royal Aquarium' 183)

This review describes Zuila's legendary act in 1902, after three decades of performances throughout the world and star billing in Sydney, New York and London. Undeniably this was a very dangerous act. Zuila would fall two years later, on 26 August 1904, while riding a bicycle across the wire at the Rotunda, Dublin (Turner 1995, 140). She was too badly injured to perform on the wire again. By then, however, Zuila was probably fifty years old and had had a long career. Zuila's available biographical details are minimal. She died on 30 January 1926 at Walton-on-the-Naze, England, aged 72 (Slout 340), which would mean that she was born in 1854. Although largely forgotten, Zuila was Australia's forerunner on the international touring circuit of Con Colleano, the Aboriginal who pioneered the forward somersault and became recognised in the 1920s as the world's greatest tightwire performer (St Leon). When Zuila debuted as a teenage aerialist in Sydney in 1872, trained by Englishman George Loyal, rope walking had been an Australian entertainment for three decades (St Leon 71-72).[1]

Zuila rose to international fame for her balancing skill doing complex actions on an exceptional high wire ninety feet up, and as one of the first woman catchers hanging from trapeze to catch Loyal in his human cannonball trick.[2] In 1876 Zuila rode a velocipede (probably with two grooved wheels) across a 500-foot long wire 368 feet above the Magani Falls, eleven miles from Pietermaritzburg, the capital of Natal (*New York Clipper* 7 February 1880, 361).[3] Zuila and Loyal had done solo and duo seasons on wire and trapeze in Sydney theatre at least until mid-May 1874,[4] and after South Africa in 1876 were probably working in London during 1877 and 1878.[5] Subsequently employed to star in American circus, Zuila was the 'Heroine of the High Wire', promoted as having performed in London consecutively for two hundred days (*Adam Forepaugh's* 3).

At the height of Zuila's fame in America in 1881, illustrations show that she wheeled a child over the wire in a barrow, carried a man — probably Loyal — on her back, poured water from one vase to another held over her head, walked the wire on stilts, with baskets on her feet and with a full body blindfold (*Adam Forepaugh's*). She is also drawn hanging upside down by her knees to catch Loyal. Zuila's work consisted of tricks of strength, balance and skill on the wire — around the time wire was replacing rope as the preferred apparatus.

Performing at Tony Pastor's Theatre in New York, and known as husband and wife towards the end of July in 1879, Zuila and Loyal had advertised themselves as 'the Australian Marvels'. They gave top billing to Zuila as

> the Australian Funambulist ... premiere gymnast of the world ... turning a complete somersault in mid-air from hand to hand, assisted by Mr. George Loyal, the Human Cannon Ball and Living Projectile, in his incomparable and original performance of being shot from a cannon loaded with powder a distance of 50 feet diagonally and catching a trapeze. (*New York Clipper* 26 July 1879, 143)

They added — probably backdating Loyal's achievement — that he 'is the original of this act, having performed it over six years'. From mid-December 1879 and into 1880, Loyal and Zuila were working in Havana with the Orrin Brothers & Co.'s Metropolitan Amphitheatre (*New York Clipper* 20 December 1879, 307).

By February 1880 Zuila and Loyal were back in New York, making the front page in the entertainment news and described as internationally known for their daring and 'graceful ease' (*New York Clipper*, 7 February 1880, 361). Loyal and Zuila's tour of North America with Adam Forepaugh's Circus in 1880 and 1881 was promoted to rival the female human cannonball Zazel, who was a protégé of Canadian showman Farini — the recognised inventor of the cannonball act — and had been brought over from London by P.T. Barnum (Peacock 265). Subsequently Zuila and Loyal worked with other American circuses touring to Mexico and Havana until 1884 (Slout 183-84),[6] before returning to London.

Zuila was to remain a major aerial star in London and Europe from 1885 until 1904, with Loyal astutely managing the act and reputedly cross-dressing as Lu-Lu in it (Turner 2000, 72). From 1885 their daughter Winifred, billed as 'little Lu-Lu' (ibid), was assisting with props for the act although when she actually performed on the wire is unclear. In 1885 Zuila was performing to thousands of people at the Crystal Palace in Sydenham, London's Canterbury Theatre, the Paragon Theatre, and touring to Antwerp and Europe in 1886.[7] She was back in London working intermittently at the Royal Aquarium from March 1890 until 1895 and Christmas seasons at the World's Fair in Islington

1891-92, 1892-93 and 1893-94. She appeared in Transfield's American Circus on 13 September 1897, and was still performing at the Royal Aquarium in 1902.[8]

Loyal discontinued the cannonball act sometime before their return to London — he had at least one accident in 1879 (Peacock 245), and Farini had been publicising his patents over the cannonball projectile mechanism *(New York Clipper* 8 April 1882, 42). The focus was Zuila's wire-walking act and her act's composition was enhanced. As well as her balancing actions on the wire, during the 1880s she introduced a mime drama with Lu-Lu. To what extent this was little Lu-Lu in the mime or a cross-dressed Loyal is unclear, and they were sometimes advertised as a trio.[9] In 1887 Zuila carried little Lu-Lu on her shoulders to mid-wire at which point Lu-Lu climbed down and they passed each other before quarrelling and making up. Zuila also executed her standard tricks of running, walking in baskets, blindfolded in a sack and for her finale standing on a chair at the centre of the wire and then riding a bicycle. She was 'Standing Still, at the same time taking the Feet off of the Pedals, and placing the same over the handles'.[10]

Advertised as the Female Blondin, Zuila was the second woman to have this title — the career of the first, Madame Geneviève, in London in 1861 was comparatively shortlived. One account of Genevieve walking a tight rope across the Thames river from Battersea to Cremorne claims that some of the supporting ropes had been cut in order to steal the lead weights, and this sabotaged her apparatus and her act.[11] Zuila, therefore, was the undisputed female counterpart of the legendary male wire-walkers; Frenchman Blondin, who first walked across Niagara Falls in 1859, and his arch rival, Farini.[12] Unquestionably, Zuila also found it advantageous to be billed as Australian since the remoteness and the newness of her nationality could be emphasised and played upon to publicise her act.

Performing empire

What were the cultural significances of this death-defying act's geographical allusions and the performer's gender identity? While Zuila's Australian identity evoked an exotic geography of untamed margins away from the European centre of culture, she legitimised her exceptional feats by an association with Blondin. The important achievements of French aerialists including Leotard, the inventor of the trapeze, perpetuated this practice whereby aerialists adopted labels to denote Frenchness and legitimise their skills. The named geographical and/or national identity of a nineteenth-century circus act often represented the type of act rather than the performer's country of origin. For example, performers in acrobatic tumbling and balancing acts were costumed as Arabs because Bedouin Arab acts pioneered important tricks (Speaight 65).[13] A number of wire acts were billed as Blondins, albeit with a unique qualification; for example, there was an 'African Blondin' and even a Blondin horse. As a female duplicating many of the feats of the leading male performer, however, Zuila's Blondin label linked the act's geographical imitation to gender identity imitation.

The visual culture of the British Empire thrived on representations of travel, geographical acquisition and the triumph of its 'civilisation' in foreign places, albeit with military conquest, and these were sought to display in London (Morris 48). Zuila and Loyal travelled extensively and by 1879 had performed across Europe, Asia, China, Japan, the Philippines, South Africa, South and North America, West Indies, Australia and New Zealand; they became celebrities and claimed medals from the Emperor of Brazil, the Mikado of Japan, and gifts from diamond-seekers of Natal and New Zealand gold diggers; Zuila received a medal for daring from the Louisville Exposition (*New York Clipper* 7 February 1880, 361). Circus daring also encompassed arduous touring schedules, so that the known risks of travel coincided with performed spectacles of danger.

Timothy Mitchell describes the nineteenth-century European practice of conceiving of the colonised world as picture-like and systematically 'enframing' it, in order to organise and reproduce an 'object-world', as the '*world-as-exhibition*' which was 'the world conceived and grasped as though it were an exhibition' (220-22). Exhibitions ranged from ethnographic displays with curiosity value, to staged representations in theatre, to detailed reconstructions of foreign places in large world exhibitions — the first being in 1851 at London's Crystal Palace. Zuila's act served the British Empire's appetite for exhibitions of foreignness, of travel and exotic adventure. She personified a far world of colonial extremes and miraculous survival. Her success in London seemed assured.

While there does not seem to be a surviving description of the reactions of Zuila or her audiences – which on a holiday could exceed 6,000 at the Crystal Palace or Royal Aquarium – Zaeo, a contemporary English aerialist, left an account of her act supposedly in her own words. Zaeo, who debuted in 1878 and become Europe's most celebrated human projectile for diving down to a net and being catapulted into the air, describes her act's first trick of walking a rope:

The first thing that struck me was the splendour of the light, as I looked down from a platform which was fixed fifty feet from the ground, and when I took my first two steps on the wire it really seemed that I was walking on the air, which was filled with the dazzle of the lamps; but I felt no fear, only a joyous exultation, and walked straight on, till I arrived on the pedestal at the other side of the vast building.

Then I heard for the first time in my life the applause of 12,000 people who had been watching me from below. The blood turned cold in my veins, for it rolled up with a sound like thunder, and I was filled with a dazed wonder as to what it might be or mean.

... I realised that it was applause, applause, for me, and I was thrilled with a sensation of triumph, which only those who have ever experienced such a moment can conceive. (S.R. 14)

As nineteenth-century circus performers traversed national borders, both as travellers and with spectacles of performed identity, they evoked an imaginary geography. In the execution of Zuila's act, actual space and a cultural imaginary of geographical spaces converge. Zuila provided a spectacle in visible space that tamed gravity while her nomenclature echoed fantasies of nature's dangerous untamed spaces. Australia was associated in the popular imagination with weird and exotic flora and fauna, and its indigenous inhabitants.[14] The execution of precarious mid-air action on the wire was enhanced by an imaginary of strange geographies. The performing body's defiance of death was refracted through a cultural imaginary of the Empire's expansionism that sought to conquer and control remote colonial geographies.

Of all nineteenth-century circus acts, wire-walking spectacles were most closely connected to cultural fantasies of the world's great geographical discoveries and wonders, as wire-walkers sought increasingly greater physical challenges. These acts, displaying human agility that defied nature's indomitable forces, are best exemplified by Blondin's walk over Niagara Falls. Monsieur Vertelli's 1865 walk across South Australia's Mount Lofty waterfall (St Leon 74), prefigured the British Empire's celebratory spectacles of conquering Australia's physical geography. Vertelli billed himself as the (first) Australian Blondin. Undoubtedly Blondin's 1874 and 1875 visits directly influenced his Australian imitators including Zuila, as well as young amateurs, one even cross-dressing as Britannia (Dunstone). Blondin was managed by Australian Harry Lyons (Braid 4), and despite the significant risks of ship travel to Australia, it was on the international touring circuit for circus performers from Dalle Case's first short-lived venture in Sydney in 1841, reportedly with Brazilian and European performers.

Significantly, two record-breaking high wire acts in Sydney followed Blondin's visit. A year after Zuila's 1876 feat in Natal, the (second) Australian Blondin, Henri L'Estrange, crossed a bay in Sydney's Middle Harbour, reportedly on a 1420-foot long wire 314 feet in the air, either on 29 March and 14 April 1877 (Braid 4), or on 18 April 1877 (St Leon 77). On 27 April and 4 May 1878, the brothers Andrew and John Le Grande crossed a wire over Middle Harbour meeting in the middle to lie down; they would later work in P.T. Barnum's Greatest Show (Braid 4). A sketch of L'Estrange performing in American three-ring circus has him walking on a wire carrying a man, with a caption that he is crossing the Sydney Harbour Heads (*Coles Brothers Advance Courier*). The conquest of a specific physical geography promoted the performer. These risky acts of wire-walking across huge physical spaces happened in the context of the nineteenth-century idealisation of spatial conquest. Perhaps though, the death-defying feats of wire-walkers in Australia masked how the Empire's occupation of its large land spaces was underpinned by a militarised geography and its technologies.

Gendered body technologies

Aerialists reflected nineteenth-century ideas of progress whereby technological advances facilitated physical mastery over nature's spaces. The aerial act is defined by its apparatus, and its history dependent on new inventions. Performing bodies on the centuries-old slack rope and mid-nineteenth-century tight rope, and subsequent copper and electric wire apparatus (Speaight 71), however, did not produce the same imaginary spaces of flight as bodies in action after 1860 on the newly-invented trapeze. Despite an associated cultural imaginary of exotic geographies during the span of Zuila's career, wire-walking acts were predominately solo demonstrations of the most distinctively quotidian aerial tricks. By 1901 wire-walking acts had completely changed as three-performer-high balances were accomplished.[15]

Although technological advances expanded the physical spaces of performance and increased the complexity of the action and thereby the dangers, most wire performances replicated movements and behaviour that could be recognised as executed on the ground unthinkingly: walking, running riding bicycles, manoeuvring wheelbarrows. Performed on a rope or wire high in the air, these everyday actions became spectacular. Wire acts needed to mark the humanness of the performing body in order to make its conquering of space through physical control and balance appear to be a great accomplishment, even superhuman. These performers did skilled balancing acts that required precision timing and footwork. Implicitly, their display challenged expectations for social identity and its physicality through their capacity to confound ideas of the socially defined body's limitations. Wire-walking purposely reoriented visible spatial geographies in spectacles of balance. Bodies moving on wires also disorientated cultural beliefs about the natural laws for the physical body and its spatial configurations.

In London Zuila's identity as an Australian from the other side of the world evoked ideas of coming up from below or down under. The performing body's spatial reorientation mimicked disorientation in imaginary geographies. At the same time Zuila's prowess as a gymnast, a field dominated by males, defied beliefs about gendered physicality. Her tricks matched those of Blondin: carrying a man on her back, stilt walking, walking with baskets on her feet, and walking blindfold. What made Zuila's tricks more impressive, however, was the cultural expectation that female bodies were weaker. The gender identity of the performing body was important, especially when a female carried the heavier male body. A female performer's appropriation of the action of male bodies became a spectacle of gender competition. Performances of physical actions that were culturally associated with masculinity disoriented gender identity.

The aerial body conveys gender identity through nomenclature, costume, stance and gesture, but its muscular action in the execution of the act often completely defies social beliefs about the physical difference of sexed bodies. Circus has always blatantly encouraged performances that blur gender and race identity (Tait). The female aerialist performed across the cultural spaces of masculinity with her muscular strength and daring. The body's signing of cultural identity was routinely manipulated to enhance the performance; the authenticity of bodily identity was always questionable.

In considering how a body is emblematic of nature and a cultural sign with and through technologies, as it does explicitly, for example, through body building, Anne Balsamo writes that as 'a social, cultural, and historical production' it functions both as an entity and a process of becoming a social identity (3). It is not only culturally represented as gendered, but its materiality is shaped through such gendered representations. Balsamo points out that femininity and nature are 'so closely aligned, any attempt to *reconstruct* the body is transgressive against the '"natural" identity of the female body' (43). In her act of muscular skill, Zuila presented a transgressive female body, and the long-standing popularity of her act in London suggests its converse impact on perceptions of female physicality. This raises the question as to whether the accumulated effect of viewing muscular acts by nineteenth-century female aerialists impacted socially on the material development of bodies.

The duplicity of circus body identities may have undermined this impact if it was known, for example, that Loyal had supposedly cross-dressed as Lu-Lu as the support person in Zuila's act. It is difficult to understand this cross-dressing other than as Loyal's pique and cheekiness faced with Farini's ownership of the cannon projectile patent, since it did not actually enhance Zuila's act — carrying a woman was a less impressive feat than carrying a male. Competition over ownership of aerial tricks and their newly invented apparatus was fierce and Farini patented the idea of five spring mechanisms behind human projectile acts (Peacock 227-28). In 1870 Farini's protégé Lulu became Europe's most celebrated trapezist when Farini's apparatus propelled her twenty-five feet vertically into the air up to an aerial platform to do her routine on the trapeze, which included a triple somersault to a net also designed by Farini. In June 1873 Lulu performed on a program that included Herr Holtum who caught cannonballs, and Farini took a steamer from San Francisco to Australia and New Zealand just after Loyal claimed to have first done the cannonball act (Peacock 213-14). Interestingly though, there is a Lulu advertised at Sydney's Theatre Royal in December 1872 when Loyal and Zuila are absent (*Sydney Morning Herald*, 7 December 1872, 4). Certainly new tricks reached Australia quickly.

By 1876 it was widely known that Farini's Lulu was actually Sam Hunt cross-dressed as female. Perhaps Loyal's later cross-dressing in London was intended to provoke Farini. Nonetheless Loyal's parody, hidden or otherwise, of the gender mimicry in the act of Farini's Lulu heightened the spectacle of gender competition in Zuila's act. Around the time Loyal's Lu-Lu returned to London it appears that Farini was off exploring the Kalahari Desert with his Lulu, Sam Hunt — their conquests in aerial, social and geographical spaces being seemingly interchangeable.

Cross-dressing in aerial acts was a performance strategy assisted by the malleability of the body's social identity, and this was also evident in nineteenth-century theatre acts. Male to female cross-dressed aerialists could be accepted in the nineteenth century because female aerialists looked comparatively muscular. The greater popularity of female aerialists encouraged duplicitous cross-dressing in the aerial body's merging of physical and social dangers.

Perhaps then, Lu-Lu's presence, played either by Loyal or Winifred or both, offsets the act's masculinisation and gender disorientation. A story about Zuila's sense of humour, however, suggests one further interpretation of the cross-dressing claim. In 1881, when circus agent Wightman of Cleveland heard that Zuila was about to perform on the wire with her baby (Winifred), he planned to ambush her at rehearsal and take the baby away. Zuila outsmarted him and climbed up to the wire with the baby, saying that there was little danger. 'In the centre, she stopped, and to the horror of Wightman lost her balance. Swaying for a moment, she uttered a piercing shriek and dropped her child to the ground below.' Zuila grabbed the wire, and running over, Wightman found that the 'baby' was canvas filled with sand. Zuila came down laughing and telling Wightman that show people were not cruel to children (*New York Clipper* 18 September 1880, 204). Zuila certainly liked to play practical jokes to make a point. Any cross-dressing by Loyal could have also been tongue-in-cheek comic play.

In the early 1880s Zuila had been in direct competition with Farini's Zazel. While Zazel's cannonball act would become a generic act owned by Farini with probably four different female Zazels, there was only one Zuila. Although Zuila does not appear to have done somersaults or similar tricks, her sustained level of skill and her nerve made her unequalled and famous. In 1902 Zuila swung up to the pedestal on a trapeze and crossed the wire with a balance pole in her hands, and then sat on a chair with 'as much apparent security and comfort as though she were upon *terra firma*'. Then she wheeled a barrow across the wire and balanced the pole across the handlebars of a hollow-rimmed bicycle and, pushed out along the wire by her assistant, pedalled quickly to the other side. ('Royal Aquarium' 183). By this time Zuila's legendary career achievements ensured that her act was a perennial attraction for large crowds. In the era of solo wire-walkers, Zuila was unquestionably one of the greatest.

References

My grateful thanks to circus historians: Fred Braid for his very helpful assistance with some of the primary research on Loyal and Zuila in Australian newspapers; Mark St Leon for help with trying to locate Zuila's photo (see Photo 6 for what is probably a photograph of Zuila); and to Steve Gossard for his ongoing invaluable assistance.

Adam Forepaugh's Annual Courier 1881. Special Collection, Milner Library, Illinois State University.

Balsamo, Anne. *Technology of the Gendered Body.* Durham: Duke University Press, 1996.

Braid, Fred. 'Tightrope Walk.' *Northern Star*, Lismore NSW, 17 February 1982.

Coles Bros Advance Courier 1883. Special Collection, Milner Library, Illinois State University.

Conover, Richard E. 'The Great Forepaugh Show: America's Largest Circus from 1864 to 1894.' Unpublished pamphlet, based on reports in forty USA newspapers, 1959. Theatre Museum Study Room Archives.

Dunstone, Bill. 'Performing Colonial Bodies and (as) Work'. *Body Show/s: Australian Viewings of Live Performance.* Ed. Peta Tait. Amsterdam: Rodopi, 2000. 29-43.

Gossard, Steve. 'A Reckless Era of Aerial Performance, the Evolution of the Trapeze.' Unpublished MS, 1994.

Mitchell, Timothy. 'The World as Exhibition.' *Comparative Studies in Society and History* 31 (1989): 217-36.

Morris, Jan. *The Spectacle of Empire.* New York: Doubleday, 1982.

Peacock, Shane. *The Great Farini.* Toronto: Penguin, 1995.

'Royal Aquarium.' *The Music Hall and Theatre Review*, 21 March 1902: 183.

Scott. W. S. *Bygone Pleasures of London.* London: Marsland, 1948.

Shapiro, Dean. *Blondin.* St Catherine's, Ontario: Vanwell, 1989.

Slout, William L. *Olympians of the Sawdust Circle.* California: Borgo, 1998.

Speaight, George. *A History of The Circus.* London: Tantivy, 1980.

S.R. *The Life of Zaeo. Diva Dell' Aria and the Story of the Vigilance Persecution.* Preface by Captain Molesworth. London: Universal Press Agency, 1891.

St Leon, Mark. *The Wizard of the Wire.* Canberra: Aboriginal Studies Press, 1993.

Tait, Peta. 'Danger Delights: Texts of Gender and Race in Aerial Performance.' *New Theatre Quarterly* 12 (45, 1996): 43-49.

Turner, John. *Victorian Arena: The Performers.* Volume 1. Formby, England: Lingdales Press, 1995.

— *Victorian Arena: The Performers.* Volume 2. Formby, England: Lingdales Press, 2000.

Notes

1   Zuila was advertised as first appearing as a gymnast at the Royal National Circus in Sydney, 23 March 1872 (*Sydney Morning Herald*, 22 March 1872: 8), and subsequently performing on a double trapeze with Loyal. Mark St Leon identifies a Blanche Zuila working with George Loyal's Combination Troupe (Gossard 109). Loyal is reported to have arrived in Australia sometime around 1868, when he reportedly rode a velocipede on a high wire at the Theatre Comique, Melbourne (*New York Clipper*, 7 February 1880: 361). He was billed performing at the Prince of Wales Opera House on single trapeze, doing a Niagara Leap with Mr Magilton, and then playing Isidore in the 'The Devil' in the great diving scene (*Sydney Morning Herald*, 21 August 1869: 4). In his 1870 outdoor act at Albert Ground, Redfern in Sydney, Loyal rode a bicycle across a wire 20 feet above the ground carrying a balancing pole, walked

forwards and backwards across the wire with a blindfold, and performed on the horizontal bar (*Sydney Morning Herald*, 1 July 1870: 5). Loyal (the Miraculous) went on to do his 'aerial bicycle feat' under the patronage of 'Earl of Belmore' in Victoria (*Sydney Morning Herald*, 15 July 1870: 8) and was advertised on both trapeze and horizontal (*Sydney Morning Herald*, 18 July 1870: 8).

2   'Zuila, besides being an accomplished high wire performer, served as the catcher in the duo's human canonball act ... suspended from a single trap high above the launcher' which came up vertically (Conover 14).

3   Adam Forepaugh's publicity reported this as 300 feet up on wire, walking over Umgami Falls, South Africa 23 February 1876, (*Adam Forepaugh's* 10).

4   The advertisement of the nightly program at Queen's Theatre during May listed among performers, Madame Zuila 'Queen of the Air' and George Loyal 'Monarch of the Air' (*Sydney Morning Herald*, 6 May 1874: 12; *Sydney Morning Herald*, 16 May 1874: 4).

5   The *Era's* annual listing of 'balancers' includes a Mlle Zuila for 1877 and 1878.

6   They were reported in Chicago to be planning to revisit Australia (*Bulletin*, 19 June 1880: 5) and in San Francisco at Woodward's Gardens (*Bulletin*, 25 December 1880: 8).

7   Zuila went to the Canterbury Theatre after twelve weeks at Crystal Palace and then continued on to Paragon Theatre (*Era*, 19 September 1885: 22). She was still at the Paragon in November (*Era*, 3 October 1885: 12). By December she was advertising a trip to Scala, Antwerp (*Era*, 5 December 1885: 22). Zuila's regular advertisement in the *Era* announces 'Grand Continental Tour commencing at Frankfurt', 16 May 1886 (*Era*, 29 May 1886: 22).

8   The Royal Aquarium advertised Zuila and Lu-Lu (*Era*, 22 March 1890: 12; *Era*, 5 August 1893: 12; *Era*, 5 January 1895: 29) as did the World's Fair, Agricultural Hall, Islington (*Era*, 6 January 1894: 26). Ella Zuila performed at the Royal Aquarium in 1902 (*The Music Hall and Theatre Review*, 14 February 1902: 183), and in 1903 (Turner 2000, 120).

9   The Royal Aquarium advertised the Ella Zuila Trio, High Rope Artists (*Era*, 18 March 1893: 12 - 1 April 1893: 12).

10   Bodleian Library, John Johnson Collection, Box 4, Canterbury Theatre of Varieties' Handbill Australian Funambulist Ella Zuila 1887 assisted by Little Lulu, Canterbury Theatre of Varieties. '1. Grand Introductory March, 2. Running on the Wire ... 3. Grand Double Act, Carrying on the Shoulders, Mounting and Standing on the Shoulders, Dismounting, Passing and Repassing, Double Forward and Backward Marching. The Quarrel in Mid-Air; now I leave you to your fate; come over here; if I do I shall fall. The making up and retaliation. Pick-a-back home, Ella Zuila and Little Lulu. 4. Walking baskets Little Lulu. 5. Blindfolded and enveloped in a sack Ella Zuila. 6. The Masterpiece, with a Chair Crossing and Recrossing, and Standing on the Chair while in the middle of the Wire, Ella Zuila. 7. Terrific and Sensational Ride on a beautiful Silver Bicycle, Riding Forwards and Backwards; Standing Still, at the

same time taking the Feet off of the Pedals, and placing the same over the handles, a marvel of equipoise, by Ella Zuila.'

11   Madame Geneviève, whose real name was Selina Young, was at Cremorne Gardens managed by Mr E.T. Smith, a 'good-natured rogue'. 'The tight-rope was raised on trestles ... but when only about six hundred feet from the end of her journey she stopped, and there was a long pause while attendants tried to tighten the remaining portion of the rope, which was sagging too much to make it possible for Madame Geneviève to continue her journey. The rope was tightened and she began to move forward, but as she moved the rope began to swing to and fro, and it was discovered that some unspeakable rogue had cut the guy ropes in order to steal the lead weights. It was of course impossible to proceed, and with the greatest of presence of mind the girl threw away her balancing pole, bent down and caught the rope with both hands, swung herself down on to one of the stay ropes, and slid down it into the river, where she was picked up by a boat' (Scott 122).

12   On 30 June 1859 Blondin crossed Niagara Falls on a rope, taking twenty minutes and '[R]unning most of the way' (Shapiro 28). Farini's wire-walking challenged Blondin (Peacock 73-94).

13   Colleano costumed himself as a Spaniard; the Spaniard, Juan Caicedo, had pioneered the backward somersault (St Leon 131). However, Colleano's earlier Arab and Hawaiian performance personae suggested that only some racial identities were acceptable (Tait).

14   By 1885 Adam Forepaugh's Federation of Nations would be advertising more exotic Australian acts than wire-walkers; 'Australia's Real Native Boomerang Throwers, Kangaroos, Emus, Birds, Reptiles in Menagerie.' (*Adam Forepaugh's Annual Courier*, 1885, Milner Library, Illinois State University).

15   See advertisement for the Zalva Trio crossing a wire as a human pyramid, 'standing erect 3 high on shoulders' (*Era*, 5 January 1901: 30). Rope acts had changed from performances of gracefulness mid-nineteenth-century, to increasingly greater challenges of balance and skill.

6.

When is an Australian playwright not an Australian playwright? The case of May Holt

Katherine Newey

May Holt achieved success in both Britain and Australia as an actress and playwright in the late nineteenth century. She was connected to one of Australia's principal theatrical managements, and her plays achieved critical success in theatres in both Britain and Australia. Yet Holt's work is overlooked by the dominant model of Australian theatre history, which values radical nationalism, egalitarian politics, deliberate anti-Britishness, and larrikin chauvinism. Holt can be offered as a counter-paradigm to this national theatrical history, suggesting that the Australian theatre industry was internationalist and open to exchange with Britain and America, not simply dominated by an oppressive colonialist ideology or an Australian cultural cringe.

Who was May Holt? And does she still exist? These are the questions I will pursue in this chapter, but there is no guarantee of a conclusive answer. Indeed, this account of May Holt's playwriting career will argue for her identity as hybrid and relational, liminal and transnational, rather than fixed. In posing these questions, I am enquiring not only about the individual woman, May Holt, and her cultural and ethnic identity, but also about the ways in which the Australian theatre is remembered. For most of the twentieth century, 'Australianness' in the theatre was defined by its difference from – indeed, opposition to – the culture of the metropolitan centre. In the wake of late nineteenth-century radical nationalism, and the anti-populist Modernism of writers and critics such as Vance Palmer and Louis Esson, earlier histories of Australian theatre focus on its developing resistance to the metropolitan centre of London, tracing the emergence of Australian theatre through local playwrights' tackling of local topics in the face of 'the ingrained belief of theatre managers and audiences that England ... was the source for the kind of drama they wished to see' (Irvin 3; Williams viii; Rees 99 ff.).

However, recent work by historians of Australian theatre has shown that an exclusive focus on the local, the distinctive, and the nationalist as indicators of 'Australianness' does not accommodate the range and variety of Antipodean cultural production, and disguises the extent to which it participated in a global culture. As Veronica Kelly argues, 'In the context of nineteenth-century popular theatre, centre-margin or colonizer-colonized dichotomies have problematic explanatory power within the commercial popular industry produced by the industrial revolution. This global entertainment culture ceaselessly circulated and hybridized texts in a heteroglossic transnational market' ('Hybridity' 43). And it is within these discussions which variously question definitions of 'Australian theatre' based on value judgements about content or genre (Kelly, 'Colonial' 32-34) and identify the internationalist connections and practices of the theatrical profession and popular entertainment in Australia that May Holt can be most usefully located.

Of course, in charting this distance from the imperial centre, historians of Australian theatre followed the cues of playwrights and producers of the nineteenth and early twentieth centuries, who gained commercial or aesthetic advantage from demonstrating the unique qualities of Australianness and its superiority over Englishness. Edward Geoghegan's *The Currency Lass; or, My Native Girl* (1844), involves marking out the difference between native-born (white) Australians – the currency lads and lasses – and migrants from England, emphasising the superiority of Australian wit, initiative, and ability over that of the English. This triumphant celebration of the white subject as an Australian 'native' is founded on the displacement of the indigenous Australian (Kelly, 'Hybridity' 44). The theatrical slipperiness and racism of this colonisation of identity was demonstrated with great wit in the Q Theatre's production of *The Currency Lass* (Penrith 1987), in which Aboriginal actor Justine Saunders played Samuel Simile, the Englishman who rushes out to Australia to stop his nephew marrying a 'native girl', a term Simile takes to mean indigenous Australian. His mistake is cause for much of the comic business in the play, and for a virtuoso demonstration of skill by the actress playing Susan, the 'currency lass' of the title. The same pattern recurs in George Darrell's *The Sunny South* (1883), where Australian-born characters outwit the migrants in courage and cunning, while Bert Bailey's adaptation of Steele Rudd's *On Our Selection* (1912) 'won instant recognition for its "Australianness"' (Webby 214). George Coppin, Clarance Holt, and Bland Holt made successful commercial careers from adapting London and New York hits, choosing carefully those plays which could be localised and interpreted as such by their Australian audiences. What Eric Irvin calls Bland Holt's 'sham' Australian melodramas had a wide following (*Australian* 60), although as Richard Fotheringham shows, their adaptation for Australian audiences was a much more complex process than previously assumed (97, 122).

However, by the early twentieth century, nationalist modernists' commentaries on Australian culture connected the features of popular melodrama and comedy with unAustralian qualities. The kind of populist entertainment presented by Geoghegan, Darrell, Dampier, Coppin, and the Holts was increasingly under fire. As 'Stargazer' wrote in the radical nationalist journal *The Lone Hand:*

> The Australian writer had better do without the profits shoddy farce and the strawboard melodrama can yield him; and, in the name of righteousness, let us keep the honest Australian brand from such ignoble goods ... [But] what hope have we of seeing ... [Australian dramas] played while the patrons of the theatres revel only in the spurious conventions and preposterous stereotyped characters of the Cockney melodrama? (104)

In the case of Louis Esson, theatrical representations of Australianness were combined with a casual dismissal of popular entertainment in his influential vision for the future of Australian theatre. His ideal was a small theatre group producing only 'local and original works ... a kind of Folk-Theatre'. The plays to be produced would be 'lively, simple, with plenty of colour, non-intellectual, without "middle-class" sentiment and drawing-room ethics' (Palmer 40). Thus, Esson reduced a century of theatrical work in the popular theatre to 'sentiment' and the 'drawing room'. This habit of erasure might now be seen as a typically Australian neurotic return to the principle of *Terra Nullius* as a founding myth of white Australia.[1] For it seems that throughout the twentieth century Australians had a love-hate relationship with their national history, and a collective attitude to the past marked by wilful forgettings and disrememberings as well as by celebrations and commemorations.

Recent cultural histories have questioned this modernist and nationalist model of Australian theatre. It is in this context that I introduce playwright and actor May Holt. Her working life is an example of the internationalism of the Australian popular theatre and of those who worked within the profession. After all, if, as Gilbert argues, late twentieth-century Australian identity is not monolithic, but fractured along lines of race, class, and gender (37), why should we assume that this was not equally the case one hundred years ago? These questions are raised by May Holt's career as an actor and playwright, and by the fact that she was claimed with great affection by both the Australian and British press and identified as a peer by her contemporaries and colleagues in both Britain and Australia. However, Holt is nearly invisible in later accounts: while she is given brief mention by Fotheringham (192) and Williams (203) as one of the few actress-managers in Australia, she is absent from the standard reference texts for Australian writing, such as Debra Adelaide's *Bibliography of Australian Women's Literature*, Eric Irvin's *Dictionary*, and Philip Parsons' *Companion to Theatre in Australia*.

Questions about the status of May Holt begin with her name. I have chosen to call her May Holt, but I could follow the practice of her contemporaries and refer to her by what seems now the rather prim title 'Miss May Holt', or use her married name Mrs Reginald Fairbairn, or Mrs R. Fairbairn, or May Holt Fairbairn. Or I could use the rather clumsy appellation 'Mrs R Fairbairn/May Holt' which Holt herself uses on her play manuscripts submitted to the Lord Chamberlain for licensing. The obvious point here is that, as a woman, May Holt was always identified in relation to her familial and marital status. This is something which usually gives us little pause, but in the career of a woman writer it compounds the issue of her near invisibility. Although Tracy Davis implies that a theatrical family might improve a woman's access to the theatre profession (70-71), and Gwenn Davis and Beverly A. Joyce find that the 'largest identifiable group [of women playwrights] is the 15 per cent who were actresses or members of theatrical families' (xi), in the case of May Holt her family connections seem to emphasise her relational, liminal position and the incorporation of her identity into a broader family enterprise, like the earlier actor-playwright, Frances Kemble (Newey 198-99).

May Holt was the daughter of actor and manager Clarance Holt and sister of Bland Holt. The Holt family were English emigrants to Australia in the 1850s, moving from Australia to New Zealand, and then back to Britain in the 1860s. Clarance Holt's pattern of travelling between north and south was repeated by his son and daughter, although Bland Holt remained in Australia while his sister settled in England. But, as is clear from Bland Holt's later career as producer of Australianised London melodramas such as *Riding to Win* (Fotheringham 122 & ff.), the Holt siblings' working lives demonstrate the extent to which movement between Britain and Australia was a constant in the theatrical industry of the late nineteenth and early twentieth centuries. Such a pattern counters both the sense of isolation underlying the 'cultural cringe' and the separatism of the Australian radical nationalists. Bland Holt's position in Australian theatre is now becoming recognised, but his sister's working life has been obscured in a number of ways. Yet May Holt's theatrical career was a success by any criterion. She worked as an actress, manager, and playwright in both England and Australia, in an industry still controlled by men. Her seven plays were feminine, frivolous drawing-room comedies of love and marriage amongst the genteel and aristocratic. They were produced between 1881 and 1885 in provincial English and London theatres and were well reviewed. Her presence in the theatrical circles of Melbourne and London was noted and welcomed throughout her career.

Holt's career began in the 1870s in Australia in her father's company, as a child performer known as 'Little May'. Apparently her 'farewell benefit at the Theatre Royal [Melbourne] ... was long remembered as a red letter day in the annals of Antipodean art' ('Miss May Holt'). Holt made her English debut at the Manchester Theatre Royal as Eponine in Clarance Holt's dramatisation of *Les Miserables*, which he called *The Barricade* ('Miss May Holt'). Her career continued in her father's company together with her brother Bland, touring the English provinces, playing the principal boy parts in burlesque, and Hecate in *Macbeth*. According to Frederick Warde, her contemporary in Clarance Holt's company, Holt was 'up to date, young, more than pretty and with advanced ideas on the conduct of woman.' Such advanced views go together, of course, with reading 'French novels, [and] smok[ing] cigarettes on the sly' (28). On leaving her father's company, May Holt was engaged by William Sydney at the Norwich Theatre and had great success there, eventually becoming manager ('Miss May Holt'). Her next step was to London, where she appeared at Sadler's Wells, the Surrey, the Adelphi, the Marylebone, Astley's, Princess's, and Drury Lane – a wide range of experience including the legitimate stages of the Princess's and Drury Lane. May Holt's London career in the 1870s as a comic actress led to her being referred to in one admiring newspaper article as 'the Nellie Farren of the legitimate stage' ('Miss May Holt'). Her career can be read like one of her own social comedies – after great success as an actress, in 1880 she married Reginald Fairbairn, son of Sir Thomas Fairbairn.

It was after her marriage and temporary retirement from the stage that she began to write plays. Her first was an adaptation of Mary Braddon's sensation novel *The Trail of the Serpent*, produced as *Jabez*

North, which was licensed for performance in Oldham in June 1881, produced in Islington, and then in 1882 toured to the north west of England and Ireland. Her next works were the frivolous comediettas *Waiting Consent*, first performed in June 1881, followed by *Sweetheart, Goodbye*, first performed in Scarborough in October 1881. She then wrote the melodrama *Men and Women*, first performed at the Surrey Theatre in July 1882; another melodrama *False Pride*, produced at Norwich in September 1883; the farcical comedy *High Art,* licensed by the Lord Chamberlain's office in October 1883 although there is no evidence of a performance; and *Every Man for Himself*, a rustic drama produced in 1885 in Great Yarmouth. All these plays are to be found in the Lord Chamberlain's Collection of plays in the British Library (LCP). The title pages of several of these plays list a further play by May Holt, *Innocence*, although that play is not in the Collection, and no evidence of its performance has been located in contemporary reviews. Likewise, a newspaper article lists yet another play, *Hands not Heads*, which I have been unable to trace further ('Miss May Holt'). The elusiveness of these plays is all the more frustrating as Holt's comedies were well reviewed and frequently revived: *Sweetheart, Goodbye* was produced at London's Strand Theatre in 1884 and revived at the Criterion in 1890; *Waiting Consent* was revived several times at Toole's throughout the 1880s. Notwithstanding the missing plays, May Holt's seven plays between 1881 and 1885 constitute a substantial and successful writing career in an industry where the norm was short playwriting careers often producing only one or two plays to indifferent critical and commercial success.

I have little evidence about May Holt's marriage, its connection with her playwriting, or her return to the stage as an actress. Certainly, marriage was often the occasion of an actress's retirement from the stage (for example Mary Anderson); but it could also be a key part of a recognised and respected public life (for example Marie Bancroft *née* Wilton). I would like to think it was as simple as the fact that May Holt liked working in the theatre, was good at it, and decided to keep on doing it after marriage. Maybe Holt was one of those women who wrote plays as vehicles for her own and other actresses' talents, in a kind of direct action against the tyrannies of actor-managers that Julie Holledge details (22-23). One contemporary account of her career explains that after marriage 'Miss Holt's indomitable energy would not allow her to remain idle, and she devoted her time to writing for the stage' ('Miss May Holt'). I would like to take that explanation at face value, but it is doubtful that in 1880 Holt's situation was as straightforward as any of these explanations. Her various names indicate the juggling of her social identities: she submitted her plays for licensing using her married name 'Mrs R. Fairbairn' but her professional name is always added in brackets to her manuscripts, and in a letter defending her professional status in the *Era* ('Dark Deeds') she signs herself as 'May Holt Fairbairn'. However, we have the fact of her return to the stage as the comic female in her own play *False Pride*, first performed with her own company at the Vaudeville Theatre in May 1884, in a company which included Fanny Brough playing the heroine. In April 1889, on the occasion of May Holt's return to London to create the leading role in George Fawcett Rowe's new play *Forward to the Front*, the Melbourne *Mirror* noted Holt's triumphant season in Melbourne in her own and other writers' plays, and her continuing popularity in Australia ('Miss May Holt'). So there exists evidence to provide the skeleton of her international career as performer, playwright, and manager, and her popularity on both the English and Australian stage.

May Holt's plays are either farcical one-act comedies, popular as curtain-raisers, or melodramatic dramas. Holt's melodramas were conceived on a large scale, and constructed around the staging of such sellable sensational events and settings as Epsom Downs and Derby Day in *Men and Women* (first performed at the Surrey, London, 1882). As well as staging these spectacular set pieces, Holt's melodramas trod a fine line between allowable sensation and outright scandal. In *Men and Women*, in the sensation style so popular at the Surrey Theatre, Holt manipulated the plot so that the heroine, a young working-class girl, must not tell her father (and indeed the audience) about her marriage. There is an extended dramatic scene in Act 4, set in lodgings in the Latin quarter of Paris, in which the heroine's father Sam (a gamekeeper), demands to know whether his daughter Daisy is an honest woman (f.92). It is only when Sam threatens to shoot Daisy's husband that Daisy admits she is married, and therefore living lawfully with her husband Ernest Wolcombe (f.94). Here Holt plays with her audience's knowledge of melodramatic conventions, and particularly their expectations of cross-class relationships between country girls (Daisy) and rich landed gentry (Ernest). In her version of the typical Surrey melodrama, where the young woman is often in danger of losing her reputation, Holt introduces a twist which invites the audience to anticipate sexual scandal and then confounds their expectations, thus confronting them with their enjoyment of the frisson of possible female sexual misconduct. This rather titillating use of sensation is complemented by the more conventional sub-plot of a spurned woman,

Nellie, and her estranged husband Jermingham, a fraudster who plots the downfall of the Wolcombe family. Nellie first appears in Act 1 at Eastwood Hall, the home of the Wolcombes, as the conventional figure of a fallen woman: weak and clinging to the garden palings, she falls prostrate as her estranged husband repulses her appeal for help. Her oath of vengeance against the 'black-hearted wretch' (f.25) is realised in Act 3 where Jermingham is trapped on a Charing Cross railway platform and publicly exposed as a fraudster and a wife-deserter, as the Dover train (represented on the stage) pulls away. Their final confrontation in Act 7 culminates in Nellie's denunciation of Jermingham; but, in contrast with the conventions of female victimhood in melodrama, Nellie makes an explicit statement of her power:

> Stand back! You've locked the door on me, & I'm only a defenceless woman against a vile unscrupulous man. Still I do not fear you. One word from me, one cry at that window, & you will find I'm not quite so unprotected as you imagine. Go – leave this house instantly, or I'll give the alarm! ... you coward – you beguiled me ... Ugh! When I think of you as you are, when I know you as you are, I shudder, abhor, & abominate you! Music. (f.144-5)

Nellie's sense of her power to defy Jermingham is striking. Although she calls herself a 'defenceless woman' she actually commands Jermingham to leave and reduces him to ineffectual pleading. Nellie remains implacable, and physically stands her ground until the act drop. In Nellie's and Daisy's defiance of conventions, there is a new vigour in the melodramatic heroine which was to be more fully explored a year later the Australian heroine, Bubs Berkeley, in George Darrell's Anglo-Australian melodrama *The Sunny South*: a young woman who is outspoken, physically brave, and able to defend herself.

The *Era* (31 October 1885) judged Holt's sensational drama *Every Man for Himself* to be 'an example of the sort of clever stage carpentry which is employed in the construction of "regulation" manufactured melodramas', but concedes that it 'contains, however, some striking situations, and the part of Dan the Wideawake is admirably adapted for the display of Miss May Holt's histrionic ability'. Interestingly, the *Era* review goes on to comment that although May Holt had 'written her own part, [*Every Man for Himself*] is by no means a "one-part piece;" and both in this particular and in her rendering Miss Holt has been commendably unselfish'. This is an unusual comment to find in a theatre review, and obviously the *Era* found the situation to be unusual enough in the profession to comment on it. However, although Holt does not write the heroine's role for herself, Dan Wideawake is a role giving Holt a range of situations and emotions. The play is set in the environs of Oaklands Hall, an English stately home and farm owned by the Armstrong family. Dan is the rustic farm boy who sees the villain, Bailiff John Roy, attempt to murder Lizzie Pringle, the working-class heroine. Dan is central in exposing Bailiff Roy and re-establishing justice and order in the final act. The situations Holt played as Dan range from comic rusticity and stupidity in Act 1, to the high drama of his denunciation of Bailiff Roy as a murderer, and the final sensation scene at Lightcombe Bay:

> Fine effect here – one rib of keel to which Dan is tied, has, during this [dialogue] broken loose – turned horizontally, and is seen floating out to sea – Dan, of course tied to it! Moonlight full on !! (f.194)

The rescue of Dan constitutes the final tableau, thus giving Holt the opportunity to play a central role in the exciting sensation scene that concludes the murder plot.

Interestingly, Dan is also one of the characters Holt ships out to the colonies: in the manuscript, Act 3 is set in the diamond mining fields of South Africa. However the physical evidence of the manuscript suggests that the colonial setting was originally that of the Australian gold fields, as Australian references have been erased and written over. Act 3 is spectacular in a different way from the set-piece sensation scene described above, as it uses the exotic setting of Australia/South Africa through which to pursue the melodramatic plot of the unmasking of the villain John Roy. This Antipodean setting gives Holt the opportunity to introduce her local knowledge of the outposts of the British Empire: in this act, set in 'Gum Tree Hill' (an Australian reference left unchanged), the 'Miners – bullock drivers – bushrangers etc' (f. 104) call each other 'mate' and 'shout' each other drinks (f.104-5). In this frontier land, Holt shows how the 'normal' behaviour of Oaklands Hall dissolves in the face of the adventure of diamond/gold mining. This is a pattern typical of the 'Anglo-Australian' drama, a genre attributed to George Darrell (Musa 183) but obviously one in which Holt participates. Unlike Darrell's plays which first appeared in Australia and then toured back to Britain, *Every Man for Himself* appeared first in Britain. The detail of the bush, the camp, and the improvised life of the miners was far removed from the Aquarium, Great Yarmouth, where *Every Man for Himself* was first performed in 1885, and Holt introduced the rough and ready life of the diggings in the colonies as a spectacle to audiences in Great Yarmouth, using her

Australian experience to enliven her managerial career in British provincial theatre.

Holt's melodramas are structurally well-made, and bear the marks of a working theatre manager. Her pragmatic managerial thinking is indicated in the notes added to the manuscript of *Men and Women* which give the running times of each act (obviously important in a seven-act play), and in the scribbled addition to the cast list of the manuscript of *Every Man for Himself*:

> Florence must play Mrs Davis – Mary – as she is – (housemaid) Nancy must be played by Deborah and Mrs Peckaby must be played by a super Act 1 Made up fat and by Lizzie in Act 2 – made up the same. Davis must double Bob Bale & play Peckaby – in Act 2 – Adam must double MacPherson and Jaggers must double Ned Handfield.

Other manuscripts are complete with notes about doubling roles, alternatives to bringing a horse and hackney cab on stage if this is not practicable (*Men and Women*), timings for acts, stock types to cast for characters, and so on. Several of Holt's manuscripts in the Lord Chamberlain's Collection contain set drawings in her hand: the set design for Act 3, Scene 2 of *Every Man for Himself* (Photo 7) is a fine example of Holt's detailed and practical work as playwright and manager. Holt's drawings, while not models of aesthetics or draughting, give clear information to producers and stage managers about the realisation of her stage directions. The visualisation of the scene is particularly important: obviously, this drawing serves its practical purpose by indicating these details, and technicalities such as the depth of field of the stage and the placing of practicable set pieces (such as the campfire) against the painted backdrop of the bush, but in the setting of a South African/Australian mining camp this drawing also gives us a hint about the Antipodean experiences of May Holt.

Recent critical discussions of nineteenth-century popular theatre have tended to focus on the genre of melodrama as carrying the weight of moral meaning,[2] but May Holt's frivolous comedies, displaying a riotous sense of fun and the ridiculous, are equally interesting. They also play with familiar stage conventions in an irreverent way which was increasingly to be identified as 'Australian'. For example, *High Art* is an increasingly over-the-top and out-of-control satire of the extravagances of the aesthetes; the one-act farce ends with Alphonso Nocturn, an artist, discovering that Mr Trallybungle, the man who has commissioned him to paint an inn sign, is his long-lost father (f.32), and that Alphonso's aesthete fiancée Miss Sunflower is Mr Trallybungle's long-lost niece, or second cousin, or cousin (the characters are not clear about this). The piece devolves into a parody of melodrama, which is carnivalesque in its performance style and dialogue. In *Waiting Consent* (1881), a one-act comedietta, May Holt carefully balances convention against impetuous behaviour and young desire, in comic scenes between a newly married couple in a hotel just after their marriage. Tom is a gentleman who doesn't stop eating during the entire piece, Grace is an actress who does not eat at all, but remembers Lady Isabel from *East Lynne* as her favourite part (f.8). The play works by a series of contrasts of tone and mood: the sexual suggestiveness of eating, combined with the hint that the couple are not properly married, plus the unarticulated background tension of the awaiting consummation of the marriage, create a frisson which, like Holt's melodramas, is on a knife-edge of propriety. The youthful energy of the characters – particularly Tom's frenetic attempts to appear respectable given the fear that his father will not consent to his marriage to an actress – is contrasted with the demeanour of the world-weary waiter:

> I wonder who they are – of course they're married, they all are as comes 'ere, of course they're spooney, they all are as comes 'ere, and of course they'll want me out of the room, they all are as comes 'ere. (f.2)

His *sotto voce* speeches to the audience underline the possibility of sexual impropriety, and invite the audience to imagine the worst and to enjoy it.

So here are several fragments of British and Australian theatre history. What is significant for Australian theatre about these traces of May Holt's life and work? One could conclude that May Holt was essentially an Englishwoman who occasionally toured Australia, but this ignores the strong ties that kept bringing her back to Australia, and caused the Melbourne *Mirror* to claim her as a 'Star of the Southern Sky' and to contemplate May Holt as a 'distinct acquisition' to the Australian stage ('Miss May Holt'). In this laudatory article there is a strong sense of ownership, and the right of Australians to comment on one of their own. This sense of proprietorship is possibly linked to Clarance Holt's remembered presence and Bland Holt's contemporary presence in the Melbourne theatre. Conversely, to assume that Holt can be regarded simply and transparently an Englishwoman is to ignore what I have argued to be a distinctively Australian style on the English stage in the intelligence and vivacity of May Holt's performing style, and the directness and energy of her writing and its tendency to irreverent humour.

It is a tenet of recent feminist scholarship that it is not enough simply to recall hitherto forgotten women and fit them into the existing patterns (Davis 63-64; Pfisterer-Smith 9). Yet, as Agnes Heller, another feminist writing interrogatively about women writers and the death of the subject, argues: 'Before someone is buried, they need first to be identified' (247). That in itself is enough to justify this brief excursion into the writing and working life of May Holt. But is naming May Holt (and tracing the complexities of her name) really only going to fill in the 'female blanks' (Davis 63) of an already established theatrical history? I would argue that naming May Holt could actually unsettle that history.

Acknowledging May Holt's career as actor and playwright emphasises the importance of thinking beyond simple nationalist and literary models of theatre historiography. Rather than discard or ignore Holt's plays and the hundreds of others like them – for that would be to discard the major proportion of theatrical production of the last two decades of the nineteenth century – we need to revalue the binary oppositions of high and popular culture, melodrama and realism, metropolitan centre and colony. Holt's plays and the pattern of her career challenge the standard accounts of the British theatre of the second half of the nineteenth century, promulgated by powerful public critics such as William Archer, Henry Arthur Jones and Clement Scott. All these writers shaped a powerful version of the development of drama as an evolutionary progression from the primitive to the sophisticated dramatic form, from the popular performance to the literary text, and from the feminised excess of melodrama to the masculinised and scientific realm of realism. This teleological model of evolutionary progress has, until recently, dominated histories of Australian theatre which narrate the progress from the crudities of melodramatic sentiment and construction derived from metropolitan models to 'realist' representations of 'Australianness'. Theatrical 'Australianness' did not encompass all of Australian life, but only specific parts of it which became ideologically overdetermined as the authentic or legitimate Australian character: masculine, working-class, contemptuous of the coercive regimes of bourgeois respectability (Kelly, 'Colonial' 34). May Holt's plays, melodramatic, frivolous, farcical, and apparently 'not-Australian' as they are, are not accommodated by these narratives. This conflict between respectable femininity and Australianness is still being played out in Australian culture and the third-wave feminist analysis of radical nationalist playwriting since the 1970s.

May Holt reminds us of the energetic and enterprising internationalist dimension of Australian popular theatre and its dialogue with the metropolitan centre. Holt's work was not primarily concerned with Australia and Australianness, but took its place in an international theatre industry; an industry focussed on the metropolitan centre of London but which had important contacts with Ireland, New Zealand, South Africa, India, and particularly the West coast of the United States (Kelly, 'Hybridity' 43). In summing up this new critical and biographical approach to Australian theatre history Katharine Brisbane argues 'it is time we stopped defining Australia in terms of a narrowing nationalism ... today's Australian culture is at every level not only an international culture but a cosmopolitan one. The seeds were sown at the beginnings of the colony. We began and have continued as an immigrant culture' (18). An immigrant culture must always be able to imagine movement between the country and culture of origin and the country and culture of choice. This is the context in which I finally place May Holt – as an Anglo-Australian playwright who 'wrote back' to the British Empire, and through whose success we can imagine an interchange between Britain and Australia without having to see this in terms only of an oppressive colonialist ideology or an Australian cultural cringe. This is the way we can ensure that May Holt still exists.

References

My thanks to Richard Fotheringham for his generosity in discussions and shared information about May Holt. Research for this chapter was supported by the Australian Research Council; my thanks to Sylvia Martin for research assistance.

Adelaide, Debra. *Bibliography of Australian Women's Literature, 1795-1990*. Port Melbourne: Thorpe, 1991.

Ashcroft, Bill, Gareth Griffiths and Helen Tiffin. *The Empire Writes Back*. London: Routledge, 1989.

Brisbane, Katharine ed. *Entertaining Australia: An Illustrated History*. Sydney: Currency, 1991.

Brooks, Peter. *The Melodramatic Imagination: Balzac, James, and the Mode of Excess*. New Haven: Yale University Press, 1976.

Butt, Peter and Robert Eagleson. *Mabo, Wik, and Native Title*. Sydney: Federation Press, 1998, 3rd ed.

'Dark Deeds'. *Era* 31 October 1885.

Darrell, George. *The Sunny South*. Sydney: Currency, 1883.

Davis, Gwenn and Beverly A. Joyce. *Drama by Women to 1900: A Bibliography of American and British Writers*. London: Mansell, 1992.

Davis, Tracy C. 'Questions for a Feminist Methodology in Theatre History'. *Interpreting the Theatrical Past: Essays in the Historiography of Performance*. Ed. Thomas Postlewait and Bruce McConachie. Iowa: University of Iowa Press, 1989. 59-81.

Day, Helen. 'Female Daredevils'. *The New Woman and Her Sisters: Feminism and Theatre 1850-1914*. Ed. Viv Gardner and Susan Rutherford. London: Harvester Wheatsheaf, 1992. 137-57.

Fotheringham, Richard. *Sport in Australian Drama*. Cambridge: Cambridge University Press, 1992.

Geoghegan, Edward. *The Currency Lass; or, My Native Girl*. Ed. Roger Covell, Sydney: Currency, 1976 (first published 1844).

Gilbert, Helen. *Sightlines: Race, Gender, and Nation in Contemporary Australian Drama*. Ann Arbor: University of Michigan Press, 1998.

Hadley, Elaine. *Melodramatic Tactics. Theatricalized Dissent in the English Marketplace, 1800-1885*. Stanford: Stanford University Press, 1995.

Hays, Michael and Anastasia Nikolopoulou, ed. *Melodrama: The Cultural Emergence of a Genre*. London: Macmillan, 1996.

Heller, Agnes. 'Death of the Subject?'. *The Polity Reader in Social Theory*. Ed. Anthony Giddens et al. Cambridge: Polity, 1994.

Holledge, Julie. *Innocent Flowers. Women in the Edwardian Theatre*. London: Virago, 1981.

Holt, May. *False Pride*. Lord Chamberlain's Collection of Plays, Add. Mss. 53301 I, British Library, 1883.

–   *High Art, a New Farce*. Lord Chamberlain's Collection of Plays, Add. Mss 53304D, British Library, 1883.

–   *Jabez North*. Lord Chamberlain's Collection of Plays, Add Mss. 53254 D, British Library, 1881.

–   *Men and Women, an Entirely New and Original Drama in 7 Tableaux*. Lord Chamberlain's Collection of Plays, Add. Mss 53275A, British Library, 1882.

–   *Sweetheart, Goodbye*. Lord Chamberlain's Collection of Plays, Add. Mss 53260 E, British Library, 1881.

–   *Waiting Consent*. Lord Chamberlain's Collection of Plays, Add Ms. 53254 H, British Library, 1881.

Irvin, Eric. *Australian Melodrama: Eighty Years of Popular Theatre*. Sydney: Hale & Iremonger, 1981.

–   *Dictionary of the Australian Theatre, 1788-1914*. Sydney: Hale & Iremonger, 1985.

Kelly, Veronica. 'Colonial "Australian" Writers: Cultural Authorship and the Case of Marcus Clarke's "First" Play', *Australian Literary Studies*, 18.1 (1997): 31–44.

–   'Hybridity and Performance in Colonial Australian Theatre: *The Currency Lass*'. *(Post) Colonial Stages: Critical and Creative Views on Drama, Theatre and Performance*. Ed. Helen Gilbert. Hebden Bridge: Dangaroo, 1999. 40-54.

'Miss May Holt'. *The Mirror*. Melbourne 5 April 1889.

Musa, Helen. 'George Darrell'. Parsons and Chance 182-83.

Newey, Katherine. '"From a Female Pen": The Proper Lady as Playwright in the West End Theatre, 1823-1844'. *Nineteenth-Century British Women Playwrights*. Ed. Tracy Davis and Ellen Donkin. Cambridge: Cambridge University Press, 1999. 193-211.

Palmer, Vance. *Louis Esson and the Australian Theatre*. Melbourne: Meanjin Press, 1948.

Parsons, Philip and Victoria Chance, ed. *A Companion to Australian Theatre*. Sydney: Currency, 1995.

Pfisterer-Smith, Susan. 'Playing With the Past: Towards a Feminist Deconstruction of Australian Theatre Historiography'. *Australasian Drama Studies* 23 (1993): 8-22.

Rees, Leslie. *A History of Australian Drama, Vol. 1, The Making of Australian Drama, 1830s to 1960s*. Sydney: Angus and Robertson, 1978.

'Stargazer.' 'The Australian Play'. *The Lone Hand* 1.1 (May 1907).

Warde, Frederick. *Fifty Years of Make-Believe*. Los Angeles: Times-Mirror Press, 1923.

Webby, Elizabeth. 'Melodrama and the Melodramatic Imagination'. *The Penguin New Literary History of Australia*. Ed. Laurie Hergenhan. Melbourne: Penguin, 1988.

Williams, Margaret. *Australia on the Popular Stage*. Melbourne: Oxford University Press, 1983.

Notes

1   *Terra Nullius* was the legal fiction which constituted Australia as uninhabited land on 'discovery' by James Cook in 1770, and by which the British Crown could claim ownership of Australia. This concept ignored the fact that Australian Aborigines had inhabited the continent for many thousands of years. The principle of *Terra Nullius* was overturned by the Australian High Court's decision on the Eddie Mabo case in 1992, which ruled that 'the theoretical basis for dispossessing Australia's original inhabitants is false in fact' (Butt and Eagleson 23). In its judgement on this case, the High Court invoked the principle of native title to describe the 'indigenous inhabitants' interests and rights in land, whether communal, group or individual, under their traditional laws and customs' (Butt and Eagleson 41).

2   Among a number of studies, see those by Brooks, Hadley and essays edited by Hays and Nikolopoulou.

7.
A tale of two Australians: Haddon Chambers, Gilbert Murray and the imperial London stage

Elizabeth Schafer

The careers of Haddon Chambers and Gilbert Murray, two Australian playwrights who often obliquely meditated on Australia and Australianness in their plays, raise important questions about negotiating Australianness through both playwriting and their performances in everyday life. Although Australia was only rarely their ostensible subject, it in fact permeated much of their theatre work.

In the colonial period 'playing Australia' for many British-based theatre workers meant a long overseas tour, with patronising overtones of bringing culture to the colonies; for many Australian theatre workers, however, 'playing Australia', in the sense of working in theatre in Australia, did not provide enough scope for their ambitions and they departed for London and Europe hoping to establish an international career. While the biggest success in terms of box office, critical esteem and star allure was Nellie Melba, many other Australians made stellar careers for themselves in London theatre: for example, the success of actor/director/manager Oscar Asche is well documented, with Asche's autobiography a particularly useful fund of information about that particular Geelong-born artist's negotiation of Australian and British cultures and stereotypes (Asche, Madelaine). At the end of the nineteenth century, success in forging a career on the Imperial London stage by writing, acting, singing or dancing was a relatively uncomplicated source of pride for many Australian theatre artists. This chapter examines the careers of two Australian playwrights who achieved great success in the London theatre, but whose writing mostly plays Australia in the sense of dealing with Australia only obliquely: Haddon Chambers and Gilbert Murray. Chambers made a fortune out of writing commercial, upper middle-class melodramas, and Murray produced translations of Greek plays which sold nearly 400,000 copies before his death (*Times* 21 May 1957), and which helped inspire new enthusiasm for professional staging of Greek plays, particularly those of Euripides. Despite their very notable successes, neither of these playwrights are included in the Currency *Companion to Theatre in Australia,* although that classic reference book does survey several expatriate artists' careers.[1] This omission is unfortunate, although it is instructive in pointing to a hesitance about these playwrights' Australianness (despite the fact that both Chambers and Murray always identified as Australian) and the slippages, equivalences, substitutions and obliqueness which make up their versions of 'playing Australia'.

In 1910 the *Stage Year Book* for the first time included a section on Australian theatre, primarily aimed at advising British theatre workers on how to get work in Australia, and supplying information on matters as diverse as theatres, digs or management practices. On the subject of playwrights, Eardley Turner (50) comments that 'the Australian dramatist has not yet arisen' but hastened to add 'I have no wish to do the most excellent native writers of melodrama an injustice by this remark'. Meanwhile Duncan Neven surveys the 'Lack of Australian Authors' (53), despite successes in burlesque, pantomime, and melodrama, and goes on to lament that:

> The greatest condemnation of the present system [in Australia] lies, perhaps, in the fact that several Australian plays have been sent to England, have been accepted and staged. These, truly, did not deal entirely with Australia, but surely if an English manager thinks them good enough, some chance should be given to them in Australia. (Neven 55)

Neven does not specify who precisely he is referring to, but Chambers and Murray certainly fit the description of 'not deal[ing] entirely with Australia', although in so doing they raise important questions about their relationship with their native country.

A tale of two Australians 1: Haddon Chambers (1860-1921)

Chambers (Photo 8) wrote plays that were so popular on the London and American stage that he was able to live comfortably on the royalties. Originally a civil servant, then a journalist for, amongst others, the Sydney *Bulletin,* Chambers wrote several plays for actor-manager Herbert Beerbohm Tree who gave Chambers his first break in the theatre. Tree's hagiographic biographer Hesketh Pearson describes Chambers, before *Captain Swift* brought him success, as 'a young Australian, who was living in rooms over a Bayswater milk-shop and trying to earn a livelihood by writing magazine stories' (52). After Tree suggested Chambers write a play for him, Chambers delivered

Captain Swift and pressed Tree for a play reading. When this took place Tree first fell asleep, and then decided he needed a Turkish bath:

> But Chambers had not rounded up refractory cattle in the Australian prairies (sic) merely to be defeated by the whims of a London actor. He followed Tree, and finished the reading in the 'hot room'. The manager consented to do the play. (53)

So despite opposition from many at the Haymarket Theatre, Tree put on *Captain Swift* for a trial matinee.

Captain Swift (1888) is full of Australian material and is quite clearly drawing on Chambers' knowledge of his home, his knowledge of which British stereotypes of Australia it would be commercially advantageous to play to, and his simultaneous expatriate sentimentality towards and quizzical distance from Australia. The doomed hero of the play is a romantic Australian adventurer, Wilding, who is visiting London from Queensland. Also from Queensland are Mr Gardiner, a wealthy squatter who was once held up by the notorious bushranger Captain Swift and who is constructed as the voice of reason and sense. A third Australia character appears in the unsympathetic Michael Ryan, a Queensland detective who has travelled to England in order to track down Captain Swift and bring him to justice. Wilding is, of course Captain Swift. The plot indulges enthusiastically in what Wilding calls the 'long arm of coincidence' and becomes extremely complicated when Wilding accidentally finds himself in the home of the woman who, unknown to all, is his mother Mrs Seabrook, a lady who was pregnant by, and due to be married to, Wilding's father when he died. We then find out that the illegitimate Wilding was fostered out, but as a boy ran away to Australia, which his aunt comments is 'a splendid country – for boys' (Promptbook I, 17).[2] Wilding's return precipitates several crises in the Seabrook family, and faced with the possibility that his newly discovered mother's indiscreet past will be revealed, he shoots himself and thus saves her honour. There is also a romantic interest as he has fallen in love with an heiress, Stella Darbisher, who has a taste for novels about Australian bushrangers and who gushes: 'Oh, I long to see all the strange things you have seen – kangaroos, wambats (sic), opossums, and the lions and the tigers and the bears' (Act III, 8). Wilding's suicide presumably saves Stella from a romantic misalliance.

The image of Australia, or more precisely Queensland, offered by Chambers is of a country full of bushrangers, gold mines, great struggles and danger. It is also a place where the heat is deadly:

The heat was fearful. Soon our faces were scorched, our tongues were parched and swollen, our lips were cracked – we could scarcely drag one foot after the other ... I gave up all hope and lay down under a tree to die. (I, 3)[3]

A variant promptbook has the following speech marked as cut, but is worth quoting as it also stresses the unbearable heat of Queensland:

The atmosphere was quite still, or if it stirred it burned. But we made fair progress for two or three days walking after the sunset, and sleeping during the day as well as the heat and the insects would allow. (I, 1)[4]

However, burning Queensland is also the home to which the sympathetically drawn and emphatically civilised squatter Gardiner is going to take his wife-to-be, the Seabrooks' fashion-conscious daughter Mabel. Gardiner is the mouthpiece for stressing the gentlemanly qualities of Captain Swift:

Swift wouldn't have stolen your pocket handkerchief, but he rode into a small township one day, with his mask on, of course, got off his horse and coolly walked into a branch of the Queensland National Bank. No one dared interfere with him, and raising his hat to all the women he passed – he had always the manners of a gentleman. (II, 7)

Gardiner also informs us that 'a Bushranger is not always the ruffian depicted in a penny novelette; this Swift, for instance, was a bit of a student. Gentleman Bill, they called him' (II, 7). This invokes something of an Australian cliché: the bush scholar, the larrikin gentleman. Although the character of Swift/Wilding is seen as romantic and capable of reform, the fact that Wilding has to die in order for others to be happy suggests Chambers' ambivalence about his hero, an attitude which was to recur in many of his subsequent plays. While Wilding, the illegitimate English boy turned Australian, cannot find a place in polite London society, the native-born Australians – Gardiner and Detective Ryan – are in different ways victorious: Gardiner gets his girl and the detective his (dead) bushranger.

Tree's production of *Captain Swift* was a huge success although it was not without its initial problems: Pearson reports rehearsals where lines were changed, the word 'bastard' was objected to, and Maud Tree commented on the fact that her husband's role of Wilding/Swift 'swamped every other part' (Pearson 53-54). Tree played Wilding as a 'comic crook' for the first matinee, but he quickly realised his mistake and changed his reading for the full run when Wilding became romantic and Tree 'became for the first time in his life a sort of matinee idol' (Pearson 54, Photo 9). Pearson also attributes the play's immense popularity to the fact that London audiences 'like to believe in the ennobling nature of British domesticity' and that 'staying in a nice English home' could convert a bushranger 'from evil to good, from irresponsibility to duty, from heartlessness to love' (54). Certainly the programmes and advertisements all carried a motto taken from *Henry V* (IV, i, 4) that promoted this idea: 'there is some soul of goodness in things evil' (Pearson 54-55).

The critical reception of *Captain Swift* was generally favourable. The *Athenaeum* (23 June 1888) felt the ensemble production was far superior to 'any specially dramatic quality in the play', but Tree's performance as Wilding was charismatic, although the *Times* (3 September 1888) was convinced that an 'Australian bush-ranger would probably have ... few opportunities of learning the nice manipulation of his hat' that Tree demonstrated. Later, discussing one of many revivals, the *Times* (14 May 1899) asserted that 'Mr. Tree's bushranger in evening dress is one of his best parts'. The phrase 'the long arm of coincidence' was much quoted and entered common parlance to such an extent that it eventually appeared in the *Oxford Book of Quotations*.

Chambers' Australianness was usefully authenticating and gave authority to the background details in *Captain Swift*, but it seems that Chambers also played out versions of Australianness in his every-day life. Pearson describes Chambers as:

> A light-hearted devil-may-care fellow, with a breezy attitude towards life which gave a tang to his work. Bernard Shaw called him 'a rough and ready playwright with the imagination of a bushranger; but it is imagination, all the same, and it suffices'. (53)

Somerset Maugham (186) provides a thumbnail sketch of Chambers as 'an Australian, jaunty, easy-going, and lonely'. A profile of Chambers published in 1901 describes him as 'a Huckleberry Finnish type' who liked fighting, but who looked ten years younger than his real age and rather like 'an unsuspecting curate – a very pale and very young curate at that'. The profile goes on to describe Chambers' life in Australia in dashing terms:

> After *several years of Civil Service, he was a boundary-rider, not only dashing* along on the fieriest and most untamed of steeds, but also putting in considerable time at bushranger-stalking. (*The Sketch* 23 January 1901)

The *Times* obituary (29 March 1921) also stressed the adventurous side of Chambers who was 'an out-of-doors-man' and 'fond of all active sports', a man who 'had the reputation of enjoying his active and various life too well to care about working hard', which would only have confirmed British stereotypes of hearty, outdoor-loving Australianness.

What interests me about Chambers' career is that, having had a smash hit with a play milking the playwright's Australian background, he then turned away from Australian material in his later plays. However, he created what I would argue are substitutes for Australianness, most notably in his use of American characters and settings. Chambers' use of American material may have been simply judicious, given the great commercial success he was enjoying in the United States;[5] nevertheless, several American characters or scenarios could easily be read as substituting for Australia. The *Times* (23 December 1891) acknowledged this possible elision of Australia and the US when it comments:

Much of his melodramatic colouring Mr. Haddon Chambers has been in the habit of borrowing from Colonial and American life, or what, on the stage, passes for such – the life that is led in jack-boots and red-shirts, and that knows no higher discipline than the 'shooting-iron'.[6]

So, for example, when Chambers initially sets *The Fatal Card* in a Colorado mining camp, with 'a view of the Rocky Mountains, through which the track of the Union Pacific Railway passes' in the background, I would argue that mining camp adventures and wild, impressive scenery could evoke Australia as well as the US (Rowell 37).[7] Another play, *The Idler*, is also full of American material which could be read as substituting for Australian equivalents: the *Times* (17 March 1891) described the play as 'a gold-digging melodrama overlaid with a veneer of fashionable London life' and the *Saturday Review* (7 March 1891) explained the scenario: 'Sir John Harding ... has lived a wild life in California before inheriting a baronetcy and a fortune and becoming a rising light of the House of Commons'.

While Chambers' plays do not all feature what the *Times* (23 December 1891) described as 'Colonial and American life', many of them do feature outsider figures, which might reflect his expatriate experience of living in London.   One of the biggest turkeys of Chambers' career, *The Queen of Manoa*, which was written as a vehicle for Lillie Langtry, features exotic and threatening non-Englishness, although the reviewers could not agree on which country the threatening outsider figure came from.   Again *The Saving Grace*, which included in the cast the young Noel Coward, focuses on a family with a divorce in their background, which renders them so outside mainstream society that the ex-soldier hero husband is having difficulty in being accepted as a volunteer in the First World War. Chambers' most thoughtful exploration of the outsider figure appears perhaps in *John-A-Dreams*, which premiered in 1892 starring Mrs Patrick Campbell as the heroine Kate.   Described by the *Times* (9 November 1892) as a sort of 'third Mrs. Tanqueray', Kate has a past that renders her an outsider amongst the wealthy yachting set with whom she now socialises.   The problem of being an outsider is eventually solved by Kate confessing to her past, which includes nobly motivated prostitution (she did it to support her ill mother), settling down with a reformed opium addict (the John-A-Dreams of the title), and being welcomed into the family by her vicar father-in-law in full knowledge of her past.   The *Times* (9 November 1892) commented: 'it would be difficult to name, even in French drama, an author of more advanced views with regard to the social claims of this class of heroine than Mr. Haddon Chambers'.   What is crucial here, however, is the outsider figure *per se*, a figure whose difficulties Chambers continued to explore in many of his plays.

Chambers' range as a playwright was extensive: he generally wrote melodramas, but he also produced adaptations of novels from the French.   He wrote history plays – *In the Days of the Duke* (1897) was set around the battle of Waterloo.   He worked in collaboration with a wide variety of co-authors and generally seemed able to adapt to the changing needs of the London theatre market.   However, apart from colonial life and outsiders, certain recurring motifs in his plays are noticeable: a crisis in the friendship between two men often occurs, sometimes because they love the same woman; protagonists are often writers; protagonists are also often villain heroes.   Indeed in reviewing *The Fatal Card*, the *Athenaeum* commented (15 September 1894) 'what differentiates [Chambers'] pieces is that his villain is generally his hero' and these characters' 'endeavours to free themselves from the consequences of their past actions stir us deeply'.   The repeated motif of characters haunted by the past is unremarkable in the period, but it is particularly suggestive in relation to an expatriate writer who left his home country, consigned it to the past, and yet seems to have continued reworking his feelings of nationhood and outsiderness.

While the *Athenaeum*, reviewing *The Idler* (7 March 1891) worried that 'Lack of humour, we fear, is Mr. Chambers' weak point', the *Times* obituary for Chambers (29 March 1921) remembered his wit and argues that 'so shrewd and finely comic a study of woman as *The Tyranny of Tears* would by itself be sufficient to ensure remembrance for his name'. *The Tyranny of Tears* (1899) featured a married couple renegotiating their marriage as the wife is pressured into behaving more acceptably. Initially she exerts 'tyranny' by crying prettily and using emotional blackmail to alienate her husband from his friends and keep his focus relentlessly on her, to the detriment of his writing career. Feminist analysis might view the predicament of the wife rather differently from the *Times* obituary and resist the argument that the reformation of the wife is entirely a victory for common sense. I would want to ask, more stringently than the play allows, what precisely would make a woman employ such 'tyranny' in the first place? However *Tyranny,* which in its first production starred Charles Wyndham and Mary Moore, achieved a very different kind of success from Chambers' more melodramatic creations; the success of frequently being attributed to Oscar Wilde (Maugham 186). This ascription is not as improbable as it first seems: Chambers' play is not as witty or as subversive as Wilde's work, but the intersection of London society, upper middle-class wealth and melodrama is not that dissimilar, and Chambers and Wilde had in common the experience of coming from a colonised country, of being always ultimately outsiders in London society.

Chambers died at the age of sixty after a long and very commercially successful stage career writing for the London stage, with international successes on Broadway and elsewhere. It is understandable why his achievements have been largely forgotten: he specialised in popular upper middle-class melodramas which stressed coincidence and kept audiences on the edge of their seats, but wrote at a time when Ibsen, Chekhov and Shaw were making an impact on English theatre and such melodramas were beginning to seem old-fashioned. Many of Chambers' successes were associated with the populist Adelphi theatre and a style of melodrama which was soon to find, and indeed help create, a new audience in film. His other major professional association, with Herbert Beerbohm Tree, links Chambers with a mode of theatrical production which entailed massive, cumbersome, detailed settings and that was also beginning to go out of fashion. Chambers did not write classic populist melodramas, the plays that have recently received most critical attention; he wrote about a social group for whom yachting and country estates were the norm. In this, his work might be contextualised by Katherine Newey's discussion in this volume of the career of May Holt. Chambers and Holt continue to be ignored because, unlike, for example, Dion Boucicault, George Darrell or Bland Holt, they did not write plays which have what many theatre historians and commentators consider to be street credibility (see also Newey, 'Women's').

Chambers presumably has not been of interest to those seeking to retrieve and mark out Australian theatre history because of his expatriate status, but there is another way in which Chambers may have contributed to the negotiation of Australianness in the international theatre: his close relationship with Nellie Melba, whom he met in 1895. The pair were presumed in the gossip of the day to be lovers but one biographer of Melba credits Chambers with teaching Melba to act. John Hetherington claims Chambers was discussing Melba with Henry Russell one day when:

> Chambers said, 'What a pity that she is so cold. Her voice is the most divine thing in the world, and if someone could only teach her to act she would be perfect.' Russell was expecting Melba for supper that evening, and asked Chambers to stay and meet her. He recalled later: 'Few people knew more about the stage at that time than Haddon, and Melba realized at once how much she could learn from her talented compatriot. The friendship grew and the diva undoubtedly benefited by the care that Haddon bestowed on every new role she learnt, teaching her gradually to be an intelligent actress. (97)

Melba then 'forgot' this when producing her autobiography thirty years later (Hetherington 97-98). The paradigm of a man instructing a woman on how to improve her acting skills is a popular one: it reached an extreme form in the Trilby and Svengali story, but the motif appeared in England almost as soon as women performers did when Restoration gossip claimed that the actress Elizabeth Barry learnt acting under the tuition of her libertine lover the Earl of Rochester. My impulse is not to attribute all of Melba's acting ability to Haddon Chambers' tuition, although it is not impossible that Chambers did contribute in some way towards Melba's stellar success. However, the link with Melba again suggests a playwright aware of the contradictions of expatriate existence – something Melba certainly lived out – and this furthers the case for taking seriously his plays' negotiations of Australianness, 'colonial life', and outsiderness.

A tale of two Australians 2: Gilbert Murray (1866-1957)

One of Chambers' contemporaries in expatriation from Australia in late Victorian and Edwardian British theatre was Gilbert Murray, although Murray's theatrical experiences took place in a rather different sphere from Chambers', that of high-art theatre.[8] Murray is now known primarily for his translations of ancient Greek plays into complex, rhyming but always dramatic verse, and for his successful promotion of Euripides, who was at the time 'commonly thought unplayable' (Henderson 136). Born and educated in Australia until the age of eleven, Murray relocated to England, became an Oxford don, Professor of Greek at Glasgow University at the age of twenty-three, married into the English aristocracy (his wife Lady Mary Howard was the daughter of Lord and Lady Carlisle) and had his ashes interred in Westminster Abbey. In later life he worked tirelessly for the League of Nations Union and became joint president of the United Nations Association. Murray's Anglification was never, however, complete and when he came to write *An Unfinished Autobiography*, Australia is featured in close up. It is the scene of thrilling and traumatising episodes from childhood, and the landscape against which Murray's beloved father, Sir Terence Aubrey Murray, lived out his life before dying when Murray was still young.

Sir Terence Murray was an unusual nineteenth-century Australian MP whose impulse was always to side with the oppressed. Murray comments of his father and Aboriginal people:

I think he really liked them. You can see in his journal how he mixes with them in a free and friendly way. He has no fear of being killed by them. [Terence Murray's] commonplace book has stories of their extreme kindness to white men who had been wounded or lost in the bush; of their unfailing gratitude and faithfulness to those whom they considered their friends. He sometimes said he would sooner trust the word of a black man than a white. (*Unfinished* 48)

Writing very much from the perspective of a Victorian classical scholar, Gilbert Murray can state that Aboriginal people 'were inevitably a nuisance to the squatters' (*Unfinished* 49) but as a linguist he also praises the skills of many Aboriginal people he has encountered in speaking several different languages. The Murray household with its anti-authoritarian stance, and its early support for the Society for the Protection of Aborigines (Wilson 3) was far more on the side of Aboriginal people than many of their mid nineteenth-century peers.

Terence Murray was a tolerant Catholic, and to his son he was 'without question, the greatest person in the world' (*Unfinished* 31). Terence taught Murray to shoot and to recognise the Southern Cross constellation (33-34). He was educated and owned a 'remarkable library for a man to have collected in the eighteen forties or fifties in the remote bush', made up of books which took six months to arrive

from London with 'the last hundred miles ... by bullock waggon' (36-
37). When the young Mary Gilmore (a year older than Gilbert) visited
she was offered the loan of books (Thorndike and Casson 150).
Although in 1841 a census listed 108 people living on Terence Murray's
station at Yarrowlumla (*Unfinished* 38) and Terence became President
of the Legislative Council of New South Wales, he eventually lost most
of his land and money and Yarrowlumla became the site for the new
Australian capital, Canberra. Murray's 'early remembrances are of
large houses and grounds in the suburbs of Sydney, especially one at
Darling Point and one at Rose Bay, but the houses grew smaller and
smaller as my father grew poorer' (33).

At school at Southeys in the Blue Mountains, Murray was so
unhappy he considered suicide (62-63) and was particularly distressed
by bullying and routine cruelty towards and torture of local wildlife
overseen by the school stable man (59). Murray found Merchant
Taylor's school, London and St John's College Oxford, far more
congenial, but nevertheless his vivid anecdotes of being lost in the
bush for a whole day as a small boy, and of his mother and his father
outwitting bushrangers on different occasions, suggest that Australia
formed an important part of his imaginative archive. While the
autobiography expects the reader to be British – 'this country' (71)
means Britain – Murray's account of his move to England in 1877
stresses his identifiable Australianness at the time. Looking back he
describes himself as an 'ill-mannered Australian cub' when he
repeatedly interrupted the Pope during an audience (73). In 'very cold
and sunless' London, faced with a bevy of aunts and uncles who
expected to be addressed more formally than his uncle in Sydney,
Murray was initially reluctant to oblige. He remembers: 'my first
months in England were depressing, and I fear I let it be known by a
certain amount of "colonial blow"' (73).

Murray's emphasis on his Australian experience in his
autobiography is important: he clearly felt that these experiences were
formative and in play during his later life. Two biographers, Duncan
Wilson and Francis West, dispute Murray's Australianness. Wilson
comments that Murray's autobiography was written 'at the end of his
long life', that 'his memory may have betrayed him at points and it was
certainly selective' (2), and in particular 'When in his old age Gilbert
talked of himself as a "little boy from the Australian bush", he was
exaggerating, and fusing memories of his own schooldays with stories
of his father's young days' (3). However, Wilson also records that the
notes for the autobiography were written as early as 1892-93 when
Murray went on a world cruise (on doctor's orders) allowing him to

revisit Australia, and when he engaged in considerable introspection and nostalgia for Australia (Wilson 7). West (1) also plays down the reliability of Murray's memory in old age and disputes the 'little boy from the Australian bush' construct, claiming Murray's 'English education' and 'the intellectual training and conviction he acquired in England after he had left Australia' were primary (West 13). However, the fact that Murray chose to construct himself as the boy from the bush is almost as important as whether or not that construction is historically verifiable.

Wilson also deduces that 'the Australian experience of his first eleven years' gave Murray 'an attitude of greater social equality than prevailed in England', and made him 'a comparatively detached observer in England and Scotland, however British he had become in many ways, and however "expatriate" he may have seemed to full Australians' (8). For many, however, Murray's Australianness was always there in his accent (Thorndike amd Casson 150), which is particularly interesting given the appraisals of Murray's translations by actors who maintained that, despite the ornate rhymes, the lines always spoke extremely well (West 102). Henderson (136) comments 'Murray's translations were not meant ... primarily for reading at all, but for sustained and rapid action on the stage' and Dodds stresses the joy students derived from hearing 'Murray read aloud and interpret a passage of Greek poetry' (16). West records that 'Murray ... cultivated a dramatic, theatrical quality, all the more effective because it was delivered without histrionics or gestures but by voice control and timing' (63). The spoken voice was crucial in Murray's work as a lecturer and translator, and the *Times* obituary (21 May 1957) speaks of Murray's 'melodious voice', something which enabled him in later life to take up a career as a frequent speaker on radio. In terms of his accent, the rhythm and intonation of his voice, it seems that Murray played Australia all his life.

Wilson also quotes Murray's description of revisiting Australia, of being seized 'with a feeling that this was really my home, my native surroundings. It was unexpected and full of thrill' (9). However, Lady Mary Murray never visited her husband's home country, and Wilson (214) records that when Murray considered revisiting Australia in 1911, Lady Mary argued strongly against it. Some tension between Murray's Australianness and his position in British society is also suggested by his renaming. 'Gilbert' spoke of his mother's prestigious family connection to the famous lyricist W. S. Gilbert, and 'Gilbert' was the name Murray was called by his wife's family, and the name he published under. However, he was christened 'George', and he 'was throughout life "George" to his family elders and contemporaries' (Wilson 4), including his father and mother. Away from Australia Murray became Gilbert, but there was still some confusion before his marriage when Murray's future father-in-law wrote to him and addressed him as 'Murray' because 'I am not quite clear as to what your Xtian name is to be' (Murray, *Unfinished* fn 1, 24-25).

This doubleness, and the sense of Murray as simultaneously insider and outsider in relation to British society, can be useful when examining Murray's championing of the Greek tragic playwright most associated with outspoken criticism of the Athenian Empire: Euripides. For Murray Euripides was a soulmate: 'I almost feel that he expresses my own feelings and beliefs: rational, liberal, humane, feminist' (West 69). The *Times* obituary (21 May 1957) suggests: 'It is possible that Murray occasionally read too much into Euripides; to drive home the theme in its English dress he sometimes pressed a parallel unjustifiably'. Certainly Murray used Euripides, and in particular *The Trojan Women*, politically, as part of his anti-war work. His translations construct Euripides as an anti-war polemicist, railing against the foolishness of Athenian warmongering. Murray's translation of *The Trojan Women* was often produced as a fund-raiser for anti-war causes – for example, to raise money for the League of Nations Union in 1919, in a performance at the Old Vic starring Sybil Thorndike (Photo 10). But by championing Euripides, Murray was also championing a critique of Empire, whether Athenian or, by implication, British.9

Given this reading of Murray's work on Euripides, Murray's defensiveness about his original play *Carlyon Sahib* sounds slightly disingenuous. *Carlyon Sahib* (1895) looks at the abuses of colonialism and was first written in 1892-93 during Murray's cruise around the world, which included visits to India, where the play is partly set, and to Australia (Wilson 60, 79. Murray himself in the Preface to the published edition identifies the place of composition as Viareggio and the time 1893 (v). The play was produced 19 June 1899 at the Princess of Wales Theatre, Kennington, London, by Mrs Patrick Campbell who also starred, and Granville Barker played Selim, the Indian who finally resists Carlyon's magnetic power. The production ran for a fortnight and was controversial, something Murray sought to address in a Preface to the published text:

> I may remark here that the Play never had the ghost of a
> glimmer of a conscious political allusion in it; nor did it occur
> to me, when I put my Napoleonic hero in the surroundings

which seemed to give most scope to his aristocratic and unscrupulous genius, that any sane person would suppose that I wished to attack the Indian Civil Service. (v) Murray complained of critics who 'adopted a high patriotic tone against this play' and argued 'their imperial sensitiveness was a little overstrained' (vi). Certainly the *Times* (20 June 1899) was incensed with the play, thought it deserved to be 'soundly hissed' for 'the detestable nature of the story' and fulminated: 'A more unfair and un-English attempt to misrepresent the great service which governs India could not have been made'. The 'un-English' taunt is particularly interesting. At the time *Carlyon Sahib* was staged, the Boer War had made imperialism and colonisation a very hot topic and reviewers were bound to react strongly. Indeed the crisis over South Africa helped to shift Murray's own politics from a belief in the possibility of a benign paternalistic empire toward radical resistance to it (Wilson 60).[10] However in his use of colonial India, Murray might be read as negotiating some of his own concerns about colonialism originating with his father's sympathy with Aboriginal people, and with what Murray frequently refers to as his Irish heritage – which he defines as sympathy with the underdog – concerns in tension with his own successful entry into the centre of Empire: the British aristocracy.[11] The fact that in the original script Carlyon deliberately had a drinking well poisoned – William Archer persuaded Murray to change this in the final script – is certainly very reminiscent of atrocities committed against Australian Aboriginal people, and it is difficult not to read *Carlyon Sahib* as some kind of meditation on Murray's anxieties about this.

Although in secondary school in England in the 1970s Murray's translations were still being used to introduce me to Greek tragedy, the translations now seem ornate, their complicated use of rhyme distracting and, judging from their stage directions, they seem targeted at proscenium-arch theatres. In 1960 E. R. Dodds describes how in 'recent years fashion has turned against their luscious rhythms and decorative Georgian style', although he adds 'for sheer technical accomplishment they still have no rival among our translation from the Greek since Pope's Homer'.[12] What was crucial was that these highly-wrought lyrics suited the moment for which they were written, they suited the theatre of the time, and they were used by directors such as Harley Granville Barker, Lewis Casson and Max Reinhardt. Murray's contacts with the contemporary theatre world also included friendship with theatre professionals such as John Galsworthy,

William Archer and George Bernard Shaw. Shaw went so far as to put him in a play: Adolphus Cusins in *Major Barbara* is closely modelled on Murray; his translations of Euripides are used for Adolphus' translations; and in the first production Granville Barker, playing Adolphus, was dressed to look like Murray. *Major Barbara* owes something to Murray's wife Lady Mary, and Lady Britomart resembles his mother-in-law the Countess of Carlisle, not least in her separation from her husband.[13] Murray also worked with Shaw on the text of Act 3 (Albert passim, Dukore xv). *Major Barbara*, of course, might also be read as a critique of empire – whether the empire of Undershaft or of the Salvation Army, and Murray as Adolphus is implicated in these imperial projects by his determination to marry Barbara/Lady Mary Howard.

Murray only wrote directly about Australia in one play: the Australian character of Sir Simon Drage appears in an 1895 tragedy *Leaves of Sibyl*, which was never performed. This character Murray thought was:

> A genuine attempt at bringing out a type which I remember among old friends of my father at Sydney – many of them Irish: courtly, ceremonious, full of 'Sir' and 'Madam', swearing smoothly – without emotion, and charged with the most outspoken *ancien régime* contempt for people they disliked, or thought beneath them. (Wilson 83)

However in *Carlyon Sahib* and in his translations of Euripides, Murray's ongoing exploration of imperial projects suggest that Australia is being played out by means of texts which never overtly invoke Murray's homeland.

I began this discussion with a reference to the *Stage Year Book*'s confidence that Australia playwrights were doing well overseas although they were 'not deal[ing] entirely with Australia'. By 1929 a rather different opinion on the subject of Australian drama and theatre prevailed in the UK. The *Observer* critic St John Ervine, quoting from a letter from an Englishwoman then resident in Australia, professes to be dumbfounded to find that the Sydney *Bulletin* is dismissing English productions as 'too alien' and 'too narrowly English' for 'local liking' (*Observer* 14 July 1929). Other horrors he reports are the monopoly on theatre in Australia by J. C. Williamson, the drain of talent going overseas, and the prevailing wisdom that productions in Australia must abide by the rule 'They won't understand that here! You must give it to them rough!', something which results in British authors' plays being doctored so much that if the authors knew about it 'they would pass from swoon to swoon'. Understandably Australians in the

UK rushed to defend their theatre and Ervine quotes from correspondence over the next two weeks. Most contributions to the debate argued the pros and cons of the J. C. Williamson monopoly; some complained that being identified as Australian prejudiced the chances of success in their home country. One correspondent argued:

If an Australian wrote a play, a topical Australian play, as good as, say, one of Bernard Shaw's best, the chances are all that it would never be staged or even read. The fact of it being on an Australian subject, as far as English publishers and managers and critics were concerned, would damn it utterly. (*Observer* 28 July 1929)

Neither the correspondents nor St John Ervine thought to invoke Haddon Chambers who had died only eight years ago, nor Gilbert Murray whose Australianness was at that time becoming almost invisible. And yet both these playwrights not only identified as Australian but in their playwriting continued to discuss Australia, empire and colonial life, even though they did this indirectly, obliquely, sometimes even in disguise. Both Chambers and Murray offer striking, contrasted and, in their own period, high-profile contributions to the discussion of what playing Australia might be.

References

Albert, S.P. '"In More Ways Than One": *Major Barbara*'s Debt to Gilbert Murray'. *Educational Theatre Journal* 20 (1968): 123-40.

Asche, Oscar. *Oscar Asche His Life*. London: Hurst & Blackett, 1929.

Brisbane, Katharine. 'Playwriting'. Parsons and Chance 446-57.

Chambers, Haddon. 'Captain Swift'. Promptbook. HBT/000035/25; Wilding Part Book HBT/000035/29; Promptbook HBT/000035/24. Bristol Theatre Collection.

Dodds, E.R. 'Introduction'. Murray, *Unfinished*. 13-19.

Dukore, Bernard F. '*Major Barbara*': *A Facsimile of the Holograph Manuscript*. New York and London: Garland, 1981.

Henderson, Isobel. 'The Teacher of Greek'. Murray, *Unfinished*. 125-48.

Hetherington, John. *Melba: A Biography*. London: Faber, 1967.

Macintosh, Fiona. 'The Shavian Murray and the Euripdean Shaw: *Major Barbara* and the *Bacchae*.' *Classics Ireland* 5 (1998): 64-84.

Madelaine, Richard. 'Substantial Pageant: Oscar Asche, Latter-day Pictorialism and Australian Audiences, 1909-24'. *O Brave New World: Two Centuries of Shakespeare on the Australian Stage*. Ed. John Golder and Richard Madelaine. Sydney: Currency, 2001.

Maugham, Somerset. *A Writer's Notebook*. London: William Heinemann, 1949.

Murray, Gilbert. *An Unfinished Autobiography, With Contributions by his Friends*. Ed. Jean Smith and Arnold Toynbee. London: George Allen & Unwin, 1960.

– *Carlyon Sahib*. London: William Heinemann, 1900.

Neven, Duncan. 'The Australian Stage'. *The Stage Year Book*. London: Carson and Comerford (1910): 51-57.

Newey, Katherine. 'Women's Playwriting and the Popular Theatre in the Late Victorian Era, 1870-1900'. *Victorian Popular Texts and Their Reception*. Ed. Emma Liggins and Daniel Duffy. Aldershot: Ashgate, 2001. 147-67.

Parsons, Philip and Victoria Chance, ed. *A Companion to Australian Theatre*. Sydney: Currency, 1995.

Pearson, Hesketh. *Beerbohm Tree: His Life and Laughter*. London: Methuen, 1956.

Rowell, George. William Terriss and Richard Price: Two Players in an Adelphi Melodrama. London: Society for Theatre Research, 1987.

Thorndike, Sybil, in collaboration with Lewis Casson. 'The Theatre of Gilbert Murray'. Murray, *Unfinished*. 149-175.

Turner, Eardley. 'Acting in Australia'. *The Stage Year Book*. London: Carson & Comerford (1910): 46-50.

West, Francis. *Gilbert Murray: a Life*. London and Canberra: Croom Helm, 1984.

Wilson, Duncan. *Gilbert Murray OM 1866-1957*. Oxford: Clarendon, 1987.

Notes

1   Chambers is briefly mentioned in Brisbane (449).

2   Unless otherwise stated, references are to Promptbook HBT/000035/25 in the Bristol Theatre Collection.

3   The Wilding Part Book (HBT/000035/29) has the same text.

4   Promptbook HBT/000035/24, which documents an enormous amount of revising, rewriting and cutting.

5   The extensive collection of promptbooks in the Billy Rose collection, New York Public Library, attests to Chambers' success in the US. Letters negotiating Chambers' royalties in the UK and North America, held in the Beerbohm Tree archive at the Bristol Theatre Collection, also make it clear how lucrative some of Chambers' plays were.

6   Katherine Newey's discussion in this volume (101) of May Holt's substitution of South African for Australian mines as the location of *Every Man For Himself* provides a parallel.

7   The portrait of Fred Terriss and W.L. Abingdon in this hit show, reproduced by Rowell, is very evocative of Chambers' work: here men impeccably attired in evening dress confront each other in a humble cottage which is just about to be wrecked by an explosion.

8   I would like to thank Maggie Collins for first kindling my interest in Gilbert Murray as an Australian playwright.

9   Murray's own adaptation of Greek myth, an original play entitled *Andromache* (1897), which was first performed in 1901, was often played by League of Nations Union associations as an anti-war play.

10   Murray's early publications include an original novel, *Gobi or Shamo* (1889) which allows for a more utopian view of empire.

11   Murray's brother Hubert was very much a supporter of Empire and became
     governor of Papua New Guinea.

12   Murray's translations are, however, still staged: see, for example, Jennifer
     Flowers' production of *Antigone* for the Queensland Theatre Company in May
     1999.

13   This extraordinary family were also imaged in Evelyn Waugh's *Brideshead
     Revisited*, which was filmed for television at the Howard family residence –
     Castle Howard.   Macintosh (77-78) suggests that Beatrice Webb was also
     behind the character of Major Barbara.   She also argues for the importance of
     the 1901 reading of Murray's translation of *Hippolytus* in the development of
     Bertrand Russell's philosophy (67).

8.
Inez Bensusan, suffrage theatre's nice colonial girl

Susan Bradley Smith

Feminist and Edwardian theatre history has much to gain by incorporating stories that go beyond the confines of English and American experiences, as this exploration of colonial Australian actress, playwright, and producer Inez Bensusan demonstrates. Famous for her work with the Actresses' Franchise League and more, Bensusan utilised her confidence as an enfranchised woman to enable feminist change within her profession and wider society.

Inez Isabelle Bensusan was not the only talented and beautiful actress who left colonial Australia for England dreaming of a life of adventure and professional fulfillment, but she was certainly one of its most glamorous successes. Yet for an important figure in British suffrage and cultural history she has little status as an Australian of note. Despite being a woman recognised as having made a 'significant contribution ... to women's theatre' (Spender and Hayman 141), Bensusan remains an enigmatic figure in theatre history. Although the basic achievements of her professional life are easily paraphrased, Bensusan as biographical subject has received no critical attention. Her acclaimed play *The Apple* has been subject to various feminist dramatic criticisms, as have the achievements of the Actresses' Franchise League's (AFL) Play Department under Bensusan's direction (Holledge, Stowell, Hirshfield). This examination pays fresh attention to Bensusan's work as an actress, producer, and administrator, and is part of a larger study that re-evaluates her feminism and theatrical career, including her writing for the theatre.[1] The inquiry into her life and work offered here represents Bensusan as a classic example of those characteristics that define Australian suffrage theatre practitioners: the embracement of 'post-suffrage' attitudes, and the enactment of expatriate feminist desire.

Bensusan as an Australian suffrage theatre practitioner whose expatriate influence on the development of British feminist theatre has not been fully realised offers an opportunity to explore how historical spaces are built, occupied, and bordered. Feminist dramatic criticism has only recently reintroduced Bensusan, swiftly and neatly placing her within the clearly defined space of British suffrage theatre history.[2] That inclusion tells its own story of exclusion, one that does not recognise the individual character of Bensusan's feminism, nor acknowledge its colonial construction – let alone how that heritage influenced her theatrical career. The very fact that Bensusan met with the kind of success that she did insists that these achievements be critically examined in a feminist context that questions the Anglo/American hegemony which characterises much theatre history (including feminist histories) of this period.

The expatriate tradition and international feminism

Jill Roe and other feminist Australian scholars have paid close attention to the interplay of nationalism and internationalism in the history of Australian women. The tradition of feminist expatriatism witnessed the displacement of talented, ambitious and enfranchised women into comparatively politically backward foreign environments. So why did they leave? Roe argues that:

> In colonies of recent settlement such as Australia, the nationalist dream of self-determination has offered women a place – sometimes. At other times the alternative of internationalism has seemed more promising ... Australian women have oscillated between nationalist and internationalist strategies in an ongoing struggle for enhanced status ... There has been a strong formal preference for internationalism over nationalism in modern feminism. (30)

When Bensusan exercised her preference for a different space and became an expatriate to meet the promise of enhanced status in an Old World (England), she took with her the gifts of the New World (Australia), and those gifts in turn played a significant role in the development of early twentieth-century feminist theatre. Australian feminists abroad enjoyed a unique status. Many historians have praised the ambassadorial qualities of Australian feminists who championed their status as enfranchised women. But one thing that suffrage histories continually neglect is the cultural content of that ambassadorship, particularly that of Australian expatriate women writers. Historian Marilyn Lake argues that 'feminist activists should be recognised as pre-eminent among the theorists of citizenship' (280). I would extend that argument to include the contribution of the artistic feminist community that so uniquely articulated those theories in cultural forms.

Bensusan's international brand of feminism was formulated in the crucible of Australian nationalism, as she experienced it in late nineteenth-century Sydney. Taking this into account, Bensusan's life and work needs to be reconsidered, and different questions about her work for the theatre need to be posed; questions that offer some distinctive postcolonial perspectives.

A nice colonial girl? Bensusan's Australian years

When Bensusan was born in Sydney in 1871 the Australian colonies had a population of over one million people and forty million sheep. In the first decades of Bensusan's life Australia experienced the growth of socialism and the union movement, nationalism and Federation, and the vote for women; thus she grew up surrounded by these social, economic and intellectual developments. By the 1880s the 'Woman Question' was popularly debated throughout the colonies with increasing focus on feminist goals, aided by the Temperance movement. These debates were mostly conducted through newspapers and journals, with publications such as Louisa Lawson's *The Dawn* proving to be invaluable for feminist education and networking (Lawson).

By the time Bensusan was seven, her mother had died shortly after childbirth at the early age of thirty-six, and she later lost various siblings including her favorite sister. While the births and deaths in Bensusan's family may be typical for colonial Australia, the fact that her father did not remarry was not. He was a wealthy businessman, constantly travelled, and had a large family. This begs the question 'what kind of community was Inez brought up in?' There was an abundance of relatives in Sydney, some of whom must have assumed responsibility. It is most likely that Bensusan's maternal aunt, Adele Haes, raised the children, but the strongest influence in Bensusan's life was her father, whose successes provided a role model for the virtues of intellectual thinking coupled with hard work. A member of the Philosophical Society of New South Wales from 1869, Bensusan's father, informed by his own professional experiences, gave and published various speeches on Australia's future ('Facts'). Whether or not Bensusan agreed with her industrialist father is not important. She was, however, to embrace his entrepreneurial spirit in her own work, and later cared for him until his death in the home they shared in London.

Jewish family life was not the only formative influence on Bensusan. She lived in a vibrant city with a theatre history all of its own, one that owed much to its Jewish traditions. In 1821 Barnett Levey came to Sydney as the first Jewish free settler, joining his brother, an emancipated convict. Remembered as 'the father of Australian entertainment', he founded Australia's first 'genuine' theatre, the Theatre Royal, in Sydney in 1832 (Brisbane 11; Bevan). There is no doubt that had Bensusan been seeking to draw inspiration from a Jewish theatre tradition, she would have found abundant examples in Australian theatre history,[3] but she was also exposed to the broader theatrical traditions of the colony of New South Wales.

Brisbane's history of Australian theatre dispels many myths, including the prevailing one of Australia's isolation in the nineteenth century. British stage successes and famous actors travelled regularly to Australia, and were met with receptive audiences. During Bensusan's time in Sydney, Australians saw the rise of many great entrepreneurs, particularly J. C. Williamson, whose firm dominated Australian entertainment of this period and went on to become the largest theatrical chain in the world (Brisbane 11). Considering Bensusan's colonial home in a world context, it is interesting to note the forces of modernism at play. Magarey argues that, because they had achieved the vote so long before their British and American sisters, Australian feminism was 'not only born modern, but was a force for modernism, at least two decades sooner than anywhere else' (96). Convincingly, she also presents the cultural argument that the English translation of Ibsen's *A Doll's House* had toured around Australia before it had received even a second performance elsewhere in the world, and that before Hollywood had even produced its first feature film, by 1911 the modern Australian film industry had developed 'no fewer than twenty-two' (108-10). Bensusan was surrounded by a wealth of opportunities as she focussed on her ambitions to become an entertainer, and was not without inspiration. Aside from noting the astounding numbers of notable international performers who visited Australia, Brisbane in particular argues that the role played by women in the developing entertainment scene was a 'striking' and 'distinctive' feature of colonial theatre. From the 1850s 'hundreds of great female stars visited Australia', and these women along with Australia's own famous expatriates including Nellie Melba, 'must have been role-models for many aspiring Australians' (4).

Although she did perform as a singer in Australia, it seems that this period of Bensusan's life was more centred on becoming an actress. One broadsheet advertising 'Miss Bensusan's Dramatic and Musical Recital' in Sydney indicates that her entertainment career in Australia was well established. On this occasion she performed scenes from Shakespeare as well as other dramatic recitations. Her concluding monologue, with its intriguing title of 'A Peculiar Attack', written by an unknown woman, could demonstrate what would later become a consuming interest in women's playwriting. At the very least it indicates what was probably an association with local playwrights.

The performance noted above took place in 1893 when Bensusan was twenty-two years old, most probably shortly before her departure from Sydney. What Bensusan's family thought of her career choice is not known, but the fact that her brother Darrell was an accompanist for the recital suggests that at least some members of the family endorsed and encouraged her decision. Emboldened by her successes at home, and sure of the reception of a moneyed and loving family in England, Bensusan was soon to join fates with many artistic Australians of her period and succumb to the allure of the expatriate tradition.

England, and a different future

Bensusan's first recorded performance on the London stage was in 1897.[4]   Unlike many Australian women who went to London, she began her professional negotiations as an expatriate with distinct advantages that contributed to her success, not the least of which was financial security. Her grandfather, a commercial broker, her brother Arthur, a mining engineer, and his wife Ethel were soon to join her in England. Bensusan no doubt enjoyed the courtesies of family and the privileges of a comfortable life as she pursued her profession. She lived in fashionable addresses and mixed with wealthy and esteemed people.

From this secure position, Bensusan utilised her solid theatrical background and developed contacts in the theatre industry. Described as a woman of 'energy and inventiveness' (Holledge 66), it was not long before she was earning her own living. Bensusan's Jewishness allowed her to make extra social connections, many of which were highly beneficial to her career. Israel Zangwill, a well-known man of letters, playwright, and a suffrage advocate, became a close friend. He was later repeatedly to cast Bensusan in his hit play *The Melting Pot*. Such contacts made for a confident professional future for Bensusan, but acting was by no means the only thing she had in mind. Before long she was directing much of her energies to the suffrage cause. How and when her political convictions were fired remains speculative, but it is clear that she was surrounded by influential thinkers and reformers, including her sister-in-law, Ethel Bensusan (neé De Lissa).[5] Bensusan formalised her political convictions in London where she joined and was active in many reform organisations, all of which were affiliated with the suffrage cause in some way. Published in London in 1913, *The Suffrage Annual and Women's Who's Who* includes a lengthy listing for Bensusan. Aside from noting her work with the AFL, it lists her as being an actress, and importantly represents her as a political creature, recording her memberships of various organisations. Aside from the AFL, these included the Australian and New Zealand Women Voters (ANZWV), the Jewish League for Woman Suffrage (JLWS), and the Women Writer's Suffrage League (WWSL).[6]

In 1910 Bensusan participated in a debate in London that took as its motion 'That the Granting of the Vote to Women Will Be Beneficial to the Nation and the Empire' (*Votes For Women* 30 September 1910: 847). Debates were used to train confident speakers for suffrage rallies, a duty which Bensusan never shirked. As an enfranchised woman in the country of her birth, and as an expatriate who was reaping the professional benefits of her exile, Bensusan felt this paradox keenly. As a result, she became a zealous advocate for feminist change. By the time Bensusan joined the political organisations listed above, she was a mature, successful, professional woman in her late thirties. She never wavered from her love of theatre, nor her belief that it was a great instrument for social change, and used her energy and influence to perpetuate this belief. Clearly, Bensusan's personal politics informed her working life.

Diversity at play: early theatrical career in London

Bensusan was supremely qualified and uniquely placed to make an extraordinary contribution to suffrage theatre history. In order to augment appreciation of Bensusan's writing for the theatre, an understanding of her wider professional life in the theatre is required. When Bensusan arrived in England she was relying on her reputation and skills as a dramatic actress and reciter, but she soon diversified into other areas. These professional achievements, though impressive, see her remembered as only a minor player in British theatre history of this time, if she is noted at all.[7] While Bensusan has received attention from some feminist scholars, most notably Holledge and Stowell, certain aspects of her work are presented here for the first time.

As an actress, Bensusan performed in over fifty productions from 1897 to 1938, including many suffrage 'classics'. She not only performed with the AFL, but with many other theatre companies including Edy Craig's Pioneer Players, the Jewish Theatre League (JTL), and the Play Actors Society. By the time of Bensusan's first known London performance in November 1897 she was twenty-six years old, and judging from pictorial evidence, a great beauty by Victorian standards. She seemed to have all the obvious requirements – talent, experience, beauty and connections – to have enjoyed every success as an actress (to use the term that was in favour then), but her acting career could be regarded as mediocre. It is evident that, for whatever reasons, she rarely played leading roles until she was much older, and usually performed more with experimental theatre groups than with those organisations that dominated the London West End. Perhaps this was a conscious decision as a feminist theatre practitioner. Regardless, she performed on the stage constantly for most of her adult life. Although Bensusan favoured, or was favoured by, alternative performance spaces such as the Little Theatre owned by Gertrude Kingston, she was nevertheless an experienced West End performer. She is probably most remembered as an actress for her interpretation of Frau Quixano in *The Melting Pot*. Produced at the Court by the Play Actors, *The Melting Pot* was such a success when it first appeared in January 1914 that it transferred in May first to the Queens theatre, and later to the Comedy. Appearing in this original production at the peak of her suffrage activities, Bensusan participated in many revivals of the play in years to come, playing the same character even as late as 1938 when she was close to seventy years of age.

Bensusan was more devoted to experimental theatres. For example, she was closely associated with the Play Actors, a society that was founded not only to produce classical English works including Shakespeare, but to present translations of well-known foreign works, and also to promote new English authors. This constant exposure to new theatre proved beneficial to Bensusan's development as a playwright, and she devoted much time and energy to this society. Perhaps of most importance concerning Bensusan's involvement with alternative theatres was the inspiration that it may have provided for other women. She certainly used her influence to promote women playwrights. For example, the Play Actors, with

Bensusan on the advisory council, was responsible for the first performance of Elizabeth Baker's *Chains* (Stowell 154). This influence meant that she provided animated leadership for other feminist theatre practitioners, continuing the sense of comradeship inherent in the suffrage movement. Participating as an actress in the production of the many new plays by new writers suited Bensusan, and eventually inspired her to take the biggest 'leading role' of her career and begin working as a producer.

Given the traditional patriarchal structure of English theatre at this time, Bensusan's sortie into the usually male preserves of producing and directing must be regarded as a highly politicised act. There is not space here to examine her 'extra-acting' career in the context of the work of other feminist theatre practitioners engaged in similar activities, such as Edy Craig of the Pioneer Players and Gertrude Kingston of the Little Theatre. This brief account of her production work is only meant to suggest that her best work for the Woman's Theatre was not necessarily solely inspired or enabled by her work with the AFL. Bensusan's professional life extended beyond those confines.

Mostly it was through this involvement with alternative theatres that Bensusan created the opportunities to expand her professional interests. To what extent her embracement of the role of producer was a self-seeking professional action aimed at fame and wealth is difficult to ascertain. Public statements about her work as a producer imply that she was more concerned with improving professional opportunities for women than with increasing her own profile, and that she chose to lead by example. As a result Bensusan has a string of successful productions to her credit, mostly comprising women's plays. Aside from producing her own play *The Apple* on more than one occasion, she also produced Cecelia F. Brookes's and Norman Oliver's *December 13th* at the Court (1912); J. M. Barrie's *The Twelve Pound Look* at the Kingsway (1912); and, for the AFL, Evelyn Glover's *A Chat With Mrs Chicky* at the Lyceum (1912). Women producers and actress managers of this period, as Gardner emphasises, 'constitute[d] a significant challenge to the traditional notions of a woman's place' ('Introduction' 10), especially within the institution of the theatre. Although Bensusan did not meet with the same kind of success of Edy Craig and her Pioneer Players or Annie Horniman's management of Manchester's Gaiety Theatre, these few examples of her work as a producer (during her involvement with the AFL and prior to the establishment of the Woman's Theatre), indicate that she shared their dreams.

At one stage Bensusan diversified into acting for film. Bensusan wrote, produced and starred in a film *True Womanhood* which no longer survives, although there are extant reviews. It was about a woman who, along with her husband, is saved from being sent to the workhouse by the fairy godmother (played by Decima Moore), who appears in the guise of a suffragette. Holledge notes (81) that the reviews indicate that it was more of a photographic record of a stage play than a film. With these and other successful productions to her credit, it is no surprise that Bensusan became such an important figure in the AFL. Along with her successful acting career, Bensusan's work as a producer provided her with a thorough knowledge of the theatre industry and a solid background to her later work as an administrator. It was her work as an actress, though, which enabled her to meet other notable feminist activists within her own profession, and led to the formation of the AFL.

Another look at the Actresses' Franchise League

If not for her involvement with the AFL, Bensusan may have gone without notice in either theatre or feminist history, for it was this organisation that brought her to prominence in the suffrage movement and created her subsequent profile. There have been various accounts of the AFL, most notably from Holledge, Stowell, and Gardner (*Sketches*), but this account is not so much concerned with the League's reputation and activities as it is with Bensusan's instrumental role in its success, and the particular qualities of her leadership.

Formed in October 1908, the League's first meeting was, as Holledge documents, a 'glittering affair as the stars of the West End stage arrived [for the first meeting] surrounded by hordes of fans and autograph hunters' (49). Almost immediately the League began performing both in public and private in support of female enfranchisement. Holledge notes that 'as the demand for suffrage entertainments increased, the AFL responded by setting up a separate play department' (62). This was run by Bensusan; her job involved overseeing the writing, collection, and publication of suffrage drama, and the achievements of the department under her leadership were impressive.

Although she organised the programs, Bensusan exercised little control over the political content of individual items. Because of the League's commitment, which was inscribed in their founding charter, to serving rather than leading other suffrage societies, her role had always been that of the 'Lord Chamberlain'. Holledge argues that she had 'no alternative but to provide non-controversial plays' (64), that is, plays which did not pit one faction of the women's movement against the other. It was perhaps because of this role that Bensusan decided that conditions for the development of a feminist theatre could be better, and began planning the Woman's Theatre project.

The importance to the suffrage campaign of Bensusan's Play Department, and the AFL in general, has been to some extent neglected by larger histories, with only feminist theatre historians arguing for its prominence. Hirshfield, for example, argues (*The Actresses'* 130) for the crucial contribution of Bensusan's work to the suffrage movement, noting that Liberal Prime Minister Asquith created a challenge to which the AFL was more than able to rise. The pressure to please the public without offence, Hirshfield argues, is the reason why the League had avoided 'the murky area of feminist politics' (133) for so many years. This situation changed when Asquith's Conciliation Bill was introduced promising to enfranchise only women householders, which of course most actresses were not because the nature of their profession compelled them to travel frequently. As a professional class threatened with exclusion, this bill forced the AFL into becoming overtly political. Consequently, at the end of 1912 AFL president Gertrude Elliot addressed the Speaker of the Commons, pleading on the actresses' behalf. The AFL also secured over 100,000 signatures after a formidable petition drive, but these bold efforts failed to move the Commons. However, by 'the flamboyant theatricality of its campaign [the AFL] had emerged in a leadership role' (Hirshfield *The Acresses'* 141). This role subsequently reduced the League's privacy and internal disagreements became public.

While the issue of the AFL's political sympathies is a fascinating one deserving more attention, Bensusan's stance as a celebrated individual within that very public organisation is pertinent to this exploration. Was Bensusan a militant suffragette rather than a suffragist? Given her public speeches, debating positions, and friendships with known militants, it is most probable that she was, but this did not unduly affect her work for the League. As Gardner points out, although there were militant members of the AFL who were imprisoned, '[m]ost actresses in the League could not, or would not ... risk their livelihoods to this extent', because '[m]any managers were ... unwilling to employ a militant with a prison record'

('Introduction' 2). This probably did not intimidate Bensusan as much as it did many of her colleagues. As her activities during this period indicate, she was working in professional areas other than acting, and may even have considered herself influential enough as a producer to be in an employer rather than employee situation.

More important than the question of whether or not Bensusan was a suffragette is the issue of how her political sympathies influence her professional work for the AFL, especially in her position as what would be recognised today as artistic director. Militant tactics employed in the suffrage campaign, although endorsed by Bensusan, had no place in her feminist campaign to reconstruct her own and other women's professional environment. With no wish to promote separatism, Bensusan's reforms were inclusive and liberal in their philosophical vision. This did not, for example, exclude decisions such as the use of male playwrights to renegotiate positions of power for women. As Holledge remarks, Bensusan 'never considered limiting the AFL productions to plays written by women, in fact nearly one third of the plays performed by the league were written by men' (84). She recognised that men had an important role to play in feminist reform. Unlike later feminist uses of theatre that rejected male voices, Bensusan had no qualms about male involvement in her enterprise.

This did not seem to hinder the development of individual feminist voices in suffrage theatre. Perhaps if Bensusan's goals as artistic director had been more focussed on exploring feminist theatrical expression, rather than on issues of humanitarian reform, then the repertoire of the AFL Play Department would have been different. As it was, Bensusan was more interested in what was said than in how it was said, or who was saying it. For feminist theatre practitioners and dramatic criticism today this is a sensitive issue: to what extent is it legitimate that men speak for women, and to what extent should theatrical forms that have traditionally worked against women be endorsed? Although pertinent to an examination of Bensusan's work for the AFL, to focus on these issues alone would be misleading. I agree with suffrage historian Patricia Grimshaw that 'An approach to women's history must first respect ways women themselves perceived their personal situations; otherwise we assess women through intellectual paradigms inherently unsympathetic to the specificities of women's life experiences' (33).

A significant component of Bensusan's subjectivity that defined her leadership of the Play Department was her liberal humanism, which envisioned all people working in harmony – after professional and political reforms had been won. Meanwhile, she adroitly chose sympathetic men to fight not *for* the AFL, but *with* them. This was partly because they needed as many plays as possible and playwrights were not always easy to find. Perhaps Bensusan's repertoire decisions were also influenced by the recognition of another historical subjectivity – that the male voice had superior authority in Edwardian England. However, Bensusan controlled those playwrights who, as men, controlled the right of women to vote. She therefore successfully manipulated male voices to speak out against corruptions of male power whilst simultaneously enlarging her potential audience.

This decision was a politically astute one, and is of particular importance to suffrage historiography. Bensusan recognised both women's 'unstable speaking position', and acknowledged men's power whilst at the same time exploiting it. 'Suffrage studies', Daley and Nolan argue, 'are no longer just concerned with how the vote was won ... a new type of political history is being embraced by feminists, political histories which do not deify male involvement but acknowledge it' (13). Such gendered approaches to suffrage history extend understanding about power relationships, and Bensusan provides a wealthy case study for how professional feminists negotiated their way to different positions of power.

Bensusan met the obligations of her position with verve and audacity, providing AFL performances for an even spread of suffrage societies both militant and non-militant. Certain evidence, however, suggests that she was dissatisfied with the constrictions placed upon her. This, along with her personal support of militant suffrage campaigns, defines Bensusan as a sympathetic if not active suffragette, constrained as she was by her prominent position in a non-aligned League.[8] This is not meant to glorify Bensusan's role in the suffrage movement but rather to indicate that although she was a 'proper' Edwardian woman in one sense, in another she represented that new breed of modern professional woman who would no longer stand to be exploited. Bensusan embraced many means to renegotiate positions of power in order to further her art for herself, for other women theatre practitioners, and for her audiences. Respecting differences within the AFL, and acknowledging the League's support of her role and the opportunities it provided, Bensusan caused no damaging rifts either within the movement or her own profession. She chose instead to branch out from the AFL.

Her reputation and respectability intact, Bensusan plotted what was hoped would become a great development for feminist theatre, the Woman's Theatre.

Beyond suffrage theatre

Bensusan was not merely a suffrage theatre practitioner, but the stories of her later professional life – including her dream project, the Woman's Theatre (Hirshfield, 'The Woman's' 123-38) – and her later work for the British Rhine Army Dramatic Company, remain to be fully told. As the work of the AFL continued throughout the war, so too did the Woman's Theatre continue to work in a special capacity, inaugurating itself as the Woman's Theatre Camps Entertainments. The war was not the end of Bensusan's story, but it proved to mark the end of her most influential years as a feminist theatre practitioner.

Tait describes a feminist theatre practitioner as 'someone who works with an awareness of the complexity of recent feminist theoretical positions and recognises the diversity and difference of women's social experiences'. Although she is here referring to a contemporary scenario, this definition, certainly fits Bensusan. Tait goes on to say that if a feminist theatre practitioner 'readily identifies feminism as an influence on her artistic expression rather than on her professional status, then she largely precludes the compromises necessary to work in mainstream theatre' (12). Bensusan devoted her professional energies to nurturing, developing, and executing feminist theatrical enterprises. Her work demonstrates the professional, political, and personal desires of an extraordinary and visionary woman who worked during the British suffrage era, and carried her desires through the horrors and barricades of the First World War, as her later work for the Women's Theatre and the British Rhine Army Dramatic Company reveals.

To what extent Bensusan still considered herself an Australian or an expatriate can only be conjectured. Her extended family was spread throughout the world, and no evidence suggests that she ever returned to Australia. Yet she bequeathed a portrait of herself, painted by a notable English artist, to the Art Gallery of New South Wales (Photo 11), and never failed to nourish her personal, professional and political contacts with Australians in London. Was identifying as an Australian a nostalgic fondness, or something more pertinent? When, if ever, did she cease to believe that Australian women had something unique to offer the world? Nevertheless, the story of her professional ambitions and endeavours is typically that of

Australian women theatre professionals of her period who could not have hoped for such career or life opportunities to manifest themselves at home.

Inez Bensusan, a privileged, educated, and talented Sydney Jewess with personal and professional support on an international level, travelled to London and made a name for herself as a feminist reformer and theatre practitioner. Without the wealth of her Australian heritage, that 'name' may have been quite different. Bensusan's death certificate cites her as being 'a spinster ... of no occupation'. In her long life – a monumental ninety-six years – it is interesting to speculate what Bensusan herself would have considered her most important occupation to be, or indeed what historical place she best occupies. It can only be said that the legacy of her pioneering efforts continues today.

References

Bevan, Ian. *The Story of the Theatre Royal.* Sydney: Currency Press, 1993.

Brisbane, Katharine ed. *Entertaining Australia: The Performing Arts as Cultural History.* Sydney: Currency, 1991.

Daley, C. and M. Nolan eds. *Suffrage and Beyond: International Feminist Perspectives.* Auckland: Auckland University Press, 1994.

'Facts in American Mining'. *The Journal of the Royal Society of NSW* 9 (1875): 73-85.

Gardner, Viv. *Sketches from the Actresses' Franchise League.* Nottingham: Nottingham Drama Texts, 1985.

– 'Introduction.' *The New Woman and Her Sisters: Feminism and Theatre 1850-1914.* Ed. Viv Gardner and Susan Rutherford. London: Harvester Wheatsheaf, 1992. 1-14

Grimshaw, Patricia. 'Women's Suffrage in New Zealand Revisited: Writing From the Margins'. Daley and Nolan, 1994. 25-41.

Hirshfield, Claire. 'The Actresses' Franchise League and the Campaign for Women's Suffrage 1908-1914'. *Theatre Research International* 10.2 (1985): 129-53.

– 'The Woman's Theatre in England: 1913-1918.' *Theatre History Studies* 15 (1995): 123-38.

Holledge, Julie. *Innocent Flowers: Women in the Edwardian Theatre.* London: Virago, 1981.

Lake, Marilyn. 'Between Old Worlds and New: Feminist Citizenship, Nation and Race, and the Destabilisation of Identity'. Daley and Nolan, 1994. 277-294.

Lawson, Olive ed. *The First Voice of Australian Feminism: Louisa Lawson's 'The Dawn,' 1888-1895.* Brookvale: 1990.

Magarey, Susan. 'History, Cultural Studies, and Another Look at First-Wave Feminism in Australia'. *Australian Historical Studies* 106 (1996): 96-110.

Pfisterer, Susan. 'Australian Suffrage Theatre'. Unpublished PhD Thesis, University of New England, 1996.

Pfisterer, Susan and Pickett, Carolyn. *Playing With Ideas: Australian Women Playwrights From the Suffrage to the Sixties.* Sydney: Currency Press, 1999.

Roe, Jill. 'What has Nationalism Offered Australian Women'. *Australian Women: Contemporary Feminist Thought.* Ed. Norma Grieve and Alison Burns. Melbourne: Oxford University Press, 1994. 29-39.

Spender, Dale and Hayman, C. eds. *How The Vote Was Won and Other Suffragette Plays.* London: Methuen, 1985.

Stowell, Sheila. *A Stage of Their Own: Feminist Playwrights of the Suffrage Era.* Manchester: Manchester University Press, 1992.

The Suffrage Annual and Women's Who's Who. London: 1913.

Tait, Peta. *Converging Realities: Feminism in Australian Theatre*: Sydney/ Melbourne: Currency Press/ Artmoves, 1994.

Notes

1 For an account of Bensusan's previously undiscussed play *Nobody's Sweetheart* see Pfisterer, and Pfisterer and Pickett. A general history of Australian suffrage theatre and a wider biographical project on Bensusan are under way.

2 Holledge notes (62) that Bensusan was 'Australian born', which information inspired this study.

3 One such example is that of ten-year-old Rachel Lazar, a dancer, who was probably the first Jewish girl to appear on the public stage in New South Wales. Another is Miss Emily Nathan, later Mrs Grundy, who began working for theatre entrepreneur J. C. Williamson in 1881, and was associated with the company for more than fifty years.

4 There is no formal record of Bensusan's departure from Australia, as there is a gap in the colonial shipping records during this era.

5 Ethel Bensusan and her sister Lillian rate a mention in the *Australian Biographical and Genealogical Records*, noteworthy because they were early Montessori educationalists in London. Born in Sydney in 1877, Ethel entered Sydney University in 1882. She was the tenth woman student and the first Jewish woman of the Women's College, graduating in 1897 with first-class honors in philosophy. She married Arthur Bensusan in Sydney in 1898, and they moved to London in 1901. Hypothetically, it could have been such influential women as Ethel and Lillian who introduced Bensusan to the suffrage cause, because education was an important issue in the women's movement.

6 To take one example, Bensusan was a founding executive member of the JLWS in 1913. The JLWS were concerned to form a Jewish League agitating for votes for women, one that 'many would join ... where, otherwise, they would hesitate to join a purely political society.' Their practice was to 'carry on propaganda on constitutional lines', and their moral tone was to 'emphasize the need for women's emancipation to secure the effective cooperation of men and women in combating social evils.' Beginning with fifty female and male members, by 1913 this had increased to 'some hundreds' with the subscriptions 'fixed at a low rate so as to enable Jewish Suffragists of all classes to join the League.'

Meetings were held in all parts of London. Bensusan's hard work for this league, though centred on the suffrage issue, was also devoted to improving the status of women in the Jewish community (*Suffrage Annual and Women's Who's Who*, 42).

7   Bensusan received critical attention for the first time in Holledge's pioneering feminist theatre history *Innocent Flowers*. Subsequent due attention from feminist scholars (Hirshfield, Stowell) has so far not aided her inclusion in 'general' histories of British theatre. This exclusion is not particular to Bensusan, but is typical of many of her contemporaries.

8   See for example *Votes For Women*, 22 May 1914: 545, where it was advertised that 'The League has undertaken a platform in Victoria Park on Sunday, May 24 where the East London Federation of suffragettes are holding a demonstration. The speakers will include ... Miss Inez Bensusan'. Bensusan was also friends with Winifred Mayo and other WSPU sympathisers.

Part III

Playing Australia abroad: the late twentieth century

9.
Cricket and theatre: Australians observed

Michael Billington

The contrast between the critical reception of Australian theatre in the UK and the critical reception of Australian cricket is stark. Despite this contrast, both areas of Australian performance are flourishing in their different ways, and the UK may have something to learn from Australian theatre as well as from Australian cricket.

I have an overpowering passion for cricket and a love for Australia which has been reinforced by half a dozen visits made over the last twenty years mainly to various arts festivals.[1] But my fascination with everything Australian has, I suspect, its origins in cricket. I remember vividly how in the freezing English winter of 1946-47 my father would get up at dawn and switch on the radio so that we could listen to Alan McGillvray and others reporting, through the hiss and crackle of the radio-static, on the Ashes series: a series that Australia inevitably won 3-0 though there were a couple of honourable draws in Melbourne and Adelaide where Denis Compton made a century in each innings. I was seven years old at the time. But there was something about the contrast between the bleak austerity of that post-war English winter and the sunlit image of those far-away places that lodged in my memory. The Gabba, the Adelaide Oval, the MCG were names that for me acquired a romance that other children may find in Timbuctoo, Istanbul or Luxor. I suspect I made a sub-conscious resolution that one day I would visit them. And I remember the thrill when, on my first visit to Australia in 1982, I found that my hotel overlooked the Adelaide Oval. I also recall the faint surprise on the part of my host when, in visiting Melbourne for the first time in 1990, I asked if we could just take a peek at the MCG on our way to the Playbox Theatre.

It all goes back to a childhood memory that began with radio cricket-commentary and that was fostered by many other things: a craftsman friend of my father's emigrating to Australia shortly after the war; movies featuring the evocatively named Chips Rafferty;

radio-comedians such as Dick Bentley, Joy Nichols and Bill Kerr who laconically announced 'I'm only here for four minutes.' There was also the potent influence of one of the greatest of all cricket books, Alan Ross's *Australia 55*, which transcends sports reportage to offer a poet's vision of Australia's cities and country-towns. How could one better Ross's description of Bunbury, 120 miles south of Perth?

> Bunbury, a timber port owing nothing, it appears, to Oscar Wilde, has recently been developing into a seaside resort: the town is a sprawl of villas, corrugated-iron shacks, gimcrack shops, petrol stations and a few hotels, but the Indian Ocean curves round it on three sides and the surf slithers in and out of a flat sea ... Next morning the cricket began, surf almost brushing the boundary edge and the ring filled with neighbouring farmers. (Ross 31)

Ross invokes Oscar Wilde; and, of course, Bunbury in *The Importance of Being Earnest* is not just a fictive device for escaping social duties but a metaphor for a whole gay sub-culture. But Ross's assumption that we all get the reference immediately raises an important issue: the extraordinary links between cricket and theatre. In Britain they go back a long way. There's the famous story of the Edwardian actor-manager Sir Frank Benson, who once put an advert in one of the trade-papers asking 'Wanted: slow left-arm bowler who can also play Romeo'. There's the well-known quiz question 'which Nobel Prize-winner appears in the pages of Wisden?' Answer, of course: Samuel Beckett. Harold Pinter, Terence Rattigan, Tom Stoppard, Alan Ayckbourn, David Hare, Simon Gray and Ben Travers are also part of a long line of British dramatists whose passion for the game ranges from the committed to the obsessive. Critics too are not immune. *The Diaries of Kenneth Tynan*, which might be described as a spanking good read, includes this passage written in 1976 about a Lord's Test:

> The patience of the game! I love the way it brings together so many kinds of human knowledge – of the weather and its vagaries, of the behaviour of turf and the earth beneath it, of human temperaments under stress, of human reflexes and their preferences, of time and how to use its passing. All these things interact in the course of a three-day match – better still in a four-or-five-day game. No wonder so many English writers love it to the point of fanaticism. (Tynan 340)

It is not only English writers who combine this love of theatre and cricket. One of my prize possessions is an anthology of writing about Australian cricket called *The Longest Game*. It was given me by

Wayne Harrison when he was director of the Sydney Theatre Company and it's edited by dramatist Alex Buzo and poet Jamie Grant. Grant indeed has a poem in the book called 'A First View of Cricket' and it begins with a wonderfully rhetorical question:

What use is this ritual, held
on a circular meadow
with men arranged in clusters, some
almost out of earshot? They
all wear cream flannel trousers: perhaps they're hospital
orderlies or homosexuals.

Buzo also has a section on 'Cricket in Australian Drama'. Not, he admits, a vast collection but still fascinating. In Bob Larbey's *A Month of Sundays* two veterans in a twilight home try to recall the names of the Australian Services Team of 1947. And there's a tantalising fragment from Timothy Daly's play *The Don's Last Innings* in which an old couple re-enact, with Ionesco-like frequency, the Don's swansong at the Oval in August 1948. That in itself is part of cricketing legend. The Don, needing only four runs to take his Test average to 100 and his aggregate to 7000 runs, was bowled second ball by Hollies. John Arlott, then commentating, suggested that Bradman, having been cheered all the way to the wicket by both the players and the crowd, was overcome by emotion and probably didn't see the ball clearly. In our defiantly Warwickshire household – and Hollies played for our county – that suggestion was quickly rebutted: the assumption was that the Don simply didn't read the Hollies googly. Whatever the truth of the matter I don't think you could have greater proof of cricket's affinity with drama. Here was the great man, on his last Test appearance, dismissed for a duck. Oedipus was punished for his pride, King Lear for his folly. And, though I wouldn't equate the reserved and puritanical Bradman with either of them, it was if he were being reminded by the gods that we are all mortal and that we can be extinguished in a moment of divine whim.

So cricket and drama can go naturally together; and on all my visits to Australia I have tried to combine the pleasure of watching both. We in Britain quite genuinely admire and revere Australian cricket: even in the 2001 rather lop-sided Ashes series the grounds were packed, partly because, before the series started, there was a naive English belief that we would give the Australian side a run for its money. But it was also because English cricket-lovers wanted to see the Waugh twins in action, possibly for the last time on English soil, and also because of the excitement of seeing the pounding consistency of Glenn McGrath, the enigma variations of Shane Warne and also the express speed of the much-touted Brett Lee who turned out to be a bit of a South Sea Bubble. Cricket-lovers will argue endlessly over whether this side was better than Bradman's visiting 1948 team or superior to the daunting West Indies sides of the 1970s and 80s. But the fact is that we all wanted to see them. Given that Warne, McGrath, the Waugh twins and Michael Slater had all played in English county cricket, we also felt we knew a good deal about their individual strengths and occasional weaknesses. In other words we analyse, argue over and talk about Australian cricket with an informed intelligence.

We cannot say the same about Australian theatre which we approach, in so far as we approach it all, with a faintly patronising condescension. Just look at the reviews of *Cloudstreet* when it opened at the Riverside Studios in September 1999 (Photo 12). In the end, the reviews were ecstatic. But Georgina Brown in the *Mail on Sunday* (19 September 1999) began thus: 'This week's starter for ten: list Australia's contributors to the contemporary theatre scene. I managed Dame Edna Everage, Rolf Harris and his didgeridoo, and Kylie Minogue before being told I was snooty.' John Peter in the *Sunday Times* (19 September 1999) led off his rave review with the confident assertion: 'You will not have heard of the Company B Belvoir, or the Black Swan Theatre Company, both of Sydney, Australia.' Well you won't have heard of Sydney's Black Swan Theatre because it's actually based in Perth. And isn't there something a touch late colonialist about 'Sydney, Australia' as if it were some far-flung outpost of the British empire? If I said that Mr Peter hails from Budapest, Hungary, I suspect he would be deeply insulted. Nicholas de Jongh in the *Evening Standard* (15 September 1999) also assured us that 'Cloudstreet shows that Down Under theatre has dazzlingly risen from the simplicities of low-level realism'. So much for Ray Lawler, Dorothy Hewett, Patrick White, David Williamson and Louis Nowra all supposedly toiling away in the realistic saltmines. My point is that no sports writer would dare write about the Australian cricket-team in those terms. So why do theatre critics feel free to be so loftily condescending?

I suppose there are several answers to that question. It has partly to do with ignorance. Not many drama critics have been as fortunate as myself in visiting Australia frequently and seeing first-hand the dynamic work that goes on in all the major centres. Also the importation of Australian theatre to Britain was patchy for several years especially after the commercial failure of a couple of David

Williamson plays. And there is more than a touch of cultural arrogance in British attitudes towards Australia: the Booker prize may go to Peter Carey and Thomas Keneally but we still like to cling to the comforting stereotype of Australia as a land of sport, sun and soaps while theatre is our particular province.

If there is ignorance and arrogance on the British side, I suspect the Australian capacity for self-deprecation is misunderstood over here. At the same time as *Cloudstreet* opened in London, *Cosi* by Louis Nowra was playing at Hampstead's New End. One of the jokes in that ran: 'You know what culture is for most Australians ...? It's the stuff that grows on stale Cheddar' (Nowra 9). In the play the line is spoken by an inmate of a mental institution in 1970 and is clearly the product of a specific place and time: it's not meant to be a general truth. But sometimes the Australian gift for self-mockery or for comically exploiting its own national stereotypes – as in Crocodile Dundee or Edna Everage – is mistaken in Britain for a literal fact. It's as if Australians were to believe that Britain is exactly represented by the image of John Cleese as a lunging, lunatic, brolly-clutching, pinstriped civil servant. Too often in Britain the comic caricature of Australia is taken for the reality.

But, since I've mentioned the epoch-making *Cloudstreet*, it might be worth asking what it is that gives Australian theatre its vitality. It's always difficult to generalise. Dramatists are driven to write plays far more by particular circumstances and temperamental pressures than by some mythical notion of the national zeitgeist. One of the first Australian plays I saw actually in Australia, in Adelaide in 1982, was Rob George's *Percy and Rose* dealing with the more sensational aspects of the private life of the composer Percy Grainger. Not to beat about the bush, though he would clearly have loved to do just that, the play was about the appetite that Grainger shared with Rousseau, Swinburne, Kenneth Tynan and many others for spanking. But clearly Grainger's private kinks were much on people's minds at the time since Melbourne was then just about to stage *A Whip Round For Percy Grainger*.

As a frequent visitor to Australia over the past twenty years what has really struck me, however, is the way theatre is constantly used to explore the question of national identity: who are we? what is our history? where are we going? how do we fit into the world? These are the questions that recur again and again in Australian plays. It is as if drama is being used as a form of self-examination in a society that seems to me in a constant state of flux. That agitation about identity is certainly very visible to the outsider. When I first went to the Adelaide Festival in 1982, everyone I met from Patrick White onwards was talking about the imminence of the republic and the dissolution of the monarchical links. When I went back to Adelaide ten years later, the agenda had shifted somewhat: it was then, possibly under the influence of Paul Keating, about the importance of establishing Australia's cultural and economic ties with its neighbours in South East Asia rather than with the UK or America. Most recently, in Adelaide and Sydney last year, I found there was only one real topic of discussion: how to overcome the sense of historical injustice towards the Aboriginal population. In the run-up to the Sydney Olympics, there seemed to be a hunger for a symbolic gesture of reconciliation.

The subject of Australian drama is Australia itself. Even when the focus is primarily domestic, the unspoken questions are invariably social and political. A good example is *Hotel Sorrento* by Hannie Rayson, which I saw in Melbourne in 1990. It's a Chekhovian play about three sisters coping with the recent death of their father and trying to discover a meaning for the future. One of the sisters runs a gourmet deli in the Victorian coastal town of Sorrento. Another is a New York-based advertising executive. And the third, is the expatriate, Meg, who has spent ten years in London, married a wet Englishman, been nominated for the Booker Prize and has given a notorious interview in the *Guardian* – no less – in which she has claimed that 'Australians are terrified of any expression of passion. Unless of course the passion is about hedonism and making money. Oh, and sport' (Rayson 73). In the course of the play we see Meg's return home and confrontation with a changing Australia. Rayson also touches on a wide variety of themes: the decaying cultural cringe, the rise of female assertiveness, the need for writers to confront the big issues rather than to retreat into studies of tortured adolescence. But finally the play is about confrontation with one's roots, the sufficiency of life in Australia itself and the challenge of the future. In the final, very Chekhovian image the old home in Sorrento is put up for auction and, as the three sisters freeze, the auctioneer cries 'Who'd like to give me a reasonable start?' (Rayson 90). The implication is that an uncertain, potentially exciting future awaits not only the sisters but also Australia itself.

This notion of a country in transition haunts most of the plays I have seen in Australia. One of the best is Michael Gow's *Away* which uses Shakespeare's *A Midsummer Night's Dream* as its starting-point and shows how the lives of three intersecting groups are totally transfigured as they head for their vacation on Queensland's Gold Coast during the summer of 1967-68. The play is partly about the way individual lives are changed through exposure to nature. But Gow is also writing about the end of the Australian holiday, about the need to acknowledge and finally discard the colonial inheritance and about the nation's entry into mature global responsibility. Watching the play, set very deliberately in the late 1960s, I was reminded of something that the late Philip Parsons said at a public forum I attended. He attributed the upsurge in Australian drama in large part to the Vietnam War. 'Australians,' he said, 'wanted to know who they were, where they were going and how they fitted into the world. Suddenly it was all right to be us.'

But if, as I've suggested, national identity is the abiding theme of Australian drama, a problem arises. Is that theme of any interest to audiences outside Australia? The short answer is 'yes' where the theme acquires a metaphorical resonance and 'no' where it doesn't. The easiest example to offer is of Australia's most celebrated dramatist, David Williamson. In a very informative, if now dated, documentary, Williamson described the imperative to write plays in the early 1970s. He vividly described the resentment that he and other young writers felt at the way Australian theatre at that time was dominated by British and American imports. 'We were locked out of our own theatre', he said. And he recalled the exhilaration of discovering, when his first work was staged at Melbourne's La Mama, that there was a voracious appetite for Australian work. His early plays, such as *Don's Party*, *The Removalists* and *The Club*, were quickly picked up in Britain because they both informed us about Australia and had a more universal application. *The Removalists*, shown at the Royal Court, is a particularly fine play and, as Williamson himself said, it's very much about the authoritarianism that lurks inside many Australians and about the confrontational nature of social relations. But it's also a play that makes sense anywhere since it relates the violence of officialdom to a guiltily repressed sexuality. A later Williamson play like *Emerald City*, dealing with the urban rivalry between Melbourne and Sydney, seemed to me about as relevant to London as a play about Glasgow and Edinburgh competitiveness would be in Sydney. And while Williamson's *The Great Man* – dealing with the chicanery and compromises of the Australian Labor Government – connected very vibrantly with its audience in Sydney, I couldn't see it having much impact in Tranmere or Tallahassee. Which, in one sense, doesn't matter a damn. Plays which deal with specific local or national issues often do important work in the community. But for a play to travel it needs to have some wider metaphorical meaning.

That is one reason why *Cloudstreet* has become the most successful Australian theatrical export since Ray Lawler's *The Summer of the Seventeenth Doll*. Lawler's play, with its story of Queensland cane-cutters and their annual festive re-union, both criticised the myth of the Australian Outback and at the same time dealt with the universal issue of dreams confronting reality. And, in a not dissimilar way, *Cloudstreet* manages to operate on several levels at once. Because it ran for five hours and because it dealt with the fractured lives of two families living in a huge old house in Perth, many British critics – maybe Australian ones too – compared it to soap opera. I think it's high time we stopped all using that as a critical term. The essence of a soap-opera is that it has no terminal point: it has action but no visible destination. A work such as *Cloudstreet* – either in Tim Winton's original novel or in Nick Enright and Justin Monjo's adaptation – does, however, have an end towards which it is moving. Indeed it has a very precise artistic shape in that it begins with the boyhood accident that leaves Fish Lamb permanently brain-damaged and it ends with his suicide. That ending still leaves me slightly uncomfortable in its implied transcendence and its endowment of Fish with a poetic sense of self-discovery. But that's a matter of taste. What can't be denied is that *Cloudstreet* has a clearly articulated structure which is a million miles from the one-damn-thing-after-another rhythm of the soaps. Nowadays it's regarded as intellectually snobbish to attack soaps: people say that they are the modern equivalent of the Victorian novel and that *Eastenders* is the Dickens of our day. Bunk. Soaps are the enemy of art precisely because of their unending quality and because character and narrative are never brought to a point of fulfilment.

But why is it that *Cloudstreet* has captured the imagination of audiences everywhere? Partly because it puts so much of Australia itself onto the stage. Katherine Brisbane once said that the recurrent theme of Australian drama is 'the past in the present, the past bearing down on the present'. That clearly is true of *Cloudstreet* where a ubiquitous figure, called simply Black Man, reminds us whose land the characters inhabit. The play is also dominated by the image of the house occupied by the Lamb and Pickles families: a house haunted by the spirit of an Aboriginal girl driven to suicide by a sadistic Victorian missionary. The house becomes a character in itself: at different times it is 'sad', 'in pain' or 'sick' and clearly needs to be restored to health. The house itself stands for the country at large. But I also take the play to be an examination of some fundamental division within the Australian character. The Pickles mob represents the easy-going, laid-back, betting-and-boozing aspect of the Australian psyche: the God-fearing, work-driven, Bible-reading Lambs embody its puritan work ethic. Of course, the division is not water-tight: Rose Pickles, for example, rejects her mother's horizontal hedonism. But between them the Pickles and the Lambs stand for the cavalier and roundhead qualities, which I have certainly observed in Australian life. If you want to see it in cricketing terms: Mark Waugh would clearly play for the Pickles team while twin-brother Steve would be on the side of the Lambs.

Cloudstreet offers a metaphor for Australia in the period from 1945 to 1965. But there are several other reasons why this play has become a global success. One obviously is the scope of the narrative itself, which embraces birth, marriage, death, separation, homecoming: all the strands that make up family life. There is also within the play a quality of charity, forgiveness and even optimism that is as refreshing as it is unfashionable in modem drama: Mrs Pickles, who moves out of the house to live in a tent in the garden where she can wrestle with her soul, concludes that 'The strong are here to look after the weak ... and the weak are here to teach the strong' (Enright and Monjo 81), which is as close as the play comes to expressing a message. The ensemble performance and Neil Armfield's production are also a major factor in explaining the work's success. I met Neil Armfield on my first visit to Adelaide in 1982 when he was a young director working on Patrick White's *Signal Driver*, and I've followed his career with interest ever since. At the Sydney Opera House I saw his remarkable productions of *Tristan and Isolde* and *The Eighth Wonder* – actually dealing with the conflicts over the building of the Opera House itself; and in London in 2000 I watched him working with a group of schoolchildren on *La Strada*, part of an English National Opera triple-bill. I believe he's a world-class director. And in *Cloudstreet* he certainly showed a greater understanding of the spatial dynamics of the Olivier Theatre than many British directors. The fluidity of the staging was what most struck me. One example that sticks in my mind is the scene where Rose Pickles goes to a pretentious literary prize-giving with her boy-friend who is an aspiring poet: the scene is both a satire on the cultural cringe and the fake Bloomsbury atmosphere of Perth prize-givings but also a sharp comment on the exclusiveness of literary coteries and Rose's sense of isolation. Armfield managed to convey all of that by showing how the little knots of Perth poetasters cut Rose out of their conversation and then formed a diagonal line across the stage as if they were an army that she had to confront. Not many directors these days know how to use choreographic grouping to convey meaning.

Cloudstreet is an acknowledged triumph. But my contention that the strength of Australian drama lies in its concern with national self-definition was confirmed by my experiences last year in both Sydney and Adelaide. As I've said, the issue I found discussed everywhere was the need to rectify the overwhelming sense of historical injustice towards the Aboriginal population. In society at large it was proving difficult: it was in the arts, in drama specifically, that some real reconciliation was taking place. I saw at the Sydney Theatre Company a lively, generous-hearted musical *The Sunshine Club*, which dealt with an Aboriginal soldier who, on returning to Australia in 1945 after wartime service, set up an inter-racial dance club in defiance of the curfew laws of the time. I had no idea that racial segregation was so strict at that time or that apartheid-like laws were in operation. But what was fascinating was the show's conciliatory tone. It was written and directed by Wesley Enoch, who has an Aboriginal father and a Spanish-Danish mother, and who ended the show with the modern image of a mixed-blood director auditioning white actors: not, I felt, in any spirit of we-are-the-masters-now recrimination but as a symbol of how far Australia had moved in fifty years. That sense of the theatre as a place where history is confronted in order to understand the present also characterised a remarkable show at the Adelaide Festival. *Ochre and Dust* consisted of two elderly Aboriginal storytellers sitting on top of a sandstone mound and recounting their battles with Prime Minister Malcolm Fraser over the land rights to Uluru in the days when it was still best known as Ayers Rock. But while the show celebrated the women's guts and tenacity it also touched on their generational sympathies with ageing white folk concerned about juvenile drug-taking and delinquency. 'Down here,' they claimed, 'they're sniffing glue, up there they're sniffing petrol.' The show suggested that the old, even when divided by race, are united by their concern for succeeding generations. It was a beautiful piece of narrative theatre that took place in the Art Gallery of South Australia along with a brilliant exhibition of contemporary Aboriginal art called 'Beyond The Pale'. The broadcaster Caroline Baum remarked that for the first time the indigenous population are being seen not as historic victims but as original artists.

On returning from my last trip to Australia in 2000, I wrote 'Australia … has an enviable knack of turning social problems into creative opportunities' (*Guardian* 22 March 2000); and that seems to me broadly true. But over the years, in talking to people like Jim Sharman, Neil Armfield, Robyn Nevin, Robyn Archer, Wayne Harrison, Carrillo Gantner, Wesley Enoch and many others I've been struck by their passion, commitment and belief in the idea of Australian theatre. They obviously welcome European comment and exposure but it's not the be-all-and-end-all of their existence. They are forging a theatre that is identifiably Australian and that confronts the problems of a society bursting with constitutional, political, racial and sexual tensions. They are also creating a theatre that, while acknowledging what's happening in Britain and the USA, is increasingly self-sustaining. The bad old days of JC Williamson's shipping out sub-West End tours featuring declining Shaftesbury Avenue stars are now happily extinct.

Talk of declining English stars brings me inexorably back to cricket. Admittedly the parallels between cricket and theatre are not exact. If Australia is successfully emergent in theatre, in cricket it is globally dominant. And, while there are lingering traces of colonial condescension in the British attitude to Australian artistic life, there are none in our attitude to Australian cricket: the mere fact of Rodney Marsh heading the English Cricket Academy is proof that the boot is now very much on the other foot. And yet when I look at the awesome power of the Australian cricket team, particularly under Mark Taylor and Steve Waugh, I do see certain parallels between sport and the arts. In a nutshell, it has to do with a certain quality of optimism, self-belief and a defiant pride in being Australian. I definitely find this combination in Australian theatre: a feeling that it neither has to live off foreign imports or subscribe to the forms and content of British or American drama. I recall David Williamson saying that he very much enjoyed seeing Tom Stoppard's *Jumpers* in London but that it seemed totally irrelevant when it was staged in Australia. And that quality of self-belief, which I constantly note in theatre, seems to me the absolute key to Australia's recent success on the cricket-field.

There was a defining moment in the 2001 Ashes series. After the First Test at Edgbaston in early July, Nasser Hussain, the English captain, once again suffered a broken finger. This posed a big question. Who should succeed him at Lords and most likely Trent Bridge as well? Alec Stewart, struggling to find his own form as batsman and keeper, indicated he wasn't interested. Mike Atherton, in what was to prove his final season, initially shrugged off the idea of taking over from Nasser. And, while voices were raised in the media on behalf of Marcus Trescothick, he didn't exactly throw his hat in the ring. Steve Waugh seized on the English embarrassment and said it was inconceivable any Australian would ever think of turning down the captaincy of his country if it were offered. There was an element of gamesmanship and psychology in all this: having just given England a thrashing at Edgbaston and having his thumb, as it were, on the windpipe, Waugh wasn't going to let go. But I'd give Waugh the credit of meaning what he said. He couldn't believe anyone would not want to captain his country; and one only has to look at his own keenness to return to the fold after the injury he sustained at Trent Bridge to see his sincerity. He worked twelve hours a day to get himself fit again for the Oval. In other words, playing for Australia is a matter of pride, and captaining it is virtually a moral duty. In contrast, captaining England has come to seem like a penance.

Gideon Haigh – the best of the current crop of Australian cricket-writers – wrote several pieces in the *Guardian* in the summer of 2001 on this theme: both on Australian pride and the ability to seize on the opposition's weaknesses. After Australia's retention of the Ashes at Trent Bridge, Haigh wrote a fascinating piece about Steve Waugh's memory of what had happened there four years previously (*Guardian* 6 August 2001). Waugh had noticed Adam Hollioake's failure to wear his England cap in his debut Test. He had also spotted Andy Caddick and Dean Headley being interviewed on the boundary while Mike Atherton and Mark Butcher were going out to bat instead of being in the dressing-room to wish their comrades luck. Waugh was not impugning Hollioake's patriotism or Caddick and Headley's team-spirit: he had simply detected a weakness which he knew he could later exploit. But, as Gideon Haigh pointed out, the problem for England in replicating the Australian collective ethic is twofold:
> First, it came with success, rather than prefiguring it. Second, it hinges on a kind of naive nationalism built on simple symbolism: baggy green cap, Bradman legend, Gallipoli sacrifice et al. The days when English birth conferred 'first prize in the lottery of life' now seem long ago.

What Haigh calls 'naive nationalism' seems to me the key to Australia's cricketing dominance and theatrical vibrancy. When

Michael Slater, in the last Ashes tour, made a century at Lords, he instantly kissed the Australian symbol on his helmet: it's a gesture everyone now copies. But when an Englishman does it it looks like affectation whereas when Slater did it it seemed to spring from some inner impulse. The trip to Gallipoli which the Australians made en route to England before the recent tour also wasn't just a pious gesture. It was a way of putting sport in perspective and of reminding these young cricketers of the sacrifices made by their forbears. Spending at least one day at four of this year's Test Matches, I was also struck by the collective spirit of the Australian side: the sense that, if someone failed, it was another player's duty to succeed. The classic example came at Trent Bridge. At the end of the first day England had been dismissed for 185 but Australia were in considerable disarray at 105-7. I felt that England had a sniff of a chance, but I reckoned without Adam Gilchrist who went on to make 54 and who, partnered by Gillespie, steered Australia off the rocks and even gave them a slight first innings lead. With a batsman as good as Gilchrist at number seven, it's hard for Australia to be beaten. If miracles do sometimes happen, it's only under the mackerel skies of Headingley.

But if any one Australian cricketer in recent years has been a source of constant pleasure it is Mark Waugh. Watching him bat, albeit fairly briefly, at Trent Bridge I was reminded of something Chekhov wrote in his Letters: 'when a man spends the least possible number of movements over some definite action that is grace.' And Mark Waugh has grace in abundance. It doesn't matter whether Waugh is simply taking guard, leaning nonchalantly on his bat at the non-striker's end or caressing a full-pitched ball off his toes to send it speeding towards the boundary, he does everything with exquisite economy and without a single superfluous gesture. Fielding in the slips, he also has the ability to pluck balls out of the air and from just above ground-height with a negligent ease. The argument against him is that he lacks application. On a flat track at the Oval this year he got out for 120 while brother Steve, severely injured, battled on for 152 not out. But mere accumulation of runs is not Mark Waugh's forte. It is the ability to bat with fluency, ease and an apparent lack of effort; to make it seem as if there is a golden inevitability about the ball's progress to the boundary after the faintest of caresses from the Waugh bat. In cricket, there are grafters and there are poets. Mark Waugh is definitely one of the latter; and, to an Englishman of my generation, the one batsman he reminds me of is Gloucestershire's Tom Graveney who had a similar kind of refined artistry.

Of course, there are bowlers who give one a different kind of pleasure. The pace of Thomson and Lillee was awesome to behold. Glenn McGrath may not have their raw speed but there's a perfectly rhythmical action and a controlled accuracy that is pure delight. And then there is the speed, the constant drama of watching Warne bowl. There is Warne triumphant, Warne indignant, Warne exasperated, Warne furious and Warne appealing. He's the Maria Callas of leg-spin: every ball seems to elicit some kind of reaction from this blond magician. By some strange fluke I was in Wellington on the very day last year that Warne passed Lillee's record as the highest Australian wicket-taker of all time and I was at the Oval in August when Warne became the first Australian ever to take 400 wickets. I hope I'm there when he gets his 500th. But, at the risk of sounding heretical, I almost enjoy seeing Warne bowl on television as much as I do in the flesh. At home you have the pleasure of seeing his grip in close-up and of getting instant re-plays of each ball. Pace bowling is more exciting when you are physically present: spin-bowling, I'd suggest, gains from the box and turns us all into armchair googly-spotters.

I could dwell on Australian cricketers for ever. I didn't see the Don but I did see Lindwall and Miller, Hassett and Morris, Harvey and Benaud, the Chappell Brothers, Thomson and Lillee and now the Waugh twins and McGrath and Warne so I can't complain. To an English cricket-lover, these men are giants and it baffles the imagination how we, the English, are even going to score more than the occasional victory against Australia in the future. Australia has many advantages when it comes to cricket: an ideal climate, a structured system that spots talent young and allows it to progress and a supportive culture. But I come back again to the quality that Gideon Haigh calls a 'naive nationalism' and what I would call internal conviction and an optimism about future possibilities. That is the quality that for me defines Australian cricket and that is also abundantly present in its theatre. I speak as an Englishman who actually enjoys living in a country that is equally defined by damp, doubt, insecurity, irony and the terrifying weight of history. The Australians often characterise us as 'whingeing Poms' and that's fairly accurate. We whinge about everything under the sun including things of which we should be defiantly proud such as the National Health Service or the social security system: better to be sick or poor in Britain than in the United States. But to live in Britain is undeniably to live in a country that is still coming to terms with the loss of empire and that even now cannot quite determine where its future lies. To visit Australia, however, is to visit a country that, while wracked with internal divisions, seems full of confidence, hope and a chipper and sometimes aggressive buoyancy.

That resilient optimism seems to me the key to Australia's theatre: that feeling, in Philip Parsons's words, 'that it's all right to be us'. It has also long been the guiding spirit of Australian cricket. My main wish, as a loyal Englishman, is that Australia's theatre goes from strength to strength and that its cricket encounters a period of mysterious and unaccountable decline. It's not that I don't love Australia. It's just that I would like to see the Ashes become a real contest once again and the most vital of all cricket series acquiring something of its ancient blood-lust and theatrical drama.

References

Buzo, Alex and Jamie Grant, ed. *The Longest Game, A Collection of the Best Cricket Writing from Alexander to Zavos, from the Gabba to the Yabba.* Australia: Heinemann, 1990.

Enright, Nick and Justin Monjo. *Cloudstreet.* Sydney: Currency Press, 1999.

Nowra, Louis. *Cosi.* Sydney: Currency Press, 1992.

Rayson, Hannie. *Hotel Sorrento.* Sydney: Currency Press, 1990.

Ross, Alan. *Australia 55: A Journal of the MCC tour.* London: Michael Joseph, 1955.

Tynan, Kenneth. *The Diaries of Kenneth Tynan.* Ed. John Lahr. London: Bloomsbury, 2001.

Notes

1   This paper was first delivered as the British Australian Studies Association annual lecture, at the Australian High Commission in London, November 2001. The event was sponsored by Monash University.

10.
What price a global culture? (or can you hope to clone a Tap Dog?)

Richard Cave

The international success of **Tap Dogs** *is analysed alongside material taken from an interview with Wayne Harrison, the show's producer. It is argued that the globalisation of* **Tap Dogs** *produced complex and new meanings for the show, but that the successive cloned productions took the event further and further from its Australian origins, and diluted important questions raised by earlier versions of the show including questions about homosociality and homosexuality.*

Two contrasting responses to *Tap Dogs* (see Photos 13 and 14), one Australian, one English, are deliberately juxtaposed here. In the first, Wayne Harrison, the promoter of the show, talks with Elizabeth Schafer and Susan Bradley Smith about its creation and his cultural ambitions for its future (Harrison). In the second Richard Cave, an English academic with a trained interest in dance and movement, analyses his own and English critics' responses to *Tap Dogs* on its first showing with the original company in Scotland and England in 1995-96, and to performances by the troupe touring in 2001-02. This discussion engages with the information provided by Harrison's interview to show how it considerably resolved ambiguities about how the production might be interpreted as 'playing Australia' for English audiences, which the performances had provoked for Richard Cave and for many other critics. While the interview elucidates much, it also raises questions about cultural communication within an international market. Though Richard Cave had the benefit of studying and editing Harrison's spoken text, circumstances unfortunately allowed Harrison no comeback to what was extrapolated from an informal conversation. No direct dialogue was possible; hence the two voices and two texts are offered openly as in part complementary and in part confrontational.

I. Wayne Harrison in interview

What was it that made **Tap Dogs** *an international success?*

Wayne Harrison: In the first instance it had to be a success in Australia to propel it anywhere. There were many elements involved; and so it's very hard to actually analyse what made it work. A lot of planets aligned to make it happen. The original pitch was interesting because the show was part of a celebration for the tenth anniversary of the Sydney Theatre Company's home, the Wharf, and I wanted to create something very special for that. There was to be a nice mix of the mainstream and the radical in the formulation; and that affected the programming. I wanted *Stomp* to come out and be part of it, and then we were looking for an Australian act to complement that programming.[1] Dein Perry was coming out of his success with David Atkins with *Hot Shoe Shuffle* and was looking to strut out on his own. He was just ready at that particular point to bring together a lot of ideas that he'd been workshopping. He got a $20,000 grant from the Australia Council to do a workshop on tap, which had led to *Hot Shoe Shuffle* and then to *Tap Dogs*. I wanted *Stomp* because I thought that they were on their way to being the most successful performance troupe in the world, and they were just reaching the point where no-one would be able to afford them any more. We managed to get in just before they went into major international status. I felt that there was some sort of trend happening based on percussion, that there was something in the popular mood, which was about a primal urge to hear these percussive sounds, and to have these sounds expressed as a form of popular entertainment. Since then with the Irish dancing shows, *Riverdance* and *Lord of the Dance*, one has seen it flower into a worldwide phenomenon that's had several branches to it. There was something going on in terms of visually-based, percussive-based entertainment forms; I could sense that, and it just so happened that there were other people like Dein Perry around saying, 'There is something going on here, let's be part of it'. So: it all just coalesced at a time when there was a worldwide interest in it. It had, too, something to do with a new generation of theatregoers, people who were bred on the visually-based MTV video clip. During the original three-and-a-half week season of *Tap Dogs* at the Wharf, forty-thousand people came through and eighty percent of them had never been to the Wharf or the Sydney Theatre Company before, which showed there was a whole new wave of people who were interested in coming and seeing shows like *Stomp* and *Tap Dogs*.

Was new marketing involved to get these new audiences?

Wayne Harrison: That was the start of Ross Mollinson's work for the STC and he went on to become what was quite a controversial appointment in that he was out-sourced. Traditionally theatre companies like STC had in-house people doing all their marketing, but I found that to be inefficient: essentially when people are there selling eighteen shows a year, they get burned out by about show four; and I needed to pitch on a much more commercial basis, so we out-sourced the position. I tried during the nine years I was at the STC to put a contemporary edge on everything, and to reach new audiences by creating non-traditional theatre fare for a theatre company. A lot of people, even a couple of board members, said what is a serious theatre company like STC doing with a tap dance show? But my philosophy had always been: it's a theatre company and you can define theatre in any way you want to. Often you get accused of being elitist, that your programming is too narrow, and only appeals to a certain percentage. And then, of course, ironically, you get criticised when you want to broaden the spectrum of the work that you do and move into other areas.

What was very helpful when *Tap Dogs* hit the stage was that it was a highly entertaining and very proficient show; it had several world class performers who were champion tap dancers; they had gone to America and beaten the best of the black dancers in the Florida championship. The show was a work of some quality; Dein Perry's ideas when they were married to Nigel Triffitt's design and directing ideas were exceptional, and so it became as successful as *Stomp* in Australian terms and went on several national tours. Why it was useful for us to see beyond the national success was that, in not being language-based, it gave us access into markets in Asia where we'd never been able to penetrate before. You find more and more when you travel through Asia that, if theatres are going to take a language-based company, then they'll go to the RSC or to the National. If they want English speakers, then they get the *real* English speakers (as they see it). So it's very hard for theatre companies like STC to emulate the success of Playbox, for example, which does very fine work in terms of co-producing with Asian theatre interests. But that's very much a part of their platform: they've spent a lot of time pioneering it, whereas large Australian theatre companies by necessity have to spend much of their time and operation just protecting their local subscription base in terms of the work that they do, which leaves not a lot of time to get out there in the field and create Asian contacts. So we were finding it difficult to get into the Asian markets and establish a presence there. This was during the later years of the Keating regime, when they were putting a lot of pressure on us (at least we *felt* that there was pressure through the Australia Council) to get out and make those Asian contacts. And we did eventually through *Tap Dogs*.

Ironically, despite our success the State government cut our subsidy by nearly $90,000, which did seem to be fairly harsh treatment after such a successful show. If you were to go to Cologne this weekend and buy a programme for *Tap Dogs* which is playing there, you would get pages of promotion for Newcastle NSW and Australian culture; and so removing the subsidy did seem to me to be hardly the reward you would expect for that sort of promotion. It's believed that the millions of dollars which they spend on the fireworks in Australia each New Year are worth it, because of the exposure we get on CNN and prime-time American TV, but I really think that something like *Tap Dogs*, which is actually at the coal face in terms of changing people's impressions of what Australian culture can be, is equally important. Maybe *Tap Dogs* is not what you want to define Australian culture by; but it's there and it's not just an image that's flashing by you instantly, it's something that is there for you to savour and to remember having experienced at first hand. I always think that live theatre is so important.

*How did **Tap Dogs** change impressions of Australian culture?*

Wayne Harrison: I think *Tap Dogs* was successful here for the same reasons that I've explained about Australia: that it is actually an excellent piece of entertainment. But it does have a political level to it, which I was always attracted to. Whether it reinforces or challenges stereotypes, I'll leave for those who are better qualified to judge. The political level I like is that there is no reason why these young men from Newcastle, which is the working-class centre of Australian steel industries, should end up being world-class tap dancers. There is a sort of incongruity there that I like. Something happens in Australia in terms of the way mothers, when they come into contact with the insensitivity of the male side of Australian culture, suddenly take these boys to tap dancing classes as a way of injecting some culture into a basically non-cultural life. And they choose tap dancing because, if you look at someone like Gene Kelly, you can actually be involved in a cultural pursuit without necessarily assaulting your masculinity: if you dance like Fred Astaire then it's getting a little bit *iffy*, but it you dance like Gene Kelly close to the ground in a very macho kind of way, then you can get away with injecting some culture into your life without having your masculinity assaulted. That seems to me what is at the core of what has produced this phenomenon. Boys, usually when they get to puberty or deeper into their teenage years, reject the dancing and leave it. Which is exactly what happened to Dein Perry and most of the Tap Dogs; under peer-group pressure they abandoned this cultural pursuit and went into trades and became plumbers and fitters and turners. Then, though a series of accidents and opportunities, Dein Perry comes back into a cultural orbit through a commercial theatre; he gets a grant from the Australia Council to workshop his dancing ideas; he brings back all the boys who had abandoned their theatrical pursuits, and he forms the Tap Dogs. The beauty of it is that when I first started (and why we had trouble cloning it in America) there was nothing theatrical about these performers, except they have beautiful, sweet feet. From the knees up they are non-theatrical. But in America, when you want to put tap dancers in to it, you end up with a Broadway tradition of eyes, tits and teeth and it's all very above the waist, whereas these guys had a very sort of untheatrical theatricality about them, which people found charming. They found it culturally exact in terms of what Australianness in a male context is all about: that, yes, it could be incredibly creative, but at the same time there was a kind of paradox there, that it was not appearing to or striving to be creative in the first instance. And that seemed to translate as an Australianness, it seemed to actually encapsulate the essence of an Australian maleness and then an Australianness beyond that. That it was cultural but non-cultural at the same time.

So how did the transfer to the US work?

Wayne Harrison: There were two *Tap Dogs* companies. They've been touring there for nearly three years now. Usually there are one or two Australians left in each company, and then we augment these with Americans; but you really have to work hard to get the Americanness out of the tap dancers. We have to rely on the director to strip it away. Many dancers are rejected: it's very hard to actually clone the companies. In fact the pool of dancers world-wide who can dance Dein Perry's style, which is now known as the Australian style, is very small, because it isn't part of the international performance style. It's very much his own style, which came from his socialisation, I suppose; and that goes a long way towards trying to define what makes it work. It's the only way that *I* can do it: when you look at it, you think: well these guys should be at the pub drinking on a Friday night, but they're not, they're tap dancing together, and you can see the tap dancing as a metaphor for the normal working-class bonding sessions of males or such. That's how Dein managed to get on stage something that was quintessentially Australian. It's not necessarily there in international eyes, but it was definitely there in Australian eyes: people recognised it and said how this was unique. And that's why this show was successful: once Dein's radical ideas for tap dancing were married with the *enfant terrible* ideas of Nigel Triffitt (it was Hilary Linstead, who is the agent for both Dein and Nigel, who brought those two together) you then get two interesting strands of Australian theatre culture coming together: Nigel, who was always on the festival-fringe of Australian culture, coming together with Dein, who was coming from a very working class non-theatrical background.

Do you have a dance background yourself?

Wayne Harrison: I trained as a tap dancer for sixteen years of my life. My mother took me off to tap dancing classes for exactly the reasons that I articulated: she wanted to put some culture into my life, and that was the only form of it that my father would tolerate. For loads of Australian guys, who come like me from that background, it's exactly the same story.

Tap Dogs' *success somewhat overshadows your production of Michael Gow's* ***Sweet Phoebe****, starring Cate Blanchett. Would you say something about the productions' comparative success?*

Wayne Harrison: If *Sweet Phoebe* were done now with Cate Blanchett in it, it would transfer easily into the West End. People would be snapping it up. Back then, the timing was slightly out, maybe. Part of my philosophy at STC is relevant here. When I went to the Warehouse early in my regime to direct Michael Gow's *On Top Of The World* (it had premiered at STC a decade before), it was to be the start of a series of works with which we aimed to establish a beachhead in London, where people would get into the habit of seeing and appreciating Australian work.   I believe habit-forming has to be involved: you have to have an investment in the culture of the country and the careers of certain playwrights before you can get to the point where something may just capture the imagination of the public the way *Tap Dogs* did. It will capture a smaller part of the imagination, because the appeal of a play is more intellectual than *Tap Dogs*, which is based on an emotional, musical, visual level. It was the late Philip Parsons, my mentor for many years, who used to say that you can't come into London with a play with all guns blazing and say, 'Here we are, we've come from the colonies to tell you how to do spoken drama', because that will not wash at all. His idea was that you should come in through the back door, establish a presence, and let them discover you. We did a lot of groundwork with *On Top Of The World*, and I felt that it was a very good production that was quite well reviewed at the time, although people found the acting styles (with a cast of Australians) very different from British acting styles. You can see this in some of the reactions to Cate Blanchett's performance in *Plenty* too, where you can see what Australian society actually does to acting styles. The acting is much more bold, more adventurous, more vivid in the space; and, when you surround it with English actors, suddenly it's thrown into sharp relief and everybody goes: 'Oh! This is very different'. Some people rave about it, some say: 'Well hold on, I don't quite get this'. And that's what happened with *On Top Of The World*. But it was an interesting exercise, and I think it was the sort of project that companies like STC should be involved in: just showing that this is what Australian acting is. How do you react to it? How does it relate to your acting styles? But more importantly we wanted to create a relationship with the critics. Some like Michael Billington have a great aptitude, an appreciation of Australian drama; and, I believe, have made a commitment, an investment, in knowing and supporting Australian dramatic work. And we got the payoff when *Sweet Phoebe* came over two years later. We had set off a rhythm whereby maybe every two years there's going to be an Australian play here by Michael Gow, and so more reviewers came this time and more of them made connections to the body of work that Michael Gow has done and to his situation in the canon of Australian work. I really believe that it was an educational thing that we had to do. When I set up the STC foundation at the theatre company, people sneered at what used to be known as extra-curricular work; but I thought it was essential to what we were doing. *Sweet Phoebe* and *Tap Dogs* have proved my point.

II. Interrogations: changing reactions to *Tap Dogs*

There is no denying that *Tap Dogs* was (and for different reasons, remains) a phenomenon. After a successful run in Australia as part of the special season to celebrate ten years of the Sydney Theatre Company at the Wharf in January 1995, the show toured to the Edinburgh Festival Fringe where overnight acclaim accelerated its move first to Sadler's Wells and then from February 1995 to London's West End. In the world of tap dancing the Empire had decidedly struck back ('struck' would seem the appropriate word, given the barrage of sound the performers galvanise with their feet). Six years and countless Australian and international awards later, the show is still on the road, touring England after an 'anniversary return' to Sadlers Wells. In the interim, to quote from Nigel Triffitt's biographical note in the current programme, '*Tap Dogs* has become one of Australia's greatest exports – having toured in over 250 cities world-wide' (elsewhere the programme lists the touring venues which, it is proudly asserted, cover four continents). *Tap Dogs* has become big business. Wayne Harrison talks of *cloning* further companies in America and Europe to replace the original team of Australian performers; he defines his objective as in line with what he saw as the tenor of the times in Australia throughout the nineties: the need to address the question, 'What is our place in the world?' In *Tap Dogs* Harrison and his directorial team have certainly given something distinctly Australian to the world. But, as the show, through multiple processes of 'cloning', sustains its place in the global cultural market, how securely has it maintained contact with its Australian roots?

It is illuminating today in 2002 to read through the spectrum of reviews of the first 1995/96 performances in Britain as anthologised in *Theatre Record*, since one would not have supposed a lengthy future for the show from such trained critical responses. The reviews make amusing reading, affording an interesting example of how little in some circumstances journalistic critical opinion would appear to influence public theatregoing. Newspapers seemed uncertain which of their critics to send to the event (the show was first seen at the Edinburgh Fringe, however, where traditional boundaries between media are often relaxed). There were many of the chief dance critics who, wedded to the ethos of either classical ballet or post-Cunningham (post)modernity, took (as might be expected) a superior and in many cases decidedly prudish stance: 'The show is about not musicality but sexy athleticism' (*Financial Times* 14 August 1995); 'Sex ... [is] not the first thing that usually comes to mind at a tap dance show' (*Guardian* 17 August 1995); 'finesse is not exactly forthcoming as they [the dancers] whack and bludgeon anything they can lay their feet on' (*Evening Standard* 21 September 1995); 'lots of energy, not enough variety' (*Sunday Express* 24 September 1995); the six dancers 'have as much charisma as six hammer drills' (*Daily Telegraph* 21 September 1995).[2] And on and on they castigated: this was not their idea of tap dancing; the feet were not those of the dapper Astaire or the balletic Kelly, nor was the show the equal of *Stomp* or of *Riverdance* (both recent London successes). When *Tap Dogs* returned for its West End season six months later, these reviewers were unrepentant in their distaste: Anne Sacks, dance critic of the *Evening Standard*, started by asserting that the show 'proves [the men] have the stamina to stamp rather than a talent for tap' and concluded patronisingly with the smug comment: 'The idea of brawny men in jeans tap dancing is novel and good fun, even if it is not dance as we know it' (*Evening Standard* 28 March 1996).

On the other hand theatre critics reviewing the show in Edinburgh (mostly male and of a pink complexion) were inclined to be more liberal, focusing on the energy, the muscularity, the surprise of finding themselves gazing at male dancers as *hunks*, the exciting slow tease of the men's strip, the 'testosterone haze' (*Independent* 14 August 1995), 'the primitive vitality' (*Evening Standard* 28 August 1995), 'the high octane of real masculine exuberance' (*Daily Mail* 17 August 1995). This is significant: finding *male* critics indulging *openly* in such rhetorical excess to communicate their unabashed arousal at the sight of male dancers. This goes some way to explaining why *Tap Dogs* rapidly achieved cult status in those early years: initial audiences at Sadlers Wells and in the West End were composed predominantly either of hen parties or groups of gay men, looking for entertainment involving all-male performers who were, in the words of one female critic, Penny Wark, 'more subtle than the saccharine Chippendales' (*Today* 21 September 1995). 'Subtle' is hardly the most felicitous epithet here, given that Wark is trying to evoke the dancers' credible workmen's machismo; but the force of the comparison still holds. Clearly the disapproval with which the dance critics wrote of the evident raw sweatiness on stage failed to deter many of their readers from going to savour the experience. And this is not surprising: the scaffolding set, the steel girders, the men's big Blundstone boots, their ripped, fraying or cut-off jeans, the heavy-duty plaid shirts, all toyed suggestively with that icon of the building-site Adonis which is a staple of straight female and gay male pornography. A particular brand of masculinity (a spot of rough trade) was frankly and joyously on display. This was not a show to further the construction of the New Man: as words like 'primitive' imply, what was on view, and unapologetically so, was the macho lad, the earthy bloke, the male sexpot, at once defiantly aloof and surly yet physically charismatic. Here were bodies with in-yer-face *presence*.

How might one get a purchase on this experience from a theoretical standpoint? One could argue that what we were watching was a deliberate presentation of the stereotypical Aussie male, the uncultured, insensitive guy with little to offer beyond his toughness. Should we be shocked at the seeming lack of any irony in the presentation? Or were the initial festival-trotting and later metropolitan audiences being offered a new version of the savage from the outback of beyond to flatter their superior, oh-so-civilised colonial gaze? Or to put it more tersely: were audiences being 'given the finger'? Queer theorists might argue that the 'other' was fighting back, glorying in the very qualities by which the establishment had determined its decentred positioning. Equally they might contend that it was all masquerade, a *playing* with cultural, gendered and sexual stereotypes, a cynical game with roles to destabilise a patronising audience. And yet spectators did not appear disturbed by the experience nor did the dancers seem propelled by the anger which fuels the finest of queer performance in this style. However, it was difficult to decide where to situate oneself *culturally* as spectator in relation to the experience; since despite the infectious fun, the brio and vitality on display, the larkiness, the amiable jockeying, the gags about peeing and body odour, there were indications that some more serious creative agenda was being grappled with.

It lay perhaps in the way the matey male bonding (which seemed to provide what scant motivation was required to give the stage-world a precise sense of *place*) was offset by a certain unease or standoffishness between the dancers. God forbid that any homosocialising that was going on should drift into the homosexual! A boundary was (mostly) observed by the gang (but that modifying 'mostly' is significant). Seemingly the only allowed form of touch between the men was a range (from the amicable to the aggressive) of different kinds of shove: a mode of physical contact that, whatever the tone and intention, instantly determines a separation of the bodies involved. A notable example was the pushing around of the one (younger) guy, Ben Read in the first cast, who early in the piece tried a little elegant spinning matched by a delicate play with his arms and hands: such cissie-stuff in the trad tap manner was definitely *off*. These guys' dancing was to be foot-work only: Astaire may have synchronised a commitment of his whole body to the rhythms of his feet, as with suave sophistication he mixed steps from jazz, ballroom and vaudeville with tap, but such a display of *style* was to prove a sustained no-go area for these lads. More disconcerting was the refusal (mostly) occasioned by the show's format to allow any of the six, except perhaps Perry himself, to evolve any degree of personality through his dancing. This was team work and individualism was also *off* (mostly).

Allied to this was a refusal (mostly) to allow any degree of narrative to develop, which might give the performance a shape. A consequence of this – remarkable in a show that flaunted male virility – was the determined avoidance of any climax. (Where one might ask was all that 'go' going to?). Repeatedly sequences fizzled out in an offhand manner so that the dancers had by a quick gesture or hoarse bark to invite applause; no episode evolved a sense of a natural ending which galvanised spectators into a prompt ovation. The steel setting was unpacked to reveal different locations within the same basic premise of a construction-site and each 'scene' demanded new kinds of expertise from the performers; yet almost before the close of one sequence the dancers were moving to rearrange the stage for the next. We were watching an entertainment (Harrison in interview repeatedly insists that this is how the production is to be viewed) but one that seemed to continually resist the structuring on which the simplest modes of entertainment are conventionally founded. The effect of this was to bring a naive innocence to the proceedings: the lads were cultivating an audience, yet were seemingly so embarrassed at their success that they were downplaying their achievement. The result was a steady undermining of the vaunted *cockiness* of it all: the *peter* petered out. Jenny Gilbert writing in the *Independent on Sunday* (24 September 1995) ended her wholly pejorative review in terms which at a first reading might seem harsh: 'A reason to stay away is that the Tap Dogs' sole motivation is to prove that they are not a bunch of sheilas. I think they have an attitude problem'. The phrasing is nasty, but the implication does offer a valid insight. Gilbert, in order to explain her dissatisfaction with the production, has searched behind the surface panache and found a controlling paradox underlying the event. For all the apparent bravura, in time (to Gilbert and to this writer at least) there did indeed seem a shamefaced, covert ideology at work in the invention of *Tap Dogs,* but one which proved difficult to define at the time without the insights subsequently provided by Wayne Harrison's interview about his life in theatre, *Tap Dogs* and its social context. Ironically in light of Harrison's comments this paradox (the felt unease which is *mostly* covered by an attempt at an easygoing manner) can be interpreted as precisely what locates the performance as Australian, as he himself readily admits.

What Harrison reveals is a social context that is far from the experience of most theatregoers or dance enthusiasts in Britain. The cast of *Tap Dogs*, he informs us, were all part of a generation in Australia where for working-class boys lessons in tap dancing were the only permitted means of introducing an element of culture into what would otherwise be a non-cultural life. It was, as he admits, the one form of cultural expression that his own father would tolerate his mother allowing him to pursue as a youth. Perry and the first cast of *Tap Dogs* were of that generation of boys, all based in Newcastle, NSW, who had undergone just such a dance training; all were expected to give up the interest on reaching adulthood and beginning their expected jobs as steelworkers. Dein Perry, unlike the rest, quickly gravitated to Sydney and a career in the chorus-line of American-style musicals, until in 1991 he was awarded an Australian Council Development Grant to workshop ideas to create a more distinctly Australian show based on tap. *Hot Shoe Shuffle*, the first all-Australian musical to play London's West End, was the initial outcome; but it attracted nothing like the interest or excitement occasioned by its successor *Tap Dogs*, for which, as Harrison reveals, Perry called back many of his old friends from Newcastle. All that first cast had experience in the steel industry; for many of them it had been extensive. They were reviving a talent for which in their earlier years they had severally won championships, though all were working-class and none came from theatrically oriented families.

Here would appear to be the source of the curiously offhand quality, that diffidence which was manifest throughout the performances, however ecstatic the audiences. Harrison encapsulates the situation more precisely when he speaks of the need in Australian theatre (and crucially in dancing) to be both 'cultural and non-cultural at the same time': performances should convey no impression of striving to be creative. That, he argues, is 'the essence of an Australian-ness'. Interestingly Harrison continually speaks of his own involvement with theatre in terms of *labour* (as if imagination and creativity never come into it). His favourite image – it recurs throughout the interview – is of working at the coalface: not the interface between performer, product and client-spectator, which European managers and producers see themselves as engaging with. Clearly within that metaphor one can infer that there is to be no truck with the idea of the artist or with the performer as part of some trained elite; the permitted alliance is with the worker, big-booted, sweaty and male. This is the culture *industry* in a very different sense of the word than is pursued in Europe and America. What Jenny Gilbert chose to interpret as an 'attitude problem', which suggests an inner uncertainty and lack of aesthetic awareness, is on these grounds to be viewed rather as a conscious, socially-propelled choice. The paradox is both necessary and intended.

It must be admitted that the concept of 'Australianness' voiced by Harrison is very limited (white, industrial working-class) when compared with the challenging re-definitions offered by Helen Gilbert in her contribution to this volume. Women are acknowledged only as spectator-receivers of this masculine display; even then the focus is chiefly inward to the bonded group. The trope of the larrikin Aussie male was never distant during the performance, though admittedly it never took on the vicious misogyny that the type can display (Holland and O'Sullivan). Though the show has played in Asian theatres, there is no admission of the multi-racial dimensions of Australian society (working class but of colour) and no reaching out to the multi-cultural dimensions of the world-wide audiences to which *Tap Dogs* is playing. The take-it-or-leave-it quality of the performance seemingly confirms a deliberate social solipsism: the gang mentality of 'us, the group' against the rest. Yet even within the gang there seems unease at the situation. The paradoxical struggle after a non-cultural mode of cultural expression has its affinities with the presentation of homosexual experience in such recent Australian films as *The Sum Of Us*[3] where, as Karen Brooks argues, the central gay working-class characters are rendered virtually invisible in being largely indistinguishable from their straight peers, a fact strengthened by the roles being played by known heterosexual actors.[4] The characters dress in conventional ways which make them acceptable within suburban society, but doing this marginalises their sexuality to confined and confining private spheres of activity. Brooks questions how challenging of the status quo such modes of representation are, when the result is gender-blending rather than gender-bending. Similarly, it may be questioned how challenging the cast of *Tap Dogs* are for Australian male spectators in daring openly, if guardedly, to display cultural allegiances and expertise. And how challenging are they for non-Australian audiences as purveyors of new impressions 'of what Australian culture can be' and of a new image of the Australian male which subverts popular stereotypes? (Harrison significantly ducks out of this question.) To the cultural critic, much can be read into the show's construction around a precise anxiety: about the elision of gender assertion with reluctant cultural expression. For the dance critic, much can be read in the bodies of these dancers about social conditioning, even when the precise details of that process are not immediately known.

Equally pertinent to the discussion here (and the statements are associated) is Harrison's claim that tap dancing as practised in Australia is an art form in which 'masculinity is not assaulted', a phrase which challengingly sees European and American styles by implication as a form of cultural rape. He repeats the words as if anxious to stress that he is deliberately choosing 'assaulted' rather than 'insulted', which would be far less aggressive in its resonances. It would appear that colonial pressures to conform in aesthetic matters to a prescribed set of norms are to be resisted, and a radical stance achieved by reconstructing the very type of the artist as theatre practitioner.   If, therefore, the colonial/postcolonial readings suggested above carry some weight, perhaps the queer theoretical readings do too? 'Masculinity' is being offered by Harrison as a site of potential vulnerability, an object of threat. What is not clear from his statement is precisely whose masculinity is at risk from assault: the performers and everyone associated with promoting the event that is *Tap Dogs*, including himself? Or a particular kind of male Australian spectator? The interview makes it apparent that from the first Harrison and the directorial team had a precise agenda in creating this show as entertainment: to attract a new-wave, previously non-theatregoing audience; young spectators whose visual stimulus had chiefly been MTV, an audience for whom the very notion of *theatre* had till then been suspect. Were these spectators also young males with a tap dancing past who might find in that past a point of contact with the performers on stage, providing the skill of tap as elevated into an entertainment had not in the process been cissiefied into *art*?

This agenda is playing with a form of nostalgia and reconstructing tap – initially and importantly a mode of black cultural expression – as a contemporary manifestation of *folk* performance, where 'folk' is to be interpreted as not rural and quaint but urban and loud. The costumes and setting, far from expressing an ideology based in masquerade or role-play, were therefore to be interpreted as relating the performance to its precise social working-class roots.   Triffitt's design-scheme reflected the work-processes of the steel industry, to which at one stage in their lives the dancers had been destined.   In terms of Australian cultural geography, *Tap Dogs* vaunted the specifics of its location.   Although the signifiers were not readily available for a European spectator to read in their complexity, the uneasy machismo which was their joint effect, as predicated on this reading, was calculated to meet and presumably allay particular (male) Australian cultural fears and fantasies. If the result was the projection through the performance of a stereotype of Australian masculinity, it was a stereotype that in hindsight, with the benefit of Harrison's comments, can be viewed, not as a risible cliché or crude caricature, so much as a socially-produced gender construct being examined experientially with some degree of insight. But it required one to read the performance with an attuned Australian sensibility to value such a subtly nuanced distinction.   In Edinburgh and London it was all too easy to critique the proceedings adversely by taking them at surface value.

From this perspective other aspects of the production can more readily be interpreted.   Triffitt's design frequently in its transformations evoked images a tap enthusiast might relate to the past American history of the medium. At one point a rising series of steel platforms suggested the glittering staircase up and down which Hollywood and Broadway staged many a concluding number; for another sequence the arrival of a water-trough for a splashy item in gumboots hinted at Kelly's singing in the rain; there was even an episode where one of the men literally danced over a ceiling (but actually upside down by virtue of a support-harness and not through the trick cinema photography that allowed Astaire to appear to achieve the impossible). But the cast did not treat these effects with a knowing manner that would suggest conscious intertextual reference, not even at the simplest level of satire to define the *difference* of their handling. The performers simply resisted any engagement with the resonances which might risk their being accused of camp frivolity. The gumboot number allowed only for some horseplay, as the lads repeatedly drenched each other and the front row of spectators with their antics; there was no 'quoting' of Kelly's choreography, as one might have expected and would have got in an American or European production today, either as homage or affectionate pastiche; instead the presence of the water was treated as a chance accident totally free of cultural connotations. And when the stage split lengthways into jagged-edged shards like a precipitous glacier, or broke up into interlacing platforms held at varying heights like rising suspension bridges (or giant waves for surfing), it required the dancers to show their manly prowess in sustaining equilibrium while jumping over the dividing chasm that resulted from the first configuration, or racing rhythmically up the ramps offered by the second. There was no place here for Astaire's characteristic display of tripping the light fantastic with accelerating footwork over varying levels of dance-floor: in fact 'tripping' was as far from Perry's choreographic vocabulary as Astaire's meticulously integrated play with top hat, cane and whirling tails. Perry's focus was on pounding feet, not on a dancer's integrated bodylines. Here repeatedly were expressions of that curious paradox defined by Harrison of a show that was 'cultural but non-cultural at the same time'; marked by an aesthetic 'innocence' which refused to acknowledge any concept of tradition, since the prevailing traditions were not home-based, not Australian. And anything smacking of artiness might have alienated the original Australian audience!

But, as implied above, there were intimations of an alternative agenda, which served to accentuate the prevailing schema as a required cultural (and by implication gendered) norm. Critics tended to write of the show as sustained at a high decibel count; the steel and wooden platforms had concealed microphones to amplify the sound of the footwork. But this was an inaccurate recall; all but a handful of reviewers chose not to note what was a carefully-paced variety of tones within the organisation of episodes. They looked only for material that confirmed their superior disdain for loud Aussie stereotypes. More interestingly, the majority chose not to refer to one sequence which was conceived in a markedly different way from the rest. This episode, situated roughly half-way through the performance so that its difference from the rest was notable, was decidedly in a quieter vein and it was for once a sustained duet, not a team piece. The inspiration followed a pattern often exploited by Astaire with one of his leading ladies; it was a kind of invitation to join the dance. He tapped a small phrase, which she imitated; so he tried another of more complex rhythms, which she again repeated; the sequence was reiterated with increasing rhythmic complexities introduced into his leading phrase, which she continually copied with sure-footed accuracy. Gradually the whole built into a dialogue between their dancing feet; intimate beginnings grew into ecstatic solo outpourings that met their match until the whole piece ended with a rapturous joint routine. It was seduction by rhythm into a joyous, shared explosion of dance.

So too was the episode in *Tap Dogs*, except it was performed by two men: the older, stockier Dein Perry with the younger, slight-bodied Ben Read. The sequence was the more telling since Perry had earlier led the other guys in shoving Read off the stage when he tried a spot of elegant 'tripping'. Perry began seated in a dusky lighting state, apparently adjusting his metal taps; Read hovered, watchful, in the shadows till he caught Perry's notice. Perry invited him into 'conversation' with the required brief phrase of footwork, playing with the model till he had seduced Read into the light, when imitation quickly gave place to a kind of friendly competition which steadily transformed into a shared delight in intricate cadenzas of tapping. Here was individuality in the dancers, a quietly evolving narrative through dance, an episode that was shaped to a fulfilling sustained climax of footwork in complete unison, and a portrayal of relationship outside the prevailing social structure of the team. Moreover the scene took a recognisable convention of classic tap dancing duos and with a beautiful, quiet nonchalance worked a remarkable inversion into the normal gender balance. The homosocial slipped elegantly into the homosexual and, for the only time in what critics relentlessly described as a testosterone-driven show, the dance was *sexy*, because it was not about self-display but depicted a couple finding physical delight in each other, even though there was no actual touching involved. It was a daring insertion within the larger format of *Tap Dogs* in being wholly subversive in its implications of the ideological tenor of the rest; implying a different style and expression of masculinity from what the show predicated as the norm, yet in terms that avoided pejorative dismissal as 'cissie'. Were those young Australian male spectators at the Wharf so indefatigably marketed for by the Sydney Theatre Company as blind to this inclusion as most of the British reviewers? Or, given the social contextualising that gave the show its ideological slant as defined by Wayne Harrison (he actually uses the word, 'political'), did it prompt a new awareness, or at the least provoke questions? Or was the subtlety of the subversion counter-productive?

It is instructive in this regard to compare *Tap Dogs* with another all-male danced event, *Enter Achilles* by Lloyd Newson and DV8, which was also staged initially in the autumn of 1995. This too interrogates a destructive masculinity, the policing of the homosocial/homosexual boundary within small communities or gangs, and the possibility of finding other modes to express male-ness. It questions why the trust, the touching, the united sensitivities required by men to perform certain skilled activities in work and sport are rendered taboo outside those specific contexts, should they become manifest in daily experience. But the subversions worked by Newson and his cast are palpably evident in the rich vein of satire that runs through the work and in sequences framed in deliberately conflicting styles of performance. That the agenda is critical, exploratory and questioning is overt within the structure of *Enter Achilles*. Newson is from Albury, NSW, and Melbourne, but he chose to leave and settle in England to further his involvement with modern dance, and to create in time a company pledged to tackling themes of social, sexual and psychological enquiry where evident risk-taking onstage is the correlative of the emotional risk-taking being asked of the audience. Questioned why he chose to work in England, Newson promptly replied in terms of the 'opportunities that were available to me' (Giannachi and Luckhurst 111), the greater choice of personnel, the larger funding opportunities, the touring possibilities, and the higher media profiling 'which proves that dance can have an effect in the wider world and act as a political force instead of reflecting the usual abstraction and 'niceness' – which speaks of little to very few' (111). He admits frankly to the value of influences (all European) and speaks most passionately of 'a rigour beyond technique' (112) required not only of performers in his work but of audiences witnessing it. This is an ideology far removed from Perry's, Triffitt's or Harrison's, made possible by the conscious decision to work within European contexts of performance, which necessitated Newson's losing touch with his roots. Or mostly so: there is no other European practitioner currently working in the field of dance or physical theatre so preoccupied with concepts of masculinity as Newson.5 Perhaps the need to return to that specific focus for his inspiration, which is the point of creative contact with Perry or Triffitt, springs as much from his Australian inheritance as from his homosexual experience.

It is the degree of Australian-ness in *Tap Dogs*, that central uneasy paradox in its confrontations with masculinity, which makes it perhaps surprising that the show has achieved international status. Harrison talks of difficulty in 'cloning' the show, particularly in America, because of its resistance to cultural conformity and the traditions of tap. As he tartly observes, the American traditions in show business are about marketing personalities, and specifically as manifest in 'eyes, tits and teeth and all above the waist' where the concern is with projection of the performer's self. By contrast he sees the cast of *Tap Dogs* as 'boys with beautiful, sweet feet' in routines which stress the group endeavour over individuality. He and his directorial team had 'to work hard to get the American-ness out of the tapdancers' because the dance idiom of *Tap Dogs* is not 'international', rather it is based on Dein Perry's specific socialisation: the local Newcastle, familial and anti-cultural pressures that conditioned his maturity.

No effort of the imagination on the part of cast members of the cloned productions can ever hope to match that background as shared by Perry and his dancers. This is evident from the current troupe touring England, where the team of eight dancers alternating on the rosta comprises only two Australians and six English guys. The physiques of the English dancers are altogether slighter and their performances have nothing like the *edge* of the original team. When the show toured to Richmond in Surrey in July 2001, the audience was predominantly made up of families (including numbers of enthralled, toe-twiddling boys) and elderly couples (the average age, despite the many children, must have been fifty-plus).6 The in-yer-face audacity had gone to be replaced by tactics for courting approval, including chatting to spectators in the stalls and ogling others in the boxes. These were likeable lads on a spree; the jokes about body odour and sweat were still there, but it was somehow all a game now; the competitiveness and the jockeying lacked tension and the high-risk stunts like the dancing on the ceiling had been cut. Though the team resolutely pursued a tactic whereby no one dancer asserted an individuality, the corporate image they presented could only be described as *cool*; with their designer-cut hair copiously gelled, they were as nice and clean-limbed as the latest fashionable boy band rather than hard-skinned, working-class steel workers. There was no hint now of that Newcastle background which Harrison outlines as essential to a proper understanding of what is being watched. Harrison may talk of 'cloning' the production but this cast were hardly the mirror images of their Australian counterparts. More crucially, though the duet was still included in the programme, it was now relocated near the beginning of the performance and was danced in an even bright light between two lads of a similar build and age. In the process the sequence had just become a conversation between hoofers, a witty excuse for a friendly exchange of dance steps; it had lost all the erotic charge that Perry and Read brought to the episode. Without the challenging tenor of their performance and its implications that tapdancing might encompass consensual pleasures, *Tap Dogs* overall lost its grit, because it lost the tensions and the paradox which originally intercut the exuberant display of manliness by questioning the basic concept of masculinity which appeared on the surface to be shaping the production.

By becoming a globalised export, *Tap Dogs* has become the victim of its own success: as a product made fit for all cultural markets it has ceased to be Australian. American and English guys cannot hope to realise Newcastle-bred physiques formed by specific social conditioning and since, on Harrison's terms, the bodies and not the faces of the performers are the focus of the show, this is a crucial difference. Ironically what his discussion of *Tap Dogs* reveals is the degree to which the Australianness of the show is rooted in much more than bodies: its agenda presents bodies driven by a particular mind-set which is the product of exact and exacting class, emotional and anti-cultural pressures. *Tap Dogs* performed by an Australian cast celebrates the triumph of physical expression over adversity (that *uncultural* culture that Harrison carefully defines). Clones may mechanically reproduce Perry's choreography, but they will not *inhabit* it, as he and his first team did; and no amount of technical training will bring those clones closer than a pale imitation of their prototypes. With an Australian cast *Tap Dogs* fundamentally re-defined the term 'culture'. Globalisation may bring welcome royalties to the coffers of the Sydney Theatre Company as the originating

178   *Richard Cave*

organisation, but on current showing it has robbed their most travelled export of its fundamental ideology, its defiance and its *heart*.

References.

Brooks, Karen. 'Homosexuality, Homosociality, and Gender Blending in Australian Film'. *Antipodes* December (1999): 85-90.

---- 'Doing' It With Your Mates: Aspects of Australian Masculinity'. *The Abundant Culture: Meaning and Significance in Everyday Australia*. Ed. David Headon et al. St Leonard's: Allen& Unwin, 1994.

Giannachi, Gabriella and Mary Luckhurst, ed. *On Directing: Interview with Directors*. London: Faber and Faber, 1999.

Harrison, Wayne. Interview with Elizabeth Schafer and Susan Bradley Smith. London, 21 May 1999.

Holland, Felicity and Jane O'Sullivan, 'Lethal Larrikins: Cinematic Subversions of Mythical Masculinities in *Blackrock* and *The Boys*'. *Antipodes* (December 1999): 80-84.

Theatre Record 1995 (10-23 September): 1273-78.

Theatre Record 1996 (25 March-7 April): 411-2.

Notes

1   Interestingly *Stomp* was playing at the Festival Hall in London at precisely the same time in 1995 that *Tap Dogs* opened at Sadler's Wells Theatre. Luke Cresswell's company are a British-based ensemble who have appropriated aspects of circus and clowning. *Stomp* was another tap show that improvised accompanying music from a variety of found objects within a junkyard setting (oil drums, brooms, radiators). Critics reviewing both shows within the same week inevitably drew comparisons between them, not always to the benefit of the Australian troupe. Cresswell and his Yes/No People had begun their careers as buskers, entertaining queues, and critics frequently remarked on their affability and direct engagement of an audience, whereas the Australian dancers were considered aggressive.

2   The reviews for the 1995 and 1996 performances are anthologised in *Theatre Record*, for which bibliographical details are given in the references above.

3   The film was directed by Kevin Dowling and Jeff Burton in 1994; it stars Russell Crowe in the gay role of Jeff.

4   Brooks quotes Peter Looker: 'Any man growing up in Australia knows that there are proscribed ways of behaving in order not to be alienated from the brotherhood of "real men" and that they risk ostracism and vilification if they do not attempt to conform' ('Doin' It' 213) . She then investigates the ways in which Jeff, the gay hero, is seen to 'conform'. The film in her view resists a potential liberating agenda, since Jeff's sexuality is not made 'a vehicle for political expression' (87).

5   This concern shaped the creativity of Newson and his casts in *My Sex, Our Dance* (1986), *Dead Dreams of Monochrome Men* (1988), *MSM* (1993), as

well as episodes in *Strange Fish* (1992) and in *can we afford this/the cost of living* (2000).

6   At first glance this might seem a typical 'Richmond' audience, though there were far more young families there than is customarily the case at performances in this wealthy suburban borough in West London. Audiences tend generally to be from the prosperously middle-aged. Interestingly *Tap Dogs* gathered an audience the night the present writer viewed a performance which was more akin to that which visits the theatre during the Christmas pantomime season. It was lively, vocal, bonded and responsive.

11.
International fault-lines: directions in contemporary Australian performance and the new millennium

Margaret Hamilton

*Australian artists are interrogating, and impacting on, conceptions of cultural identity, history and performance in many different ways in an international context. Crucial here is the relationship between European presenters and producers, and the strategies of Australian policy makers abroad. This relationship is examined by means of a focus specifically on music theatre works currently in repertoire, the Performing Lines' production **The Theft of Sita** and **Moon Spirit Feasting** by the Elision Ensemble, and by reference to a range of recent international presentations by Australian companies including the Marrugeku Company, Urban Dream Capsule and Phillip Adams' BalletLab.*

Tradition, according to French philosopher Jean François Lyotard, is a matter of time, as opposed to content. Australia, as the composer Liza Lim has pointed out, is 'known as "the antipodes", a place diametrically opposed to other regions on Earth (specifically Europe) ... a place where one is often made conscious of one's relationship to *somewhere else*' (Lim). It is a location that precludes the claim to cultural authority. Australia's borderline 'newness', based on the subjugation of Aboriginal and Torres Strait Islander peoples, disavows a culturally significant past. How then are Australian artists interrogating, and impacting on, conceptions of cultural identity and history – the very terms of reference underpinning artistic practices and directions at the outset of the twenty-first century? How are Australian artists demonstrating a growing awareness of, and engagement with, Australia's positioning in the Asia Pacific region? At issue in this chapter's discussion of contemporary Australian performance is the very process of translating cultural forms and differences in an international context.

It is a process that is increasingly attracting European presenters and producers re-negotiating questions of cultural value and its location. This point is emphasised by the following quotation from a letter by Maria Magdalena Schwaegermann, Artistic Director of the Zürcher (Zurich) Theater Spektakel and Deputy Director of the Hebbel Theater Berlin,[1] to the Australia Council, the Federal Government's arts funding and advisory body:

> After my visit to Australia I arrived back to a Europe that ... appears less open minded towards the future. There is a lot to do here if we really want to step into the 21st century. It is my impression that the next generation of Australian artists will be free to create new forms of expression. In contrast, the 'weight' of cultural systems and traditions in Europe is at times limiting.

This is significant praise given that the Hebbel Theater has presented and produced projects involving a range of critically acclaimed artists: the Wooster Group, Jan Lauwer's Needcompany, Heiner Goebbels, Richard Foreman and Robert Wilson, to name just a few. In music theatre the Russian-born Australian composer Elena Kats-Chernin and the Australian Cathy Milliken, a founding member of Ensemble Modern, add to the Hebbel's list of artists, and a model of production that 'is not tied in any traditional way to the business of theatre' in Germany (Herkenrath 9). What distinguishes the Hebbel in Germany is a program based on 'on-going collaborative work with international artists and companies, work which grows out of experience and mutual trust' (9). This contrasts to short-term guest performances and a fixed ensemble; the latter underpinning Germany's international theatrical reputation. The ensemble tradition is, of course, rare in an Australian context. What dominates Australia's state theatres is a text-based repertoire largely dependent upon developmental time, causally related events and psychological speculation. This is not the prerogative of the Hebbel's artistic program. What, then, are venues presenting and/or producing international work, like the Hebbel in Berlin, the Kaaitheater in Brussels, Théâtre Vidy-Lausanne ETE, T & M Nanterre in Paris, Rotterdamse Schouwburg, Kampnagel in Hamburg and the Archa in Prague interested in programming? More precisely, what is the relationship to Australian companies and artists, the potential for domestic artistic development and export and the reception of Australian cultural product in Europe? And how are Australian cultural policy makers 'playing Australia' on the continent, as distinct from Britain?

The theatres cited above are venues that see themselves as contemporary forums facilitating artists to 'explore the boundaries between dance, performance, theatre, music and the fine arts in new and unexpected ways' (Herkenrath 7). It is an artistic policy that describes what in Australia is 'loosely referred to as performance, or contemporary performance or live art', to use Keith Gallasch's words (38). In Australia, performance developed a presence in the 1980s with the emergence of a body of work based on artistic collaborations between arts practitioners working in a variety of disciplines; practitioners predominantly interested in an anti-illusionary aesthetic. Performance, to quote Philip Auslander, reflects 'a re-consideration of the very activity taking place on stage' and this contrasts with the preoccupation with innovations in acting that characterised modernist and avant-garde theatres in the nineteenth to mid-twentieth century (1). In Australia this re-evaluation coincides with a shift in contemporary culture as Gallasch, co-founder of the performance company Open City and editor of *RealTime*, a national journal of innovative and contemporary arts, has observed. Australia's convict, working-class roots, 'reticent and wary of high culture and the intellect', have given way to what Gallasch identifies as the culturally complex Australian body: a body rich in its diversity; a body increasingly accommodating indigenous Australians, the influences of immigrants, the female voice and gay and lesbian Australia' (38). These are influences underpinned by diverse aesthetics; temporal, spatial and political as well as cultural. The result is a dramaturgical landscape that is profoundly impacting on our conceptions of the theatrical experience. The non-linear performance traditions of Aboriginal Australia and of the East, for example, as well as the counter-hegemonic decentralisation of political space articulated in postcolonial and postmodern theories of contemporary culture, are redefining the relationship of marginal artistic practices and peoples in the context of (dominant) cultural production.

It is precisely the culturally complex Australian body that has attracted Maria Magdalena Schwaegermann to contemporary Australian performance, given that she is 'convinced that we have to open more than borders between countries in order to collaborate in a way that maximises the richness of diverse cultures' (Schwagermann). As the Deputy Director of the Hebbel Theater, Berlin, since its re-opening in 1989 she has been responsible for its artistic program in conjunction with the theatre's director, Nele Hertling. In a European context, cross, inter and intra-cultural artistic explorations are clearly of interest to a range of leading festivals and venues apart from the Hebbel. The Performing Lines presentation *The Theft of Sita* exemplifies this trend. Rotterdamse Schouwburg, the Aarhus Festival in Denmark, Zürcher Theater Spektakel and the Hebbel Theater selected *The Theft of Sita* for their 2002 programs. This tour follows successful seasons at the Brooklyn Academy of Music (BAM) in New York, the London International Theatre Festival (LIFT), and other venues in the United Kingdom in 2001. *The Theft of Sita*, which is the result of collaboration between Australian composer Paul Grabowsky in association with the Balinese composer I Wayan Gde Yudane and director Nigel Jamieson, opened the Theaterformen Festival in Hanover in 2000. 'Theaterformen', as the word suggests, literally translates as a festival of theatre forms. For critic Ronald Meyer-Arlt *The Theft of Sita* was an astute choice as a premiere by the then artistic director, Marie Zimmermann. In Meyer-Arlt's words *The Theft of Sita* is 'a declaration for a different theatre, instructions for seeing (anew) and an occasion to think about what should stand at the centre of theatre, when actorly expression and the words of the dramatist have disappeared from it'.[2]

This 'seeing anew' is the result of more than one hundred and fifty shadow puppets accompanied by a jazz-infused gamelan score, which retell the ancient Indian Ramayana Sanskrit myth against the backdrop of the contemporary socio-political climates of Australia and Indonesia. It is an adaptation that was welcomed by *Die Welt* critics Matthias Heine and Martin Jaspar, who commented: 'How good that in the visions for the twenty first century, the oldest virtual model of the world still appears'. It is a vision specifically contextualised by the political situation leading up to the overthrow of the Suharto regime in Indonesia and the political tension between Australia and Indonesia surrounding the East Timor crisis.[3] In this modern account of Ramayana, which is told from the perspective of Twalen and Merdah, the servant clowns of the Wayan Kulit, the images of the puppeteers consist of forest-devouring factory dinosaurs, a rhinoceros battling an excavator, river-rafting rubber dinghy crews, corrupt and aggressive policemen, prostitutes and skyscrapers. At various points in the ninety-minute performance the screen dramatically sweeps down to reveal the puppeteers and musicians at work. This is a self-reflexive device that foregrounds the process of representation and by extension the (political) agency of the theatrical sign. In Nigel Jamieson's words,
> While *The Theft of Sita* is broadly located in a mythic
> Indonesia, the tale it tells of the costs of environmental

destruction, the sacrifice of the natural world in pursuit of power, profit and the demands of economic globalisation could be located anywhere. Indeed it would find a fitting home in the denuded forests, river systems and salt encrusted pastures of a country with the world's highest per capita green house emissions – Australia.

The thematic concerns of *The Theft of Sita*, although spectacularly folkloric and comically presented, confirm the sophisticated treatment of politically and culturally sensitive subject matter in contemporary performance practice in Australia. *Die Welt* critics Heine and Jasper remarked in their review of *The Theft of Sita* that the production stems 'from that part of the world which the geo-economists insistently repeat will have a determining influence both economically and culturally on the century which has just begun'. What then is distinguishing Australia culturally in the context of international artistic production? *Yuè Lìng Jié (Moon Spirit Feasting)* by the Elision Ensemble interrogates artistic and cultural boundaries in such a way that it is perhaps the most pertinent example in repertoire of Heine and Jasper's remark. Like *The Theft of Sita*, *Yuè Lìng Jié*, which premiered on a barge on the River Torrens, was commissioned by Robyn Archer for the 2000 Adelaide Festival. With a libretto in English, Mandarin, Cantonese and a colloquial English-Malaysian dialect by novelist Beth Yahp and a score by composer Liza Lim, Elision Ensemble's *Yuè Lìng Jié* draws on the mythology of South East Asia to present the legend of the Moon Goddess, Chang-O, in the context of the Chinese Hungry Ghost Festival. The annual month-long Hungry Ghost Festival seeks to pacify the ghosts of blighted souls following the opening of the gates of hell. These souls seek other souls to take their place in hell. To appease them and protect themselves for another year communities offer various forms of street entertainment, including opera. With puppets, riddles, song contests, a karaoke session and a Daoist sex manual scene, *Yuè Lìng Jié* is a seventy-five minute performance that juxtaposes the divine and the profane, which are important points of intersection for Lim (Davenport 49). *Yuè Lìng Jié*, directed by Michael Kantor, explores what Lim describes as the 'fault-lines of cultural hybridity'.

This 'hybridity' is precisely what is interesting European presenters and producers who are in a process of artistically renegotiating questions of identity and history, and, in doing so, of cultural value and its location at the outset of the twenty-first century. The seven scenes of *Yuè Lìng Jié* performed by three singers and nine instrumentalists act, according to Lim, 'as a series of "tools" or "instruments" ... to access different levels of story – mythic, symbolic, comic and contemporary' (Elision). It is a ritual street opera inspired by the various and conflicting versions of the Chang-O legend throughout the Chinese diasporas. The linguistic complexity of *Yuè Lìng Jié's* libretto and the disjunctive play between the celestial and the desecrated – the Queen Mother character, for example, is visibly naked beneath a transparent plastic chong sam – produces a jarring of meanings that foregrounds what Homi Bhabha discusses as the performative nature of cultural communication: the process of cultural interpretation or 'the potential archaeology of the story':

> The opera conjures up the figure of Chang-O to re-tell her story from a number of angles: Chang-O as a woman who is transformed into a goddess; as a figure of psychic nightmare; as a wish granting heavenly creature (associated with fertility). The stories can be understood as projections of a society's anima in terms of symbolic interactions between cosmic forces. (Lim, qtd. in Davenport 48)

In *The Location of Culture* Bhabha points out that hybrid sites of meaning expose the process by which the repetition of the sign functions differentially according to its specific social practices, despite the similitude of the symbol. Lim makes the point in Rhana Davenport's review of the performance that the countless versions of the Hungry Ghost story maintain the symbolic presence of a cultural form. However, this presence is continually reinvented by the contemporary dialects of the Chinese diasporas. In *Yuè Lìng Jié* the Elision Ensemble foregrounds this process of cultural negotiation, the very acts of translation constituting cultural signification. Or in Lim's words,

> As soon as one starts looking closely at what that culture is [Chinese] and what it might comprise, one sees that it is not a unitary thing at all. The rough and ready contemporary opera performances offered to the spirits in Penang are a world away from the perfections of Beijing opera and their ritual context would certainly be regarded as a relic of feudalistic superstition in modern China. From a European point of view, this very hybridity would perhaps be regarded as an impurity, less 'authentic' and less 'Chinese' than something coming from mainland China. In reality, there are many 'Chinas' and Chinese cultures.

To return to Schwaegermann's quotation in the opening paragraph, the question of authenticity, or more explicitly, the legitimating presence of culturally-historic artistic forms, is precisely what

Schwaegermann identified as 'at times limiting'. The hybrid approach and styles evident in *Yuè Lìng Jié* constitute an in-between space, or the cutting edge of translation and negotiation that Bhabha describes as carrying 'the burden of the meaning of culture' in his discussion of critical theory (38-39). It is a hybridity that negates what he calls the exoticism of multiculturalism on the basis that it 'engages with culture as an uneven, incomplete production of meaning and value, often composed of incommensurable demands and practices'. These are the artistic fault-lines that the four main characters, Chang-O (soprano), Hou Yi or the Archer (baritone), the Queen Mother of the West (mezzo-soprano) and the Monkey King (baritone), apply to interrogate the symbolic textuality of cultural signification. Divine icons as well as a statue of a drunken monk and cigarettes adorn the shrine in *Yuè Lìng Jié*. This is not simply an example of pastiche, a polyvalent aesthetic pushed to the limit. Instead, *Yuè Lìng Jié* opens up a differential space dedicated to the translational, intersecting and transitory basis of cultural signification; its historicity.

I am reminded here of the attitude of one of Australia's most controversial and critically significant performance companies of the late 1980s and early 1990s, the Sydney Front. In Nigel Kellaway's words the Sydney Front 'forgot about ... history, we just say it's words. They mean this to us and we did them' (Kellaway). The words 'belonged' to Heiner Müller, arguably Germany's most significant post-dramatic playwright, to use Hans-Thies Lehmann's term.[4] The Sydney Front overlooked the historical context of Müller's words in order to interrogate the question 'Where do we place ourselves in our cultural history?' (Kellaway). Or to quote Schwaegermann,

> We are used to giving answers in Germany, you are used to asking questions ... Germany is still very connected to the last century while you are very much expanding into the future ...
> (Litson 5)

The growing geographic point of reference for Australia has been its proximity to Asia. This is contextualised artistically by what Lim describes with reference to Peggy Glanville-Hicks as 'one of the great cultural shifts of the twentieth century in the West, namely that of looking to other cultures outside of the Western canon as a source for creative renewal'. *Sonorous Bodies*, another Elision Ensemble production, exemplifies this shift. In addition it demonstrates the blurring of boundaries between institutional spaces, the museum and theatre. First performed for the Asia Pacific Triennial of Contemporary Art in 1999 at the Queensland Art Gallery, the work was presented in the Hebbel Theater in Berlin in September 2001. A traditional proscenium arch stage theatre, the Hebbel was converted into an installation space for this meditative inquiry into 'the potentiality of silence (absence) and the dimensions of its touch (presence)' (*Sonorous Bodies*). Composer Liza Lim, visual artist Judith Wright and Koto master Satsuki Odamura explored the resonance of the body. The Chinese classification of musical instruments by physical materials (stone, silk, bamboo, metal, wood, skin, gourd and earth) structured the eight video sequences created by Wright. The diegetic space of one of the videos, for example, refers to the invisible act of eating, an imaginary elsewhere, which was suggested by a pair of hands and chopsticks delicately lifting pieces from a paw-paw out of the frame of the projection. Lim's music, in Rex Butler's words, 'goes against the assumed immateriality of Western music, its status as the most ideal, abstract and non-referential of the arts. Its constant impulse is towards the "earthly" rather that the celestial, the elemental rather than the metaphysical'. *Sonorous Bodies*' eight-part musical score, which was written in traditional Japanese music calligraphy, emphasised this disjunction, given that as opposed to the result, the imaginary sound indicated in western music, actions and gestures are notated in the score for the installation. The use of traditional music calligraphy examines not simply the conjunctions between an ancient and a modern practice of performance, but re-figures this relationship as an in-between space or site of negotiation. In doing so, it introduced the complexities and juxtapositions that audiences experienced in *Yuè Lìng Jié*, performed at the Hebbel Theater in June 2002.

With these artistic complexities in mind, how then are cultural policy-makers promoting contemporary performance in Australia to European presenters, producers and audiences?

Around thirty-five million people annually attend performances in theatres and concert halls in Germany. As the world's third largest economy and with a population of over eighty million, Germany is a key production, co-production and presentation market in the international arts industry. The expenditure on the arts by its capital, Berlin, represents the largest investment of any European city on arts and cultural activity.[5] Australian contemporary cultural product is still relatively unknown in Germany. The presence of Australian artists at Theater der Welt 99 in Berlin, and Laura Ginters's article 'From White Australia to Black Theatre' in the catalogue produced by the International Theatre Institute to accompany the festival, have raised the profile of Australian work; and this has been augmented by the cultural activity organised by the Australia Pavilion at Expo 2000 in Hanover. However, a real knowledge of the breadth of Australian arts is yet to be established. As a consequence, the Australia Council's Audience and Market Development Division in conjunction with the Australia International Cultural Council (AICC) has targeted Berlin as a centre from which to promote Australian arts to German, and by extension European, presenters, producers and audiences in 2002-03. What distinguishes this promotion is that it has been conceived of as a sustained program of activity as opposed to a discrete festival, and that its program will be largely determined by local artistic directors, in particular Maria Magdalena Schwaegermann from the Hebbel Theater. This approach allows artistic directors to select Australian work as part of their normal program; work which is appropriate for their audiences and touring networks. In addition, it is based on a clear financial investment by the presenter in Australian cultural product. This implies a risk on the part of presenters, and in doing so attests to a belief in the quality of Australian arts and its ability to attract audiences and impact culturally in Europe.

This raises the question of how European artistic directors are developing their knowledge of contemporary Australian performance, given the tyranny of distance that isolates what Peter Sellars, who resigned as the artistic director of the 2002 Adelaide Festival just four months before its opening, has described on the basis of land mass in comparison to population as both a big country and a small one (Sellars). Schwaegermann visited Australia for the third time in February 2001, and embarked on a fourth trip to Australia for the 2001 Melbourne Festival. In 1998 she attended the Australian Performing Arts Market along with Markus Luchsinger, then director of the Zürcher Theater Spektakel and now director of the Berliner Festwochen (Theatre and Dance) run by the Berliner Festspiele, the largest festival organisation in Germany. The following year Schwaegermann programmed three Australian groups – Five Angry Men, Bambucco and Ranters Theatre – for Theater der Welt 99. In 2000 Schwaegermann returned to attend the Perth Festival and the Gay and Lesbian Mardi Gras Arts Festival in Sydney. As a result of that trip she invited the White Cockatoo Performing Group from Arnhem Land in the Northern Territory to perform at the Potsdamer Platz festival in Berlin. As a consequence Schwaegermann, in conjunction with the Australia Council's project manager based in Berlin, is in a position to provide targeted artistic advice to European presenters about Australian performing companies, and this is contextualised by the growing interest from presenters in travel to Australia. What is striking about a high percentage of the work attracting Schwaegermann and Luchsinger is that it challenges the very concept of theatre and the theatrical infrastructure that dominates Europe; its proscenium arch auditoria.

Legs on the Wall, formed in 1986 and arguably Australia's leading physical theatre company, creates performances for a range of sites or situations. The aerial spectacle *Homeland*, which was performed on the AMP skyscraper at Circular Quay in Sydney as part of the Olympic Arts Festival, is a poignant example of the site-specific work drawing international attention to the theatrical forms being developed in a country neither famous for its proscenium arch theatres, nor noteworthy for the work staged within these structures. In 2001 Marrugeku toured its latest site-specific production *Crying Baby* to Ireland, Holland and Belgium, as well as to other destinations abroad. The Marrugeku Company, which formed in 1994 specifically to develop the performance *Mimi* for the Perth Festival, is

a milestone in Australia's advance towards a more pluralistic artistic and cultural identity. At Marrugeku's heart is a process of reconciliation, not in the sense of searching for a universal theatrical language, but rather through the process of making performances which respects our differences while we work together to tell stories.[6]

The Marrugeku company consists of Western Australian urban indigenous dancers, musicians, physical theatre practitioners from Stalker Theatre Company, and Kunwinjku dancers, story-tellers and musicians from Kunbarllanjanja, a remote community in Arnhem Land. *Crying Baby* is based on Thompson Yulidjirri's story from birth to displacement, and by extension colonisation and its continuing impact. It is visually about two worlds: the everyday, recognisable and immediate physical environment; and dreaming, 'a world that we can "see" in our minds when we're told about our history, or of a time that once existed, or that we may once have experienced'.[7] The stories of the company's non-indigenous members complement the narratives that weave through and weave together *Crying Baby*. A large-scale outdoor performance that incorporates traditional and contemporary images and music, *Crying Baby* is part of Marrugeku's desire 'to push further into issues of cultural identity, of blurred edges between story, history and Djang (or dreaming) which challenge our understanding of ourselves as a nation at the edge of the 21st century'.

This is a challenge that impacts profoundly upon the way in which Australia is not simply received, but perceived in an international context. Are policy-makers endeavouring to build an artistic reputation on the basis of existing repertoire from the perspective of competition, which binds us to the cultural cringe that plagued Australia in the past? Or are they supporting the creative development of artistic projects that forge directions on the world stage? This question implies an additional challenge; that is, knowing the international stage and taking risks which may not always produce the hoped-for result. The work of the 'new wave' of British playwrights, Mark Ravenhill and Sarah Kane, for example, has in recent years developed a significant profile in Germany and specifically in Berlin. It was against this backdrop that Raimondo Cortese's *Features of Blown Youth* failed critically as part of Theater der Welt 99. Joachim Fiebach remarked that he found a sense of acuteness or coarseness lacking in the production (109). In contrast, *Amplification* by Phillip Adams' BalletLab was critically well received by *ballet-tanz international* critic Klaus Witzeling at its German premiere at the IndepenDance Days Festival at Kampnagel in Hamburg in January 2001. Witzeling responded positively to Adams' decision to focus on the theatrical, interdisciplinary dimensions of the performance as opposed to technique, which is highly significant in the context of European dance with its emphasis on developments in the movement vocabulary. The fifty-minute work for five dancers by choreographer Phillip Adams included a live turntable composition by the Melbourne-based composer Lynton Carr. Based on 'the 1.6 second "disassociation" time freeze, which occurs at the moment of impact during a car crash'[8] and inspired by David Cronenberg's film adaptation of J. G. Ballard's *Crash*, *Amplification's* engagement with death, ritual, burial and torture in the form of an art installation exemplifies the diverse and challenging preoccupations of Australian artists developing a profile internationally.

In 1995 Sarah Miller, the current director of the Perth Institute for Contemporary Arts (PICA) wrote:

It is inadequate to treat the British text-based repertory model as the be all and end all of the performing arts. The influences of circus, music hall and Commedia dell'Arte for instance, as well as theatre practitioners such as Tadeusz Kantor, Antonin Artaud, Robert Wilson etc should not be underestimated (9).

Urban Dream Capsule, a performance consisting of four actors living in the windows of department stores for a two-week period, is perhaps the extreme end of this equation. In many respects this marathon production, which attracted over 300,000 spectators to Sears in Chicago in 2001, is suggestive of people's theatre, as Schwaegermann has noted:

It's amazing because it's not voyeurism – though when people have a shower it's always an event. But it's much more about a dialogue that they are creating with the audience in the street. (Litson 5)

There is undoubtedly an extraordinary breadth in contemporary performance practice in Australia, and the body of work emerging is challenging just what we mean by theatre and culture in the twenty-first century. 'History', as Peter Sellars stated in his *New York Times* article 'Australia's Arts Unfettered', published ten days before his resignation from the Adelaide festival, 'is moving on'. In Sellars' words,

Perhaps Australia is the country that can help usher in a new era of global leadership that is less about high-profile proclamations and more about low-key negotiations, shared destinies, mutual obligations, collaborations and cooperation. Open dialogue and radical inclusiveness are the prerequisites for any global security arrangement, which will have to be based on tolerance, and basic respect.

The sensationalist advertising campaign making references to Adolf Hitler, which was designed to promote Sellars' community-based program, did not unite the heterogenous histories of peoples in cultural production in the eyes of Telstra, the Festival's main sponsor, which threatened to withdraw. Sellars did not attend the launch of his program. In addition, according to John Morphett, the Chairman of the Adelaide Festival Board, Sellars had been asked to broaden his program in response to poor ticket sales, which he felt was impossible without a significant injection of financial resources, and he therefore resigned. The production of meaning, as Bhabha has pointed out, requires a third space involving the performative and institutional strategies inherent in communication. A team of Australian associate artistic directors – Waiata Telfer, Lynette Wallworth, Angharad Wynne-Jones, Catherine Woolcock, Rose Wight, Karl Telfer, Jonathan Parsons, Amanda McDonald Crowley, Bridget Ikin, Gay Bilson – was appointed to facilitate Sellars' process of cultural interpretation in an Australian context. In response to Sellars' vision of cultural experiences designed to inspire audiences to question their ways of thinking and to encourage participation, the associate directors, according to the official final program, 'developed a web of meaning where themes, projects and processes are intertwined' based on ideas, as opposed to art form.[9] What Sellars' experience in Adelaide publicly illustrated is the contending discourses and unequal interests in the expression of cultural value within a festival framework. However, beyond the controversy and the debate about the role of festivals, contemporary Australian performance has emerged as a vital site in the articulation of new cultural demands, meanings and strategies in the political present, domestically and internationally.

References

Auslander, Philip. From Acting to Performance: Essays in Modernism and Postmodernism. London: Routledge, 1997.

Bhabha, Homi. *The Location of Culture*. London: Routledge, 1994.

Butler, Rex. *The Heart's Ear*. CD cover notes. ABC Classics: 1999.

Davenport, Rhana. 'Elision, Yuè Lìng Jié (Moon Spirit Feasting).' *Eyeline: Contemporary Visual Art* 42 (2000): 48-49.

Elision Ensemble website: www.elision.org.au.

Fiebach, Joachim. 'Gespräch zwischen Raimondo Cortese, Joachim Fiebach and Christel Weiler'. *Theater der Welt Arbeitsbuch*. Berlin: Theater der Zeit, 1999. 108-114.

Gallasch, Keith. 'Australian Contemporary Performance: An Introduction'. Repertoire: A Guide to Australian Contemporary Performance – Circus, Physical Theatre, Outdoor, Multimedia, Site-Specific, Performance. Strawberry Hills: Australia Council, 2001. 38-40.

Ginters, Laura. 'From White Australia to Black Theater'. *Theater der Welt Arbeitsbuch*. Berlin: Theater der Zeit, 1999. 115-124

Heine, Matthias and Martin Jasper. 'Bilder von heute im Schattenspiel von gestern.' *Die Welt* 9 June 2000.

Herkenrath, Kirsten, ed. *tanz.musik.theater HEBBEL*. Berlin: Hebbel Theater, 2000.

Jamieson, Nigel. Director's Notes. *The Theft of Sita Press Kit*. Sydney: Performing Lines .

Kellaway, Nigel. Interview with author. 14 August 1995.

Lehmann, Hans-Thies. *Postdramatisches Theater*. Frankfurt am Main: Verlag der Autoren, 1999.

Litson, Jo, 'Following the Flame.' *Artforce* 108 (2001): 4-5.

Lim, Liza. Third Annual Glanville-Hicks Address, Sydney Opera House Studio, 15 September 2001. New Music Network for the Sydney Spring Festival. Transcript of paper provided by Liza Lim.

Lyotard, Jean-François and Thébaud, Jean-Loup. *Just Gaming*. Trans. Wlad Godzich. Minneapolis: University of Minnesota Press, 1985.

Meyer-Arlt, Ronald. 'Träume vom anderen Theater.' *Hannoversche Allgemeine Zeitung* 9 June 2000.

Miller, Sarah. 'A Question of Silence – Approaching the Condition of Performance'. *25 Years of Performance Art in Australia*. Ed. Nick Waterlow. Sydney: Ivan Dougherty Gallery, 1995. 7-12.

Sellars, Peter, 'Australia's Arts Unfettered.' *New York Times* 30 September 2001.

Sonorous Bodies. Official Programme, Third Asia Pacific Triennial, Queensland Art Gallery, 1999.

Schwaegermann, Maria Magdalena. Letter to Philip Rolfe (Director, Audience Development and Advocacy, Australia Council), 22 March 2000. Provided to the author by Schwaegermann.

The Theft of Sita. Director's Notes, Press Kit. Performing Lines, Sydney: n. d.

Witzeling, Klaus. 'Die Zeit vor dem Zeitstillstand: BalletLab aus Australien: Adams' Amplification.' *ballet-tanz international* 3 (2001): 48-49.

Notes

1   Schwaegermann continued to act as the Deputy Director of the Hebbel Theater until August 2003, as well as artistically direct the Zürcher Theater Spektakel.

2   This quotation refers to *The Theft of Sita*, as well as Marc von Hennings's production on the opening day of Theaterformen 2000.

3   The tension between Australia and Indonesia in relation to East Timor followed Indonesia's military take-over and the killing of five Australian journalists in East Timor in 1975. However, it was Australian Prime Minister, John Howard's letter to Suharto's successor, B. J. Habibie in December 1998 that preceded the crisis that took place during the development of *The Theft of Sita* production. Howard's letter urged Habibie to consider autonomy for East Timor and an eventual referendum on East Timor's future and contributed to the announcement of an immediate referendum in East Timor. The ill-prepared proposed referendum lead to attacks by pro-integration militias associated with the Indonesian military against pro-independence Timorese in March 1999, and the establishment of the UN Assistance Mission for East Timor (UNAMET). Australia contributed significantly to UNAMET and Indonesian officials and military leaders accused the Australian government of bias towards the pro-independence movement in East Timor. The referendum, which took place on 30 August 1999, under the supervision of the UN, favoured independence with a majority of 78.5%. This was followed by a massive wave of violence by pro-integration militias and Indonesian security forces were accused of inaction. A largely Australian led and manned International Force for East Timor (INTERFET) authorised by the UN Security Council arrived in Dili on 20 September 1999. In September 1999 Indonesia cancelled its security treaty with Australia and the dispatch of Indonesia's new Ambassador to Australia was postponed.

4   Hans-Thies Lehmann coined the expression 'post-dramatic theatre' to describe the emergence of highly self-referential forms of theatrical practice that suggest, but depend upon, the erosion of the concept of traditional drama. That is, dramaturgical forms that are not driven by the dramatic literary text, forms of theatre that lack conventions of character, dialogue, action, story and conflict. Lehmann's use of the term 'post-dramatic' explicitly articulates the dialectical relationship inherent to these forms of theatre, given that they are emergent in so far as they respond/are read in relation to the framework of tradition (Lehmann passim).

5   Berlin's ruling coalition collapsed in June 2001 as the result of financial scandal and the disclosure of significant debt. The government deficit stands at €38 billion in 2002. As a consequence, Berlin's €373 million cultural budget is

under constant threat of reduction as part of major cut-backs in public spending.

6   'Marrugeku Company History' provided by Sofia Gibson, Company Manager, Stalker Theatre/Marrugeku Company.

7   ibid.

8   Programme Note, *Amplification*.

9   Official website of the 2002 Adelaide Festival: www.adelaidefestival.org.au.

12.
Rhetoric, reconciliation and other national pastimes: showcasing contemporary Australian theatre in London

Susan Bradley Smith

Australian theatre enjoys a new prominence in the United Kingdom, one where critics and audiences alike are showing an increased enthusiasm for our drama. But that enthusiasm is limited to reading/seeing Australia within a colonial paradigm whereby the exotic 'other' prevails as the preferred mode of relationship. Consequently, offshore performances of 'Australia', particularly dramas dealing with contemporary politics such as reconciliation, need to be scrutinised in that light.

How we think about ourselves as Australians, and how the rest of the world perceives us, are fundamental questions at the dawn of a new century that is witness to our failure to reinvent ourselves as a republic, leaving us entwined in the past with the ongoing quest for the never-never land of reconciliation between black and white Australia. If this quest (for postcolonial serenity?) must be our national pastime, then despite how tired we may be of analysing 'nation' and 'identity politics', to move beyond rhetoric we must try harder to understand what is at stake: what matters, and how to secure it. As ever, cultural history provides an opportunity not only to explore these vital issues, but to assess how in recent times cultural practitioners have themselves revealed and interrogated Australianness.

Because this essay examines Australian cultural politics at play in an international marketplace, the question that most insistently demands an answer is: 'are we really what we write ourselves as?' Specifically, what stories have Australian playwrights circulated about Australia and Australians, and to what import? In other words, what impact do performances of Australianness have on the way that others perceive us: our identity, our reputation, our ranking in the global status of desirable nations and peoples when the criteria are measured in terms of human rights and quality of life? For if theatre and performance are entertainment, like any art form they are also an opportunity for others to steal glimpses of the (fictive) inner lives of Australians and the machinations of our nation, and to form (non-fictive) opinions on such matters. I argue that it is not only the performers and practitioners on stage, but rather, or also, the creative worlds audiences are asked to enter that are scrutinised and judged. This is perhaps a peculiar problem to which colonial nations are subject when telling their stories to the 'motherland'. It is a curious liberty, funded by an anthropological interest, that reads theatre as reality, or insists on culture as dialogue rather than investing in mature political relations, but as a liberty taken it demands a different approach to theatre history than might otherwise suggest itself.

Reconciliation, whiteness, and cultural politics: the reception factor

There remain many unresolved issues in the landscape of Australia's imaginations; the republic is one, and reconciliation is another. This inability to resolve the dilemma of reconciliation may be symptomatic of our lack of national maturity and indeed linked to the republican debate. By national maturity I mean a nation of people with a sufficiently shared dreaming (philosophical world view) reflecting an inner coherence of morality that fosters harmonious progress and prosperity; the possession of a sense of culture informed by a shared sense of justice. As Inga Clendinnen argued in her 1999 Boyer lectures, Australia currently has what she terms an inauthentic culture because it is marred by systemic injustices to a specific group of citizens – Australian Aborigines. If you believe that authentic Australian culture is distinguished by a distinctive element of egalitarianism, of a commitment to 'a fair go', then this injustice makes our culture inauthentic, and reconciliation remains a dream rather than a reality. At the same time that theatre, along with other Australian cultural exports, aims to 'perform' cultural authenticity, it highlights this most undistinguished part of Australian life and society and denies our authenticity as a mature culture, which is one reason why performances of Australian theatre in Britain are so intriguing to witness.

In October 2000 the journal *Australasian Drama Studies* devoted an issue to 'Australian Aboriginal Performance', and many contributors paid attention to the topic of reconciliation and theatre's role in that process. The majority echoed Aboriginal director and writer Wesley Enoch's sentiments regarding the need for the heart to be involved in the performing and receiving of stories. This desire is complicated in offshore performances of Australian theatre. Why and how is not always so simple to explain. Wayne Harrison offers a technical explanation, arguing that reception problems can be viewed in terms of an Australian acting style that has partly developed in response to the demands of Australian scripts, a style that can be so different as to be alienating to offshore audiences (see Chapter 10). So if the message of Australian performance material is a political one, how do offshore audiences receive such messages, 'screened' as they might be by the differences of subject, culture, geography and style?

Perhaps the problems with reception have less to do with style and other cartographies of meaning than they do with political perceptions. As Whiteness theory reminds us, being white defines us more than we have often cared to admit (Dyer). Therefore, theatre critics and historians need to be more aware of the politics of reception, one that is informed by a desire to increase white accountability in race relations. For that to happen, we must accept that white people's position in the hegemonic ideology of the West automatically places white people in a supremacist position that belittles peoples of other races. This notion of supremacy underlies the balance of power in all postcolonial societies such as Australia, which is why reconciliation is such an important issue; one that Australian theatre explores and often exports for the scrutiny of foreign sensibilities. Consequently, the focus of this examination is on cultural Australia and how the contemporary Australian performing arts, particularly the theatre, participate in political processes. That possibility is explored by examining instances of recent Australian theatre in London. Two main events are scrutinised: the performance of *Cloudstreet* in London in October 1999; and the 'HeadsUp: Australian Arts Come to London' festival which was part of Australia Week in July 2000. The exploration/survey is meant to be impressionistic, not exhaustive, and of course these are by no means the only examples of Australian theatre in the UK in recent years.[1] Nevertheless, these examples collectively reveal ways in which offshore performances of Australian culture affect the project of reconciliation, or at least exercise the rhetoric of Australia as a desirable (or otherwise) nation, and Australians as likeable (or not) people.

Australian history and theatre have not only a long tradition of racism but also of white activism protesting the crimes of colonisation. As a nation we have our harsh critics, but Australia also has great admirers. Indeed *Neighbours*, *Home and Away* and other soap exports do a convincing job of marketing Australia as a pristine paradise. For indigenous Australians paradise was lost long ago. For many

Australian women living in a rampantly masculinist society, utopia has always eluded them. Similar disappointments are felt all too frequently by post-World War Two immigrants living bewildered lives in an often racist society. These sentiments of loss, disappointment and exclusion are located with embarrassing regularity in the identity-politics plays that form a rich vein in Australian theatre history. Yet perversely, the notion of Australia as paradise persists, sanctified by the soaps, our largest cultural export. Australian theatre on the world stage, showcasing our talent and our stories, is also not always innocent of seducing audiences with notions of paradise. *Cloudstreet* is perhaps the most recent and stunning example of this.

Hangovers from *Cloudstreet*

Should a play as profoundly successful as *Cloudstreet* go unchallenged for its international performances of Australian nationhood? And can one criticise a play on an intellectual level yet praise it on a performance level without compromising the theatrical genius at work – a genius which clearly had London audiences, as elsewhere, spellbound?

Tim Winton's novel *Cloudstreet* was adapted for the stage by Nick Enright and Justin Monjo to great acclaim (Photo 12).[2] Under Neil Armfield's direction, this production of the award-winning novel performed to sell-out houses at both the 1998 Perth and Sydney Festivals before repeating this success on its 1999 European tour. *Cloudstreet*, the play, is now acknowledged as being an international critical and commercial success – no mean feat in the history of Australian theatre. At the London performances expatriate Australians were weeping in the aisles, and notable theatre critics were declaring that Australian theatre had (finally) come of age. But slowly, softly, some 'anti-*Cloudstreet*' sentiment surfaced, raising significant questions about Australian culture and its international receptions.[3]

Why is it that this play is so celebrated as a vision of paradise when, for example, every single Aboriginal character in it is dead? Is the play so popular because, as Fallon argues 'it delivers on [Australia's conservative Liberal Prime Minister] John Howard's promise to make "Australians" feel comfortable and relaxed again' (28)? Set in post-World War Two Perth, *Cloudstreet* is hardly a contemporary story, but has nevertheless come to represent what most people seem to want to embrace about contemporary Australia: it is a white, English-speaking country; safe, conservative, colourful in language, landscape and history, with the odd exotic feature (read Aborigines). What is the value of a cultural commodity that reinforces such unsophisticated stereotypes of Australia? Exploring the play's critical reception in

London ultimately poses questions about performances of nationhood in the heart of the not-so-dead empire.

The plot of *Cloudstreet* is simple, yet the stage performance takes between five and six hours. It is an epic narrative following the story of two families who inhabit the same rambling old house in Perth, the Lamb family being large and religious, and the Pickles family being large and representative of that larrikin, gambling, ocker element of the Australian working classes. The house is haunted by the ghost of a dead Aboriginal girl cruelly abused by her protector, the white woman who once ran the place as a home for lost children. The play's narrator is simply named 'black man' and his function throughout the tale is to explain the world of 1940s, 50s, 60s Australia to the audience – or more pointedly, the confusing ways in which the families both live, love and lose themselves in their own history.

The main character is Fish Lamb, (central for the reconciliation between black and white Australia at the heart of the narrative) who is left both simple and Jesus-like after an accident prawning on the river. He is the one who sees all. But it is the 'Black Man' who does most of the explaining for us; for example, telling why and how the house in Cloud Street had been boarded up after the scandal, presenting a metaphor for how White Australia in general shut the doors on atrocities committed against Aboriginal Australians and refused to deal with them.

Cloudstreet airs this history. It is celebrated for so doing. It is precisely because Winton's text and its adaptation engages with issues of such central importance to the processes of reconciliation as the stolen generation, that the play has won its reputation as writing a map for Australia's (positive) future. But that reputation needs to be questioned. To do that, it is necessary to consider *Cloudstreet* as a cultural export that engages with the process of nation-building through identity formation. Critical reviews of the play in London can generally be described as euphoric, but many also possessed a surprising critical and political alertness.

Paul Taylor writing for the *Independent* (15 September 1999) noted that the house has a haunted past 'not unlike Australia itself', whereby the respectable (does he mean British representatives of the Crown or later immigrants to Australia?) abused those under their care. But while he was 'troubled by certain strands of emotional furiousness in the material', and did not particularly warm to the character of Fish Lamb (less Jesus-like, more Forrest Gump), Taylor seemed to reserve his major criticism for the hype that surrounded the play – '[t]hrowing national understatement to the wind, one British journalist described the ending as "transcendental"' – rather than the play itself. Taylor was left with a 'healthy admiration' for the staging and the fourteen-strong cast, but felt 'as much manipulated as uplifted' by the narrative, which Taylor nonetheless recommended for 'the heart-warming nature of its message'.

Writing for the *Daily Telegraph* (15 September 1999) Charles Spencer's review was headlined 'All the way from Australia – a haunting, moving *Nicholas Nickleby* for the Nineties'. He hailed *Cloudstreet* as providing proof to jaded London theatre-goers that it *was* possible for interesting things to happen on the contemporary stage. He declared both the writing and the actors to be 'blessed with a ... generosity of spirit ... giving their hearts and souls' and praised the design for capturing 'a sense of the wide open spaces of Australia'. Initially Spencer likened *Cloudstreet* to a 'theatrical soap' but later suggested that '[t]he story could be an allegory of Australia itself'. But rather than develop this notion of guilt and persecution he instead discussed the Christian symbolism of the play, arguing that it 'beautifully suggests the possibility of forgiveness and redemption in a harsh world'. Interestingly he commended the 'delicacy' with which such a message was conveyed, pleased that the plot was sufficiently non-confrontational as to allow audiences freedom to find 'as much, or as little, in the narrative as they want'. Spencer's conclusion, though, wrote precisely into the gullible sentimentality that has been so criticised for its lack of awareness: '[t]his is a deeply engaging and emotionally open production about the meaning of home and the urges of the human heart. It sends you back out into the world feeling better about life and I cannot recommend it too highly'.

Are criticisms of gullibility warranted, especially when one of the functions of theatre as entertainment is to uplift? It is treacherous territory to answer such a question definitively, but this discussion is as much about theatre as it is about the politics of culture, international receptions, and postcolonial relations. And many of the British reviews ran the risk of being offensive in this area, writing into dangerous stereotypes whilst gallantly advocating things Australian, as Jasper Rees's article for the *Evening Standard* demonstrates (14 September 1999). While he displayed generosity in declaring *Cloudstreet* an export providing a 'new cultural high from Down Under' that 'looks like changing a few of our preconceived ideas', he could not escape the pitfalls of both paying sloppy attention to Australian theatre history and explaining things Australian in derogatory terms. He characterised the entire history of Australian theatre on the English stage as receiving only 'sniffy' responses, concluding that 'perhaps the culture doesn't travel as well as the wine or the cricket team'. That is, of course, until Australian movie stars like Cate Blanchett and Nicole Kidman proved that they could sell tickets in the West End so long as they could play at being what Rees calls a 'movie siren' with a convincing 'fake pommy accent'.

Despite the predictable stereotyping language of Rees's praise ('certainly the most Australian show ever to show its honest, grinning, sunblasted face on the London stage'), the review developed into something more interesting, and went on to explore cultural relations between English and Australian theatre rather than the play itself. Declaring that '[o]ne of the quieter themes running through *Cloudstreet* is a wariness of Anglo-Saxon condescension', he related director Neil Armfield's anecdote comparing his attempts to bring a Company B (*Cloudstreet*'s producers) production of *Hamlet* to London some years before, with staging *Cloudstreet*. Unlike *Hamlet*, with *Cloudstreet* Armfield was not 'throwing' himself 'up against the source place'. The message remained that success was potentially dependent on not trespassing upon what is commonly regarded as sacred territory. Although Rees acknowledged more the press release's insistence than the play's presentation of the political metaphors at work in the play, and that the 'action of the story is to find a cleansing', he concluded that '[f]or our part, we will inevitably view *Cloudstreet* as a play about the state of Australian theatre'. When he put this idea to Tim Winton, Winton responded that 'I don't think a piece of art should have to travel with that weight'.

Yet writing cultural history is inevitably an exercise in assessing the bearing of weight, and it would be negligent to underestimate the import of a play whose real subject is 'Australia itself' (Michael Billington, the *Guardian*, 15 September 1999). Clearly, considering the play purely as a national saga, one that supposedly takes us on an epic journey from despair to hope, critics and audiences alike saw atonement at work where arguably it was and is not. *Cloudstreet* ultimately performed a masterful 'Emperor's-new-clothes' trick with English audiences: they trusted what they were told. Who can blame them, for the play unfolds its tale in such a magical and theatrically spellbinding way? Whereas the wilful ignorance of Australian audiences is located in a different psychological space, the performative power of *Cloudstreet* in an offshore setting involves creating a sense of awe in the audience that inspires an unquestioning trust in the factual accuracies of the reconciliation rhetoric. This trust suspends critical disbelief as the political (is there only one side to this story?) is overwhelmed by the sensuality aroused by the spectacle of the performance: this story is being so spectacularly told! To put it bluntly: when considering differing levels of maturity that relate to political sensibilities, (comparatively) ignorant English audiences should not be blamed to the same extent as their informed Australian counterparts, who are regularly exposed to the politics of reconciliation.

For critics such as Kathleen Mary Fallon (23-28) writing from Australia, the play failed to sweep her away on waves of euphoria. For her *Cloudstreet* as a saga of reconciliation and renewed national identity, and its subsequent overwhelming praise, was completely unbearable because it legitimised white occupation of Australia as benign and benevolent, dispensing gnomic Aboriginal spiritual advice about place and belonging which was seductive and exotic but ultimately harmful. The play, as the black narrator states, leaves a 'warm clean space amongst the living', and for Australians, perhaps more so than foreign audiences, we are hard pressed to locate that space in reality. Reconciliation is arguably being fought for in spaces very different and far removed from the simple world insinuated by *Cloudstreet*. But for foreign audiences, one of the absolute charms of the play is to believe the lie that racist Australia is capable of being seduced, calmed, and altered by such spirituality, and that a happy ending is inevitable.

As Fallon (23-24) insists, despite being hailed as a 'saga of reconciliation and renewed identity', *Cloudstreet* does not strive to find a shared history with black Australia. Such wilful innocence enforces an unbecoming naivety on a nation that ought to be struggling for maturity. That when Australian cultural products are performed in offshore settings this maturity can not be located (or falsely presumed) is doubly harmful. It is important here to note that in the drama of reconciliation Britain has far more to worry about than other European nations. Of all heads of state, only the Queen was sought out in October 1999 by a delegation of Aboriginal elders, specifically to ask her to recognise that Britain should shoulder some responsibility for the consequences of colonialism.[4] While an audience was held with the monarch, the Australian High Commissioner of the time refused to welcome them.

Nevertheless, *Cloudstreet* presents us with an Australia that we know and love, the one that evidently holds most purchase at home and away: the larrikin paradise, bereft of lasting aggression and full of goodwill. Comfortable. Relaxed. Reconciled. But is this what Australia really is, and if not, is it fair to condemn *Cloudstreet* for misrepresentation? I would argue no on both counts. Nevertheless, like Fallon, I believe that 'it is imperative that cultural works of all kinds should be guiding audiences and readers through these perilous places' (26); the seat of pain and confusion that must be confronted if reconciliation is to move from rhetoric to reality. Is this achieved in *Cloudstreet*? No. Is *Cloudstreet* the most exciting piece of Australian theatre I have seen in London since first working here as a theatre critic in 1988? Yes. For all my liberal reservations about *Cloudstreet*, perhaps my sorrow-filled criticisms are nothing more than manifestations of white-girl guilt, demonstrating yet again that the sites of the ongoing struggle for reconciliation are very different for indigenous Australians than they are for people like me.

'HeadsUp' or thumbs down? Arts festivals and official stories

Cloudstreet's critical and commercial success augured well for the *HeadsUp* Australian Arts Festival that descended upon London with Australian talent in July 2000. Audiences and critics alike were expecting big things, and there was a buzz surrounding the events that indicated a generosity of spirit that perhaps had not hitherto been extended to Australian theatre. This positive anticipation generated good press and good audience attendance, but importantly there was a significant shift in the kind of critical reviewing that was taking place. Leading London theatre critics engaged directly and often expertly with not only the style of theatre that was on offer but the political content of much of the drama (and by extension Australian politics and society); suggesting, for example, that it is in the arts that the real racial reconciliation is taking place.

Before examining the plays themselves, a little about the rationale for the celebration that facilitated the festival in the first place. Unlike *Cloudstreet*, with the backing of Sydney's Company B and the likes of Nicole Kidman and Baz Luhrmann,[5] the fare offered by *HeadsUp* came through the less entrepreneurial but no less prestigious route of the Australia Council for the Arts, who were directly engaging with a dual English and Australian Government initiative that came to be known as Australia Week, running from 30 June-9 July 2000 (although the plays ran beyond these dates). Australia Week was conceived as 'a significant program of contemporary arts presented in London to mark Australia's Centenary of Federation', as the Federal Minister for the Arts and the

Centenary of Federation, Peter McGauran, put it in the official launch programme.

In fact the agenda for the entire enterprise was very precise in its focus and intention. Australia Week in London commemorated the hundredth anniversary of the Commonwealth of Australia Constitution Act, passed by the UK Parliament and later Queen Victoria in July 1900. But this commemoration of the foundation of modern Australia caused much outrage, both at home and abroad, mostly to do with the costs involved and the perceived exploitation by Australian dignitaries and politicians of Australian public money spent on a pointless 'party' in London. So although Australia Week itself was not without controversy, the *HeadsUp* festival seemed mostly immune from such criticism. The program, however, was selected with major ambassadorial goals in mind.

While the Chair of the Australia Council, Margaret Sears, simply called the festival what it was, 'a unique opportunity for Australia to present a diverse and rich showcase of its best contemporary arts in one of the most significant cultural capitals of the world' (*HeadsUp*), others were more intent on extending the agenda to include showcasing Australia itself, using the festival as a kind of propaganda machine. The Australian High Commissioner, Philip Flood, welcomed the opportunity for Australia to 'showcase' its artists as they represented 'the vibrant strength of modern Australia', that is, 'the unique country that we have become over the last century'. He praised the fact that Australian artists find inspiration from many sources, 'including the rich vein of indigenous culture, the old world traditions of the early settlers, and those of the many societies and countries whose people have followed them'. He argued that this variety is what makes Australia unique, and that that uniqueness is given expression 'perhaps most essentially through the arts' (*HeadsUp*). Peter McGauran was more direct:

> From a country that is both ancient and modern, reflecting voices from the rural heartland to the urban centres, and embracing waves of immigrant cultures, Australia reveals its cultural soul through new forms of artistic expression.

He insisted that that 'cultural soul' is not a hybrid one, but rather one that is 'a collision of ancient cultures and contemporary edginess' (*HeadsUp*).

HeadsUp was a festival encompassing Australian dance, literature, painting, music, fashion, film, and more, as well as incorporating many associated events and exhibitions, some of which had been years in the planning. But the leading talent of the festival appeared to be

Australian theatre, judging from the amount programmed and the publicity it received. Aside from the staged playreadings conducted by the Blue Tongue Theatre at Australia House of Jack Hibberd's *Stretch of the Imagination* and Beatrix Christian's *Spumante Romantica*, the programme included the following: Leah Purcell and Scott Rankin's *Box the Pony*; Deborah Cheetham's *White Baptist Abba Fan*; Jane Harrison's *Stolen*; Andrew Bovell's *Speaking in Tongues*;[6] and Tyler Coppin's *Lyrebird: Tales of Helpmann*. The plays which generated the most press coverage were the three 'Aboriginal' dramas *Stolen*, *Box the Pony*, and *White Baptist Abba Fan*: it appears that despite the 'assimilation-speak' in the official programme – confidently boasting about the rich culture of Australia's multicultural society – offshore audiences are not as interested in our diversity as we are. In the current climate of postcolonial relations between Britain and Australia, anything Aboriginal captivates, and most else is considered second-rate in the entertainment stakes in the sense that nothing on offer is unique. Perversely, perhaps, this somewhat condescending attitude has the curious effect of enhancing political and cultural awareness between Britain and Australia and has subsequently improved the quality of postcolonial relations – that is, if you accept that theatre can effect social change. Many of the reviews seem to suggest precisely that.

Stolen is a play that explores the crime of indigenous Australians being forcibly removed from their families and brought up 'white', a policy endorsed by the Australian Government of the time. It received the most critical attention, and its politics were an essential part of the play's marketing, as the following demonstrates:

> *Stolen* is an extraordinary testament to the endurance of the Australian Indigenous culture and the strength of the Indigenous family. It is an overtly theatrical piece of storytelling powered by the strongest tool in the fight for reconciliation: the truth. (*HeadsUp*)

As a play that engages directly with history, its agenda is a fierce and direct confrontation with white Australia, its colonial constructions, and the political machinery that wreaked such damage:

> If there is one feeling that you will take away from this play, it is an understanding of the generations of Indigenous Australians who were forcibly taken from the arms of their families. (*HeadsUp*)

So what did the critics do with this understanding?

It is important to note that journalistic reactions to the fare of the festival and its (often) political content did not occur in isolation.

Australia was big news in London during Australia Week, and heightened coverage was given in the press to all matters Australian, from the upcoming Olympics to Prime Minister Howard's refusal to offer an official apology (recommended by a Royal Commission) to Aboriginal Australia. While Howard insisted that it was meaningless to apologise for things his Government and his generation of Australians did not do, others felt differently, insisting with Aboriginal activist Charles Perkins that 'saying sorry is a psychological, spiritual, symbolic thing that will act as a catalyst for us to discuss all the problems between us' (Chandrasekran 4). Such debates in the press meant that an increased political awareness was brought to bear when critically engaging with Australian theatre performed in London during that period.

Kate Kellaway writing for the *Observer* (9 July 2000) said that the material of *Stolen* 'is written to cut to the quick' and relates director Wesley Enoch's tale that not only had thousands of people signed a 'sorry' book after seeing the play in Australia, but three people suffered heart attacks. Though some criticisms of the style were offered, Kellaway concluded that the play 'works'; that 'no one could fail to be moved by the testimony of the actors'; and that it is 'extraordinary' that Australia's Prime Minister feels 'unable' to sign his name in the sorry book. Writing for the *Times Literary Supplement* (14 July 2000) Nicola Walker better captured the relationship between art and politics when she noted that the point of the play was not to shame or name, but 'the desire to be heard out'. She found the play to be 'mordantly acute', and places the narrative squarely in the tradition of such writers as Herbert 'Nugget' Coombs, Katharine Susannah Prichard, and Henry Reynolds who all 'worked hard to raise awareness of the wrongs done to Aborigines'.

Dominic Cavendish's review in the *Independent* (11 July 2000) began with a detailed description of the sorry book, and what was meant by signing it at the Tricycle Theatre as part of the experience of seeing *Stolen*. His two main points are interesting. Firstly, it is noted that the play 'doesn't examine racism in its institutionalised forms' and that this has the striking effect of creating deeper sympathy (a guilt-free association?). Secondly, but not unrelated, Cavendish concludes that the play felt 'like a rudimentary first step towards examining a terrible wound. We can bear witness to the pain, but it is premature to expect us to supply the balm that will make it heal'.

Michael Billington's review for the *Guardian* (8 July 2000) adopted no such 'all knowledge and no responsibility' posturing. He began somewhat slyly by noting that the Australian Prime Minister had met with his British counterpart earlier that week asking for help in repatriating the remains of more than 2000 Aborigines. Billington suggested that 'before making a decision, Blair and the museum bosses could visit some of the shows in the Australian HeadsUp season', mentioning in particular *Stolen, Box the Pony* and *White Baptist Abba Fan*: 'At the very least, the shows will tell them something about the wrongs aborigines have historically endured and about their sacred relationship with the past'. In common with all the reviews of Aboriginal theatre in the programme, more critical space was devoted to explaining black and white relations in Australia and revealing the flawed nature of reconciliation politics, than to the actual performances or productions themselves. This review was not alone, for example, in making comparisons with South African theatre, pronouncing that 'good theatre is the best way of recording social injustice', insisting that political messages packaged so entertainingly, ('it is not worthy, it is not preachy'), will succeed in their mission.

Box the Pony and *White Baptist Abba Fan* were mostly reviewed in tandem, both being one-woman shows performed back-to-back at the Barbican Centre. They were billed as dramas with 'Aboriginal actors ... telling their personal stories of growing up, desire, and the weight of cultural heritage' (*HeadsUp*). Ian Johns writing in the *Times* (10 July 2000) praised the shows for their skilful performances, 'well-aimed punches' and the fact that pleas for 'universal respect' were 'made with a light touch', involving an endearing humour and candour. Humour is an essential element in Aboriginal drama. Although *White Baptist Abba Fan* has as its lead the true life character/performer who was taken from her mother as an infant, both plays are celebrations of survival and Aboriginal identity that educate and entertain.

In the same review that covered *Stolen*, Michael Billington had the final word on the value of experiencing these performances: 'true stories vividly told' where you could not fail to be 'moved by the authenticity of the experience'. He ended by saying that he had been reading a book (Jonathon Bates' *The Song of the Earth*) that offers an ecological reading of literature and makes a powerful plea for engaging with poetry as the place where we save the earth. Seeing these plays suggested to him 'that drama may have a parallel function. It is the last place, in a high-tech world, where we gather to hear stories and possibly redeem the past'. Billington felt that, just as for Bates where poetry becomes 'the original admission of dwelling', 'in the case of these exhilarating Australian shows' theatre becomes 'a vehicle for reconciliation' (*Guardian*, 8 July 2000).

Theatre, illusion and final stories

In the tradition of realism, much contemporary Australian theatre holds a mirror up to our society; one that in *Cloudstreet*'s case, along with the other examples explored here, have been reflected on to the larger world. Like those Aborigines looking for the first time at their reflections in mirrors – implements of European refraction[7] – the colonial past, refracted by Australian cultural products, enables us to see ourselves differently. It is not enough to beg the imperialist gaze to look elsewhere, to stop constructing us as the ultimate victory of colonisation – paradise – and leave us alone to examine our own flaws with an authentic dignity befitting a reconciled nation. Performing Australia in the United Kingdom requires its own finely-crafted politics simply to share our stories with dignity. As Wayne Harrison said when recalling the advice of a mentor, Philip Parsons, 'you can't come into London with a play with all guns blazing and say, "Here we are, we've come from the colonies to tell you how to do spoken drama", because that will not wash at all. His idea was that you should come in through the back door, establish a presence, and let them discover you' (see 164).

Does such advice depend on the oft-criticised practice of marketing culture in nationalistic terms? Can political theatre ever avoid this conundrum? When Wesley Enoch was asked about the ambassadorial qualities of *7 Stages of Grieving* and its huge success overseas, his response suggested that to be stereotyped as either having purely Australian or political agendas was a dilemma for theatre:

> when it comes down to it, when it went overseas people didn't see it as a piece of Aboriginal theatre. And that's both a good and bad thing. What they saw is a piece of Australian theatre about this particular issue, and it just happened that there was a black woman performing it. So it was an important piece in that way, that it wasn't seen within a sheltered political environment. It actually had to make its mark in a different way, and it did. And that was really exciting.

Regardless, the term 'Australian' as a defined descriptor operates as a shorthand when critics and the public alike relate stories concerning their experiences of Australian theatre. 'Australian' does not mean what it once did, however, and it is not automatically a term of derision implying an inferior theatrical experience. Occasionally and increasingly, it is a term used to denote what is cutting-edge, bold, exciting and well worth seeing. It is demonstrably clear that a more sophisticated understanding of 'Australia' exists in the UK today than it did a few decades earlier.

Nevertheless, in terms of global marketing and the politics of reception, Australian cultural exports that reveal the 'secrets' of contemporary Australian society continue to be read within a colonial paradigm: are we forever to be explained in comparative terms? Perhaps not, as some of the examples cited here suggest. It seems, though, that audiences (if not playwrights and other theatre practitioners) have a limit when it comes to mixing entertainment and politics, and it is this ultimately that confines the role of theatre and social change. Meme McDonald (a white woman) captured this sentiment perfectly when she recently explained the success of her partner Boori Pryor's cultural practice. She said of Pryor, an Aboriginal educator and storyteller who works a lot in Australian schools, that: '[h]e tells stories, plays the didgeridoo, gets the children up to dance. He has a way of talking about this very sorry history of ours in a way that didn't make you feel so guilty you couldn't move' (Sullivan 5).

Immobility in human relations is not good for business, whether it be the business of reconciliation or commerce. The theatre examined in this essay is ultimately a commercial enterprise, perhaps more so when it ventures offshore. The arts are a significant commercial component of Australian exports. For example, any discussions concerning postcolonial relations between Britain and Australia should heed the fact that our historical and habitual closeness is reflected in hard cash: Australia is one of the top four investors in Britain, and Britain is one of the most important investors in Australia.

Arts companies are business, and like any businesses they aim to increase their stakeholding. Performance success, ultimately, is measured by box-office success; even if plays merit and receive outstanding critical praise this hard commercial fact remains the final determinant. And what seems to work best for Australian theatre in Britain are dramas about how varied our people, history and country (and maybe performance styles) are compared with England and the English, which so dominate what constitutes 'British'. Arguably, theatre-goers in Britain, particularly in London's West End, are not interested in white bourgeois Australia and its dilemmas, as demonstrated by the recent short run of Hannie Rayson's *Life After George*, and prior to that the mediocre responses to productions of David Williamson's works.[8] There is a distinct feeling that the market in middle-class angst has been cornered and that Australian experiences have nothing unique to add to this Universal. Such attitudes demand a critique, particularly from the standpoint of the postcolonial critic, but – and this is a generalisation demanded by the need to make a commercial forecast – it appears that these attitudes are steadfastly held. But if a play offers a look at something exotic, something that might even permit non-Australian audiences to feel superior about such issues as white Australia's shoddy reconciliation record whilst thoroughly entertaining them with the high standard of writing, direction, and performance offered by most Australian drama in London, then that is Australian theatre's best hope of success. It appears that only certain types of Australian stories are worth performing overseas; certainly in the current climate Aboriginal theatre (for the wrong reasons perhaps) has a higher currency.

But performance has a value beyond the commercial. For me, the best production covered in this essay was *Stolen*, performed as part of *HeadsUp* at London's Tricycle Theatre. I was there crying my way through *Stolen* (they really were my farming-family ancestors on that riverbank doing what the play said they did). Sitting in the audience on one of the last nights of the run, and throwing a reception afterwards for the cast, was the same Australian High Commissioner who twelve months earlier had refused to receive the delegation of Aboriginal Elders. If you believe that the old-world orders suppress the power of resistance and redefinition demanded by postcolonial times, and if you believe that Australia might never reconcile, this was one of those moments that charges hope. The whole world might march across Sydney Harbour Bridge in support of reconciliation, but seeing that man receiving the play, its stories, and its performers, gave me more hope for Australia's future than I could fathom.

Politics continue, the shows go on, paradise awaits.

References

Bradley, Lynne. 'Choosing Good Ground: A Forum Interview with Kooemba Jdarra Artistic Directors Lafe Charleton, Wesley Enoch and Nadine McDonald'. *Australasian Drama Studies* 37 (October 2000): 59-67.

Chandrasekran, Rajiv. 'Sorry for a "Stolen Generation"? Australia Debates an Apology for Aboriginal Policy'. *International Herald Tribune* (Washington Post Service) 8 July 2000.

Clendinnen, Inga. *Boyer Lectures*, November-December 1999 (transcripts at http://www.abc.net.au/rn/boyers/index/BoyersChronoldx.htm).

Dyer, Richard. *White*. London: Routledge, 1997.

Enoch, Wesley. Interview with author. London, August 2000.

Enright, Nick and Justin Monjo. *Cloudstreet*. Sydney: Currency Press, 1999.

Fallon, Kathleen Mary. 'A Close Look at *Cloudstreet*. *Australian Book Review* (October 1999): 23-28.

HeadsUp. Programme, Australia Week, 30 June-9 July 2000. Australia Council for the Arts.

Marshall, Anne and Gordon Beattie, ed. *Sun Sisters and Lightning Brothers: Australian Aboriginal Performance*. Spec. Issue of *Australasian Drama Studies* 37 (October 2000).

Sullivan, Jane. 'The Two of Us: Meme McDonald and Boori Pryor'. *Good Weekend* 4 September 1999.

Notes

1   For example, London's Australian theatre company, Blue Tongue (with Lucy Skilbeck as artistic director and Gale Edwards as patron), deserves serious attention.

2   *Cloudstreet*, Winton's fifth novel, has been a huge literary and commercial success since its publication in 1991. Awards include the Deo Gloria Award (UK), the Miles Franklin Award and the National Book Council Banjo Award. After sell-out performances at the 1998 Perth and Sydney Festivals, the stage adaptation met with similar success on its European tour.

3   *Cloudstreet* met with some disapproval due to the 'infantilism' of its reconciliation politics, which influenced certain European theatre managements (who prefer to remain anonymous) not to program the production.

4   The meeting took place on Wednesday 13 October 1999. A report of the meeting can be found at http://news.bbc.co.uk/hi/english/uk/newsid_474000 /474036.stm.

5   Kidman, Luhrmann and Jane Campion, among others, were financial backers of Company B's tour of *Cloudstreet*. See *Evening Standard* 14 September 1999.

6   Subsequently developed into the successful feature film *Lantana*.

7   From Clendinnen, Boyer Lecture 1, 'Incident on a Beach', 14 November 1999.

8   Large audiences but mediocre reviews greeted the 2002 London production of Willliamson's *Up For Grabs*, starring Madonna.

13.
Playing Australia in the theatre: an interview with Cate Blanchett

*Cate Blanchett was interviewed by Elizabeth Schafer on 30 June 1999 during the London West End run of **Plenty** by David Hare, in which she was playing the demanding lead role of Susan Traherne.*

*You played Helen in **Sweet Phoebe** by Michael Gow both in Australia and in the UK.[1] What were the differences between playing it in Sydney and Melbourne and then in the UK?*

Blanchett: I'm a great fan of Michael Gow's writing and I feel that he places himself in the public arena in a very dangerous and provocative way. In Australia people come to Michael Gow's work with a knowledge of him as a personality and so people are not only receiving the play but are receiving him as a figure. This happened when we performed *Sweet Phoebe* at the Sydney Theatre Company's Wharf theatre. Then we went to Melbourne with it and it got a different response because it was a play from *Sydney*, and I experienced that rivalry. Finally it was such a relief to be performing in a really intimate space in England where the play came with no baggage and I felt that it really found its audience. There were some very suburban references, very specific references to place when Helen's going out to look for the dog, but the actual humor of it was received better in the UK than in Australia. It was a great ending to the production that it actually found its audience here.

*How does that experience compare with **Plenty** which has had more mixed reviews?*

Blanchett: As a practitioner I have become less and less interested in what the few male gazers who come and supposedly critique what goes on have to say because they have little interest in what the people are actually trying to do, especially when they are pushing the envelope in terms of what theatre can be. My obsession at the moment is that theatre is actually in danger of becoming elite in the way that opera is elite, and probably as irrelevant. I feel that increasingly theatre will go into small spaces.

In reviewing *Plenty* no one has made any mention of *Sweet Phoebe* at all or mentioned that it was received incredibly well. That was only three years ago and the production was reviewed by all the main papers but suddenly I'm now a film actor and I am perceived incredibly, and therefore judged incredibly, differently. It's affected the whole fabric of the way people are coming to watch this play. That's not something that I've spent any time dwelling on but it's just been thrown back in my face a little bit, and while I don't want to wear a T-shirt saying that 'I trained at Drama School and worked primarily in the theatre, I've made five films but I've been in double the number of plays', I have become pigeon-holed, and with high-profile actors in film there's sometimes a sense that you move into theatres for credibility or something.

I'm not up there to be liked but the reason why I don't find reviews particularly helpful is because if they are fantastic then you puff up like a peacock, which is not helpful, and if they are terrible and destructive then you still have to go out and do it, and yet it's just someone's opinion. The greatest strength that you have to have, and that's why it's so important who you're surrounded by, is the people you are working with.

Overall being a little adrift and coming here and working in the theatre were useful. The more baggage you accumulate as an actor, and the more public you become, the harder it is to shed that off. I was grateful for not doing *Plenty* in Australia in some ways because the challenge for me was greater *because* I was less known and I didn't know the other actors and so could take risks.

You were giving a big, full-throttle performance while there were some people on stage who were by comparison very withheld. Your performance had a very different energy. Could this be related to an Australian acting style as opposed to a British tradition?[2]

Blanchett: It's hard for me to be objective about this particular play but this is also to do with the character of Susan Traherne. She is somebody who is living her life in descent, she is outside, is delving into dangerous areas of thought and action which actually exist outside the Noel Coward role which she sometimes inhabits. The play has never been in completely British hands: the first Susan, Kate Nelligan, is Canadian, Meryl Streep who played the role on film is American. The director of this production, Jonathan Kent, is South African and Fred Schepisi, who directed the film, is Australian. I do feel – and it's not a criticism, just an observation – that often when I go to theatre in Britain that I'm receiving a very polished, intelligent reading, a moved reading of a play. I'm speaking in general terms but if there is a difference it is that the British don't engage their bodies as much – but then you get people like [Théâtre de] Complicité who do. Something that the English do have they is that they respect language.

What was your experience of playing the West End?

Blanchett: The West End holds little attraction for me and nor does Broadway. Sure if you're in a good space with good group of people with a wonderful piece of writing it doesn't really matter where you are, but it's a funny thing that when watching plays in the West End I feel like I'm in a certain demographic, like people are on a bus tour a little bit, and people truck themselves out to see these things because they feel they should. I don't know what these proscenium arch theatres will turn into. Those West End theatres can feel a bit like Old Sydney Town. Everything's propped up by tourists, it's becoming like Pompeii, we are seeing how people used to do things rather than finding our own way of doing it again. I originally thought *Plenty* was going to be at the Almeida which was more appealing. I do prefer spaces like the Wharf, like Belvoir Street, like the Almeida. I have never been in a production like this before. It's like working on a musical. There's twenty crew trucking things around.

You've played some very demanding and strong roles. Do you choose them for their strength?

Blanchett: I've played Miranda and Ophelia and I don't actually know what the term 'strong' means with them. Maybe that's my presence and I don't know if I can comment on that, and I don't want to stamp myself. I don't make early decisions about characters. I try to leave the points of conclusion as late as possible and keep them open ended so they can change and mutate throughout the run because that's why people come and see it, to see the cogs shifting in different ways every night and because we have painfully few weeks' rehearsal time, five weeks usually.

I'm very fatalistic about work, I don't read plays and think 'I really want to play Hedda Gabler or Helen in *Sweet Phoebe*'. It depends completely on who you're surrounded by, who's looking at you, who's designing the surface you are walking on. One of the most important things in designs is the surface on which the actors are walking. That's really important and in my mind's eye when I conceived of *Plenty* I imagined Susan Traherne to be walking on the soil of France.

Do you feel politics, gender and cultural politics, inform your performances?

Blanchett: People are frightened of anything that sounds vaguely extreme or passionate, but of course I'm a feminist but I'm a postmodern feminist. I've been brought up in an environment where I've been afforded luxuries that people have fought for, and frankly I think we are going progressively backward. I am just constantly amazed watching female actresses on film and on stage play up to the male gaze because they know that's what they are being looked at for. The way we relate to each other is of course, on a basic animal level, sexual, but it's not interesting when that's all people are playing. Of course my politics inform what I do, the choices I make, but I also don't think that theatre is an educative space, I think the theatre and education mentality is a dangerous one. Obviously Theatre in Education has an important place in schools but it's not what *we* do it for. That was what was so wonderful being in *Oleanna*. I had the most challenging and aggravating and inspiring conversations after the play because it was thought-provoking. And I feel that particularly in the West End there are a lot of people who don't want that. It's their right.

Oleanna for the Sydney Theatre Company was directed by Michael Gow and starred you and Geoffrey Rush [see cover photo]. It was also one of your earliest professional productions. Was the controversy surrounding that play a baptism by fire?

Blanchett: I came out of Drama School and didn't do very much. Then I did *Top Girls* and *Kafka Dances* and then I did *Oleanna*. When I first read the play I threw it across the room and thought it was the most misogynist crap and I couldn't understand it. Then I kept coming back to it and I thought 'Why am I frightened of something that's provocative?' If it provokes people to talk about it then that's fantastic. Also to be sparring with Geoffrey Rush was inspiring. What was also important about the production was – and this is different to how it was done in England where it had an interval – was that we barrelled straight through. By having an interval in that play you actually let the audience off the hook, you let them go and discuss it and try and intellectualise their emotional responses and then they come back and they have taken their sides for the second half. It works much better when you barrel straight through, and then let them out with a gasp.

We were in an elevated space, it was like a boxing ring, and so Geoffrey and I would literally lock in every night. It was all about the other actor and trusting that you've done all the work, you don't need to over-inflect, you just need to look the other actor in the eye and progress from there. It's quite Zen in that way, quite paring down. I did find the rehearsals difficult because I was trying to impose my own politics. I was trying to tell the audience how to be sympathetic towards the character and it was just disastrous, so Michael Gow and I had an enormous fight, one of the biggest fights I've ever had in the rehearsal room, and then from that, from actually getting rid of my fear of my *own* politics being judged by being in it, the play actually opened up because I did my job. And that's really important: you've got to know what your function is when you are working on good writing like *Plenty* and *Oleanna*.

Focussing specifically on the notion of playing Australian and playing in Australia, what difference has it made that you were trained and began your career in Australia?

Blanchett: I've been only been working professionally for around five years and now I'm suddenly talking about my career and having to cross-reference myself when I've only got a few strands to cross-reference. I thought when I did *The Seagull* that I wanted to work in the theatre in a way that really pushed me but because it's such a small pool in Australia you tend to be cast in the same vein. And I didn't want to be (and that's one of the downsides of a great idea about having a loose ensemble of actors at Belvoir Street) always the Juve[nile].

I started first with drama classes at primary school where we used to put on little plays, but I never really took theatre seriously as a career. I thought I was not strong enough to cope with all the unemployment and the rejection. I still think I don't have the right temperament to be in this profession. I find a lot of the extraneous stuff difficult to deal with, it's distracting. I was so pleased to be engulfed with *Plenty* when all the Oscars were going on because it meant that it could be just the enjoyable froth that it was.

I was fortunate in my third year at drama school [the National Institute of Dramatic Art, Sydney] to work with director/teacher Lindy Davies who now runs the Victoria College of the Arts (VCA) and that for me was a life-changing experience. I played Electra in a production she directed: we had seven days, and I had to throw myself into it. What I try to do, which is difficult, is to be fearless in the rehearsal room. Lindy's method is working with, not fighting with, your surroundings and turning them around to use them in a positive way. Metaphorically that's what I carry with me, and that's where the theatre medium is collaborative and that's what I love. It's not always the way in film.

Is there anything about Lindy Davies' method that you can identify that is particularly useful?

Blanchett: She's got a very specific way of working; it's characterised by confusion primarily. One stage is abstract and you do your work at home and I sometimes do this, I sometimes don't. It depends on the project. You do dictionary work, you literally look up every single word in the text. You make a connection with the text away from the rehearsal room, you put the text up in front of you, you drop it in, and make an intellectual and emotional connection with each line. So when you come into the space you have actually in some way inhabited the words. The words are projected onto the wall and you then do the abstract work. Lindy fills the space with junk and you literally might find the line 'O brave new world' and for example, pick up a bottle and find the light shining through it and that might attract something. You connect with the spaces and connect with the other actors. Then the junk is cleared and she does what is called a blue print, which is basically blocking. It's a very, very slow process and often in the tech you still haven't blocked it which means the lighting and the design evolve from what happens in the space. It's a nightmare for the technical people! So things often aren't ready and it's very messy, but it means that the actors are secure in what they are doing and in the layers of their connection to what they are saying, and their connection to the other actors is very deep and hopefully profound. In the end it's about working with the other actors and finding a way of working together so I tend to use just some of those things when appropriate. It's problem solving.

Lindy's training at the VCA now, and she trains actors so thoroughly and makes them really connected to their bodies and their spirits and the way they think, and also to the way of working with other people. At NIDA (National Institute of Dramatic Art) they train people to be show ponies and the people who look like they are being show ponies get pushed. It's also scary that, because we're so incredibly youth-obsessed, NIDA take people who are eighteen and they don't know who they are (who ever does know who they are?) but they are completely unformed and don't have a lot of life to bring. And the students are so terrified of being kicked out that they don't actually take risks. It's quite a brutal place in some ways. It wasn't until my third year that I met Lindy and she encouraged me to explore the way one needs to rehearse, how to take time and use time productively.

So what do you want from the rehearsal process?

Blanchett: What I like about rehearsal time is that you have to humble yourself to what it is that you're doing and I don't think there's a lot of humility in the way most films are made, although I've been lucky enough to work with people and on projects where it does feel collaborative and respectful.

To me theatre should not be a polite space and the more bourgeois it becomes, the more expensive and elite, the less government money there is the more you have to justify what you're doing in terms of dealing with people politely – because you don't want to offend people, you want to market something that appeals to all people – and that is the death of theatre. The rehearsal room is not, nor should it be, a polite space. One of the liberating things in going to and training at drama school is that you lock yourself away in an impolite often quite destructive environment to stretch things to the edges. I'm not saying 'place actors in danger', I just mean that it needs to be a space, like the actual performance space, where things are transgressed and boundaries are pushed.

I am eclectic and what I've been afforded is the luxury or the opportunity to cross-fertilise, hopefully in a productive way, between my experiences in film and television, radio and theatre, Australia and the UK. You obviously accumulate different things that work at different times.

What would you to do in the future in the theatre?

Blanchett: My sister Genevieve is a designer and we talk a lot about space. I love her designs because she's interested in acting and she creates spaces that don't draw attention to themselves, but focus in on the action. I get very excited at seeing large numbers of actors on stage and I much prefer space, things to be sparse, and to watch people moving through. That's partly me being interested in dance as well. I'd love to work with Pina Bausch.

Notes

1   The play premiered by the Sydney Theatre Company on 2 November 1994, directed by Michael Gow and starring Cate Blanchett and Colin Moody. Gow directed the same cast at the Warehouse, Croydon, 26 March-23 April 1995.

2   On differences between Australian and British acting styles see also Wayne Harrison's comments in Chapter 10 of this volume.

Index of Proper Names

230